# Revitalising Teacher Education in India

# Revitalising Teacher Education in India

***NEP 2020***

Prospects and Challenges

*Editors*

Jasim Ahmad

Aerum Khan

Ansar Ahmad

SHIPRA

And the project is funded by ICSSR, New delhi



₹795; US$ 26.50
ISBN: 978-93-91978-73-0

2024
First Published in India

Revitalising Teacher Education in India
*NEP 2020—Prospects and Challenges*



Published by:
**SHIPRA PUBLICATIONS**
LG 18-19, Pankaj Central Market
I.P. Ext., Patparganj, Delhi 110092, India
91 11 2223 5152; 96500 28065, 98105 22367
info@shiprapublication.com
www.shiprapublication.com

# Foreword

In the dynamic landscape of education, the importance of teacher education, encompassing both pre-service and in-service training, has become indispensable in realizing the objectives outlined in India's National Education Policy (NEP) 2020. This policy places strong emphasis on holistic development and the delivery of quality education, recognizing educators as pivotal agents of transformative change within the educational framework. By equipping teachers with contemporary pedagogical methodologies and up-to-date subject knowledge, teacher education seamlessly aligns with NEP 2020's overarching vision of fostering an environment conducive to innovation and continual enhancement within the educational sphere.

Understanding the multifaceted dynamics inherent in the swiftly evolving landscape of teacher education within the context of NEP 2020 underscores the imperative of our endeavor. It is within this context that the present book '*Revitalising Teacher Education in India: NEP 2020—Prospects and Challenges*' compiled and crafted meticulously to illuminate critical themes and pressing issues pertinent to contemporary teacher development in India.

The chapters contained within this volume offer a rich tapestry of viewpoints, research discoveries, and pragmatic insights contributed by esteemed scholars, educators, practitioners, and researchers alike. Each chapter serves as a testament to the transformative potential inherent in teacher education, delving into a spectrum of topics spanning from the perspectives of novice educators to innovative pedagogical methodologies, from the integration of digital technologies to the cultivation of socio-emotional learning competencies.

Central to this volume is our commitment to bridging the chasm between theoretical discourse and practical application, offering actionable strategies, evidence-based practices, and policy recommendations aimed at informing and inspiring educators, policymakers, researchers, and stakeholders vested in the future trajectory of education in India. By anchoring discussions within the overarching framework of NEP 2020, this volume not only elucidates extant challenges but also proffers concrete pathways for progress and transformation within teacher development initiatives nationwide.

The chapters enshrined within this volume epitomize the heterogeneous tapestry of teacher education, broaching pivotal topics such as conceptions of science pedagogy among pre-service educators, the ramifications of the COVID-19 pandemic on teacher training modalities, the importance of fostering scientific acumen among elementary school teachers, and the implementation of constructivist methodologies in mathematics instruction, among myriad others.

Furthermore, this volume transcends mere academic discourse; it functions as a pragmatic compendium, offering tangible insights and recommendations for fortifying teacher education programs, fostering inclusive learning milieus, and advocating for continuous professional growth. Whether one assumes the mantle of educator, policymaker, or researcher, this volume furnishes a treasure trove of resources designed to edify and embolden individuals invested in the evolution of education in India.

By synthesizing diverse perspectives, bridging theory with practice, and furnishing actionable insights, this volume endeavors to galvanize positive transformation within teacher development initiatives throughout India. I extend a warm invitation to readers to embark upon this odyssey of exploration and enlightenment, secure in the knowledge that this volume shall serve as a guiding beacon, empowering individuals to navigate the ever-evolving contours of teacher education with sagacity, resilience, and purpose.

As educators grapple with the complexities of preparing students for an increasingly interconnected and rapidly evolving world, the role of teacher education becomes ever more critical. The chapters presented in this volume offer practical strategies and evidence-based insights to empower educators in their quest to nurture the next generation of learners. From innovative pedagogical approaches to strategies for fostering inclusivity and diversity in the classroom, each chapter provides valuable guidance for educators striving to meet the diverse needs of their students.

Beyond its immediate relevance to the Indian context, this volume also contributes to the global discourse on teacher education and educational reform. Its insights into effective pedagogical practices, technological integration, and socio-emotional learning have implications for educators worldwide. By fostering cross-cultural exchange and collaboration, this volume advances the collective effort to enhance the quality and equity of education on a global scale.

I extend my deepest appreciation to all the contributors who have generously shared their expertise and insights, as well as to the editors and readers whose engagement and commitment to excellence drive the ongoing evolution of teacher education. I believe that this volume will spark dialogue, inspire innovation, and catalyse positive change in teacher education, ultimately contributing to the realization of a more equitable, inclusive, and impactful education system for all.

**Prof. Mohammad Shakeel**
Officiating Vice Chancellor
Jamia Millia Islamia

# Acknowledgements

It gives us immense pleasure to recall all the university officers, faculty members, and the funding agency who helped at all stages of Jamia International Conference on Education (JICE-2024), whose final product is in your hand in the form of this book.

We first and foremost thank Prof. Eqbal Hussain, Vice Chancellor, Jamia Millia Islamia for guiding us at all stages of the conference. Prof. Nazim Husain Jafri, Registrar, Jamia Millia Islamia has been very supportive during the conference preparation and organization.

We are indebted to Prof. H.C.S. Rathore, Chairperson, NRC, NCTE & former Vice Chancellor, Central University of South Bihar, and Prof. Dhananjay Joshi, Vice Chancellor, Delhi Teachers University for gracing the occasions of Inaugural and Valedictory sessions respectively as chief guest. We thank Prof. Jyotsna Pattnaik, California State University, Long Beach, USA, Prof. Theodoros Karakasidis, University of Thessaly, Greece, for delivering the keynote address during inaugural and valedictory functions; and Prof. Joey Martinez Dela Cruz, University of Abra, Philippines, for his plenary talk in the valedictory session of the conference.

The Dean, Faculty of Education, Prof. Sara Begum and Head, Department of Teacher Training and Non-formal Education, Prof. Jessy Abraham have extended all kinds of support throughout the conference planning and execution. Without their support, it could not be materialized in the grand way it went on.

We acknowledge and thank our superannuated faculty members Prof. Mohammad Akhtar Siddiqui, former Chairman, NCTE, for delivering the keynote address, Prof. Najma Amin, Prof. Shoeb Abdullah, Prof. Ahrar Hussain, and Prof. Ilyas Husain for chairing the technical sessions and guiding us whenever we approached them for their support and guidance. We also thank Prof. Mohd. Miyan, former Vice Chancellor, MANUU, and Prof. Talat Aziz, former Dean, Faculty of Education, JMI for their benign presence in the inaugural session and the moral support they provided throughout the preparation of the conference.

We acknowledge and thank the key members of the conference organizing team — Prof. Sara Begum, Prof. Jessy Abraham, Prof. Naheed Zahoor Prof. Kartar Singh, Prof. Kaushal Kishore, Prof. Savita Kaushal, Prof. Roohi Fatima, Dr. Dori Lal, Dr. Ajit Kumar Bohet, Dr. Sameer Babu M, Dr. Raisa Khan, Dr. Sajjad Ahmad, Dr. Andleeb, Dr. Sarita Kumari, Dr. Shadma Yasmeen, Dr. Aysha, Dr. Saman Zaki and Ms. Nazneen for their constant support and contributions towards the organization of JICE-2024.

Thanks are due to all faculty members from both departments, Department of Teacher Training and Non-formal Education (IASE) and Department of Educational Studies for their cooperation in reviewing papers, convening/ chairing/ co-chairing technical sessions and doing all the associated work during the entire process of JICE-2024.

I must thank the Indian Council of Social Science Research (ICSSR), the agency which funded the organization of the international conference JICE-2024. Without the financial support of ICSSR, it would not be possible to organize the conference on such a big scale.

It is important to mention that we decided to publish ISBN books instead of publishing papers in the form of proceedings with a vision to make the researchers' work wider dissemination. It is generally observed that proceedings are read by a fewer number of people, but books are more read as they reach in the form of course material for certain programmes and are useful for teachers as well as students. This book will be very useful for teachers and students of Education in the specified area of study. We thank and acknowledge the worthwhile and important piece of work contributed by researchers and faculty members for their presentation in the conference and allowing us to publish it in the form of a chapter in an edited book with ISBN. We thank them all and wish to have the same support, motivation, and encouragement in our future conferences.

We acknowledge the utmost efforts and untiring day and night work of our scholars—Mr. Md. Ashique Husain, Ms. Zahra Kazmi, Ms. Soumya Panigrahi, Ms. Ambrin Khanam, Ms. Aditi Tiwari, Ms. Sehar Nigar, Ms. Shahla Naz, Mr. Sajuddin Saifi, Mr. Haroon Salmani, Mr. Mohd. Noor Alam, Ms. Sania Noor, Mr. Dhananjay Kumar, Ms. Humaira Khatoon, Mr. Dheeraj Kumar, Ms. Maria Waseem, Ms. Samra Jamal, Ms. Shaista Tanweer, Mr. Mohammad Haider Raza, Mr. Nisar Ahmad, Ms. Khushnuda Bano, Dr. Noor Alam, and Mr. Taj Mohammad in timely completion of all necessary preparations of the conference and its publication work including this book. We wish them all great success in their future endeavours.

Special appreciation is due to Ms. Aditi Tiwari, research scholar, IASE for her sincere, dedicated, and rigorous efforts towards the content management and proofing of the manuscript.

We would like to extend our sincere thanks to all the contributors for their insightful work in the area. We would also like to convey our gratitude to those who have put great efforts and supported us during the publication of this book.

Editors

# Contents

# 1

# Introduction

Teacher Education, both pre-service and in-service, is integral to the implementation of NEP 2020 in India. It aligns with the policy's emphasis on holistic development and quality education. By ensuring that the teachers are equipped with updated pedagogical approaches and subject knowledge it supports NEP's vision of transformative education. Additionally, investing in teacher educators enhances the capacity to implement NEP reform effectively, fostering a conducive environment for innovative and continuous improvement in the education system.

In this edited volume, we bring together a diverse group of scholars, researchers, educators, and practitioners who have contributed their expertise and insights to elucidate the multifaceted dynamics of this rapidly evolving landscape.

In their chapter titled "Digital Competence among Pre-service Teachers," Soumya Priyadarsani Panigrahi and Jasim Ahmad emphasize the increasing importance of digital competence for pre-service teachers. Through a quantitative approach, the study examines pre-service teachers' perception of digital competence across five dimensions outlined in the European Commission's framework. Findings suggest that while information literacy and communication skills are relatively strong, digital content creation, problem-solving, and safety competencies lag. The study underscores the need to integrate digital competence training into teacher education curricula.

In response to the challenges posed by the COVID-19 pandemic, educational institutions worldwide have been compelled to innovate and adapt to new modes of teaching and assessment. The chapter, titled "Unprecedented Walk in the B.Ed. Term-end Examinations during COVID-19 Lockdown in India: A Case Study" authored by Muddam Yochitha Reddy, explores a notable case study of a higher education institution in India that successfully conducted term-end examinations for its B.Ed. program amidst the pandemic using a blended approach. The focus is on maintaining the quality of teacher education during unprecedented times, emphasizing the institution's resilience and adaptability. In the chapter "Scientific Temperament among Elementary School Teachers: Awareness and Application," Ambrin Khanam and Aerum Khan, the significance of scientific temper, emphasized by Pandit Nehru in 1946 and later enshrined in Constitution of India in 1976, remains paramount.

Fostering scientific thinking among citizens is pivotal in dispelling superstitions and societal biases like casteism. This chapter investigates the scientific temperament of elementary school teachers. Through a descriptive survey method involving 30 educators in South Delhi, the study uncovers varying levels of awareness and application. Notably, science teachers demonstrate stronger inclinations towards logical reasoning and the application of scientific principles compared to their non-science counterparts.

According to Tashnim Ferdaus and Roohi Fatima, in the chapter titled "Teachers Perception and Implementation of Constructivist Approach in Teaching Mathematics", the constructivist teaching approach in mathematics emphasizes active knowledge construction over rote memorization, aligning with NEP 2020 goals. This study investigates middle school math teachers' views and implementation of this approach. Findings reveal barriers such as lack of instructional materials. Recommendations include initiatives by the Ministry of Education to enhance its implementation.

In her chapter titled "Changing Contexts in Global and Indian Teachers", Shumaila Saif Siddiqui emphasizes the importance of educating future generations with global attitudes promoting gender equality, peace, and respect for all. With evolving human development, education in the 21st century demands broader subject-specific knowledge and skills from teachers. The chapter delves into the shifting landscape of teacher education in both Indian and global contexts to address these demands effectively.

In the next chapter titled "Teacher Education Institutions in Kashmir: Recent Developments", Bashir Ahmad Khan discusses the challenges faced by the teacher education system in Jammu and Kashmir. The lack of a unified monitoring system like the NCTE led to unchecked growth until 2015-16, particularly with the introduction of a one-year B.Ed. program. However, the declining quality of school education has diminished interest in teacher training programs. Using a Descriptive Survey Method, the study examines the status of teacher education institutions, revealing alarming deficiencies in basic facilities. Despite challenges, there is optimism for improvement with the implementation of national governing bodies post-article 370 revocation.

Priti Sangray, in her chapter titled "Need for Culturally Responsive and Relevant Teaching Today", highlights the intrinsic link between culture and education, as well as the importance of cultural diversity in India's educational policies. The National Curriculum Framework (NCF) 2005 and the Kothari Commission 1964–66 prioritize diversity, reflecting India's commitment to inclusivity. With the National Education Policy (NEP) 2020 aiming for universal access to quality education by 2030, Cultural Relevant Pedagogy and Culturally Responsive Teaching emerge as crucial theories. They advocate for understanding and respecting students' diverse cultural backgrounds to create inclusive learning environments. Despite India's multicultural emphasis, this chapter underscores the need for teachers to structure classrooms and teaching methods based on students' cultural experiences, supported by Culturally Sensitive Teaching strategies.

In "Current Trends in TPACK Research in Teacher Education: A Systematic Literature Review ", Kaushik Sarkar highlights the increasing importance of integrating Technological Pedagogical Content Knowledge (TPACK) into teacher education programs to meet the demands of modern classrooms. TPACK, introduced by Punya Mishra and Matthew J. Koehler in 2006, emphasizes the intricate interplay between technology, pedagogy, and content. The systematic literature review, comprising 111 peer-reviewed journal articles, reveals emerging trends in TPACK research, including its implementation in classrooms, strategies for developing teacher TPACK, and the relationship between TPACK and other components.

In the chapter titled "Conceptions of Pre-service Teachers regarding Science Teaching and Learning", authored by Kothai Nayagi N, the focus lies on understanding the perspectives of novice educators regarding science education, particularly in line with the inquiry-based approach endorsed by the National Education Policy (NEP) 2020. Through qualitative analysis of interviews with first-year secondary pre-service teachers, the study uncovers their inclination towards teacher-centric approaches in science education. The chapter delves into the factors influencing these conceptions and discusses implications for teacher education programs.

Ashu Threja Malhotra, in her chapter titled "Developing Reflective Practitioners in Pre-Service Teachers", illustrates how pre-service mathematics teachers engage with the Knowledge Quartet framework during their school experience program, fostering reflective practice. Through facilitated reflection on foundational knowledge, transformation, connectedness, and contingency in mathematics classrooms, pre-service teachers analyse dilemmas and enhance their teaching skills. Data analysis from class observations and reflection sessions demonstrate how the Knowledge Quartet equips pre-service teachers to reflect on and improve their mathematical teaching practices.

Reena Kumari addresses the challenges teachers face in managing professional and personal responsibilities amidst technological, social, and economic changes in her chapter titled "Work Life Balance Strategies in Teacher Education". She emphasizes the importance of employee well-being for student success and suggests incorporating work-life balance strategies into pre-service teacher education. These strategies, including self-care, physical health promotion, social connection, mindfulness, and time management, aim to equip teachers with the resilience needed to navigate the demands of both domains effectively.

Vandana Laishram's chapter titled "Self-efficacy of Higher Secondary School Teachers: Study of Chandel and Senapati Districts of Manipur", examines the self-efficacy levels of teachers in the region using the Teachers' Self-Efficacy Scale (TSES-SVSS). The study, conducted in eight secondary schools with 80 teachers, reveals a moderate overall level of self-efficacy. Gender, marital status, and teaching experience show no significant impact on self-efficacy, but there is a notable difference based on teaching training.

In his chapter titled "Popularising Science and Fighting Superstition: Exploring Student Mindset by Using Writeup and Diagram Approach", Pradeep Gusain discusses the importance of student homework in understanding their mindset. The research methodology involves a mixed approach, combining qualitative and quantitative methods. Assignments were given to 58 IXth-grade students, seeking their ideas on popularizing science and combating superstition. Responses, obtained in both written and diagrammatic forms, were analysed quantitatively and qualitatively. The study yields valuable insights into students' perspectives on science popularization and superstition reduction, shedding light on their understanding of the Indian knowledge system and concerns regarding superstitions.

Mridula Bhardwaj and Raisa Khan underscore the importance of socio-emotional learning (SEL) in contemporary times in their chapter titled "Social and Emotional Learning through Work Education in D.El.Ed. Curriculum". They highlight the significance of SEL in teacher education, emphasizing its role in fostering academic success and social well-being. The paper analyses the Work Education curriculum in Delhi District Institutes of Education and Training (DIETs), examining its alignment with SEL principles and emphasizing the cultivation of skills like empathy and collaboration to shape socially responsible citizens.

In her chapter titled "How do Teachers Perceive their School Heads", Shadma Absar discusses the significance of school leadership in India's educational landscape. With initiatives like the Right to Education Act and Samagra Shiksha focusing on quality interventions, effective school governance becomes crucial. The study explores teachers' perceptions of their school heads' leadership functions and their influence on teachers' work behaviour. Through quantitative analysis of data from 240 teachers using SPSS, the study reveals the impact of school heads on creating a positive school culture.

Mohd ZiaUl Haq Rafaqi in "Transformative Impact of Classroom Observations on Teacher Development", attempts to explore the significant role of classroom observations in enhancing teacher development. Through a survey-based approach, the study aims to empirically demonstrate how observations catalyse improvements in instructional strategies, classroom management, and student engagement. By gathering self-reported data from teachers, the survey delves into their perceptions of observed feedback and the influence on their teaching practices. Additionally, contextual factors such as school culture and administrative support will be examined to understand their impact on teachers' experiences. This qualitative approach aims to provide rich insights into teachers' professional growth, contributing to effective professional development strategies.

Amanpreet Kaur delves into the imperative of Continuous Professional Development (CPD) for educators in alignment with the National Education Policy (NEP) 2020 in her chapter titled "Continuous Professional Development for Teachers amidst the NEP 2020 Landscape". The NEP underscores the centrality of teachers in the education process and emphasizes their CPD. This paper explores the essence of CPD in NEP 2020, highlighting its expected changes and requirements for teachers at various levels. It scrutinizes how CPD differs from INSET in previous education policies, aiming to assess whether NEP 2020 enables its effective implementation in the education system.

In their chapter titled "Perception of Teacher Educators towards Implementing ITEP", Mohammad Kaif Farooqui and Sajid Jamal delve into the pivotal role of teacher educators in shaping prospective teachers' competencies and attitudes. With the National Education Policy (NEP) 2020 emphasizing the enhancement of teacher education quality, a specialized Integrated Teacher Education Programme (ITEP) has been proposed. This program aims to provide a holistic approach to teacher training, serving as the minimum qualification for aspiring school teachers. However, successful implementation of ITEP presents challenges, necessitating effective strategic planning and the commitment of teacher educators. This study explores the perspectives of 100 teacher educators on implementing ITEP, revealing intriguing findings with implications for educational stakeholders.

In "Teachers' Perception on Impact of Flipped Teaching on Students' Achievements", Ashoshika Bhadoria and Aerum Khan explore the effectiveness of flipped teaching from the teacher's perspective. Traditional teaching methods often foster compliance rather than innovation among students, while modern methods, such as the flipped classroom, prioritize learner-centered approaches. This study focuses on the impact of flipped teaching on student achievement, surveying Class 12 students from selected Delhi Government Schools. Interviews with teachers revealed that flipped teaching was highly effective, fostering self-study habits among students and aiding in preparation for college entrance exams. The findings suggest that modern methods like flipped teaching lead to better understanding and time-saving benefits compared to traditional methods.

Mohd Haroon Salmani and Dori Lal in their chapter "Awareness of TPACK Framework among Pre-service Teachers" suggests that in the digital age, especially post-COVID-19, teacher education programs are evolving to prioritize technology and future readiness, aligning with the emphasis on digital education in NEP 2020. This study investigates pre-service teachers' awareness of the Technological Pedagogical Content Knowledge (TPACK) framework, which integrates technological, pedagogical, and content knowledge for effective technology integration in teaching. Employing a mixed methods approach, the research assesses pre-service teachers' levels of awareness through surveys and interviews. The findings aim to inform teacher training programs and curriculum development, contributing to a more technologically adept and pedagogically skilled teaching workforce.

In the dynamic field of education, continuous professional development (CPD) for teachers is crucial for adapting to pedagogical advancements. Blending traditional face-to-face methods with online elements addresses the diverse needs of educators. Aligned with the New Education Policy 2020, this chapter, titled "Blended Approaches in Teachers' Continuing Professional Development" by Kiran Joshi, identifies NEP 2020's focus on teachers' professional development and examines the effectiveness of blended learning approaches in CPD. It explores various models of blended learning, assesses their benefits for teachers' CPD, identifies implementation barriers, discusses current research trends, and emphasizes the role of technology in supporting teachers' ongoing growth.

In the realm of Indian teacher education, diverse pathways and modalities have shaped its trajectory. Masooda Haseeb's chapter titled "Concerns regarding Teacher Education in Indian Discourse from B.Ed. to ITEP" delves into the evolving landscape, particularly with the implementation of ITEP under NEP 2020. The shift from one-year B.Ed. to two-year programs in 2015, compounded by post-COVID-19 challenges, presents uncharted territory. This thematic exploration addresses concerns such as meeting 21st-century demands, fostering school-community coherence, and aligning with NEP 2020's holistic education vision. It advocates for transforming teachers into learning facilitators, emphasizing professional development and peer support to meet modern learning needs.

In her chapter titled "Science Educators' Perspectives and Practices on Integrating Art into Science Teaching", Shaista Tanveer explores the growing significance of incorporating art into STEM education, known as STEAM. Recognizing the interplay between artistic expression and scientific inquiry, this study delves into the multifaceted benefits of art integration in science teaching. It emphasizes the utilization of diverse art forms, such as visual arts, music, and literature, to enrich learning experiences and deepen scientific comprehension. Aligned with the National Education Policy 2020's vision of multidisciplinary education, the integration of arts into STEM fosters creativity, critical thinking, and holistic learning in students.

Priyanka Singh delves into the growing recognition of teachers' creative problem-solving abilities in education in her chapter titled "Elevating Teachers' Creative Problem-Solving Skills: Capacity-Building Strategies".

Acknowledging the significance of capacity building and problem-solving skills in pedagogy, particularly in light of the National Education Policy 2020's emphasis on holistic education, the paper explores how capacity-building techniques can enhance educators' problem-solving abilities. Through a mixed-methods approach, the study investigates various professional development initiatives aimed at fostering creative problem-solving skills among teachers. By integrating capacity building with a focus on creative problem-solving, educators can better navigate the complexities of modern education with resilience and adaptability.

Shama Norien Major, Ayushi Sinha, and Anwesha Rai explore the implications of the National Education Policy 2020 on alternative education systems in their chapter titled "Reflections on Alternate Education in Contemporary Context: A Study of Digantar Institute, Jaipur". The paper presents a case study of Digantar, an educational institution in Rajasthan, India, which offers alternative education. Data was collected during a field visit as part of the practicum for the Bachelors of Elementary Education program. Through qualitative analysis of observations and interviews with stakeholders, including teachers, administrators, and community members, the study examines various aspects such as curriculum, pedagogical approaches, and community-school relationships considering NEP 2020's emphasis on educational reform.

In their chapter titled "NCERT's Instructional Material: Role in School and Teacher Education", by Pooja Jain and Meera explore the significance of NCERT's role in educational research, curriculum revision, and the development of instructional materials for school and teacher education. The study investigates the various types of instructional materials produced by NCERT for different educational stages and subjects over a five-year period from 2017 to 2022. This research, conducted as part of a Ph.D. study, aims to evaluate NCERT's academic contributions towards enhancing the quality of school and teacher education through the development of teaching materials.

# 2

# Digital Competence among Pre-service Teachers

Soumya Priyadarsani Panigrahi
Jasim Ahmad

## Introduction

We have access to information from all over the world by connecting to the Internet, and all we need to utilise it to its best potential are digital skills. A collection of skills that are necessary for humans to thrive in the digital age are collectively referred to as "digital competence". As technology continues to play an increasingly essential part in both our personal and professional lives, digital competence is becoming more and more crucial in today's society. It refers to the capacity to utilise technology successfully and efficiently in a variety of settings and includes a broad range of abilities. In the year 2006, the European Parliament and the Council mentioned digital competence as a competence for lifelong learning. It explained that while employing new media and ICT to carry out tasks, create and share content, collaborate, communicate, manage information, solve problems, and build knowledge appropriately, autonomously, creatively, critically, effectively, efficiently, ethically, flexibly, and reflectively for participation, socialising, work, learning, leisure and conventions, this knowledge and skills are collectively referred to as digital competence (Ferrari, 2013).

The areas of digital competence are the following:

The above mentioned five areas of digital competence are given by the European Commission. The five competencies are information and data literacy (DC1), communication and collaboration (DC2), digital content creation (DC3), safety (DC4) and problem-solving (DC5). Figure 1 depicts the five areas and the keywords related to these competencies.

## The Study

### *Problem Statement*

Teacher plays a central role in the education system. Teacher education is a program that aims to equip future teachers with the required set of skills, attitudes, and knowledge. Teacher education has a direct impact not only on

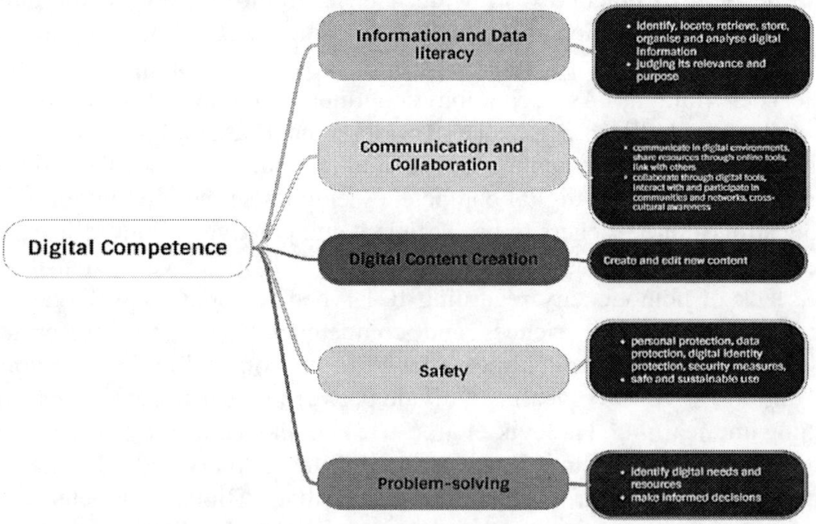


**Figure 1:** Areas of Digital Competence as recommended by the European Commission

the teaching-learning process as well as on the learners (Panigrahi & Naaz, 2021). Therefore, teacher education must be aligned with the learner's needs. Youth are frequently referred to as digital natives. Any child will be able to navigate any device given to him without any instruction. We live in a digital culture where sharing, uploading, and streaming are all possible anytime, anywhere. Even if children are not required to be taught how to navigate the Internet, if we do not teach them how to stay safe online, they are at risk. To do that pre-service teachers must be trained for the same.

This study focuses on two research questions:

1. What is the perception of the pre-service teachers on their digital competencies?
2. Do pre-service teacher's perceptions of digital competencies vary according to gender?
3. Do pre-service teacher's perceptions of digital competencies vary according to their level of education?

## *Related Research: Digital Competency of Pre-service Teachers*

Throughout the years teacher education in India has experienced various changes to prepare the teachers for educating the future generation. Linking teacher education with school education so that our teachers are well equipped to educate the next generation. Following NCFTE-2009, there is a widespread belief that teacher education must reflect what is going on in the field of practice worldwide. Hence, to close a few of the gaps between teacher education and actual school settings, ICT (information and communication technology) must be prominently stressed in the curriculum for teacher training. As technology continues to play an increasingly essential part in both our personal and professional lives, digital competence has developed into more and more crucial in the modern world. The studies of pre-service teachers' digital competency emphasise the vital importance of educating future teachers to be proficient and creative in their utilization of technology in the classroom. Chen et al., (2010) discovered that there was a lack of homogeneity regarding ICT when researchers in Singapore examined the ICT experiences and competencies of 1554 pre-service teachers. The study dispelled the widespread misconception that everyone is a "digital native" by revealing a divide between personal use and that for teaching and learning. Hatlevik et al. (2015) conducted a study "Predictors of Digital Competence in 7th Grade: A Multilevel Analysis — Journal of Computer Assisted Learning" which reveals that, "Digital competence is frequently ignored or relegated to more superficial and utilitarian activities, including learning to use a computer or doing Internet searches in the teacher preparation program." Elstad & Christophersen (2017) in a research on the student teachers' perceptions of digital competence: influencing the improvement of pre-service teachers' instructional self-efficacy inside technology-integrated classrooms infer that, it has been received a lot of criticism of current teacher-training programmes, leading some to claim that "the development of professional digital abilities is routinely insufficiently implemented in teacher training". Some have questioned the ability of those who conduct such courses to create campus-based education in topic didactics and pedagogy in a way that fosters professional digital abilities in future teachers. Howard et al. (2019) conducted a study titled "Seeing the Wood for the Trees: Insights into the Complexity of Developing Pre-service Teachers' Digital Competencies for Future Teaching". In this paper, they mentioned that, in order to be successful in the classroom, pre-service teachers must develop their digital competencies. Although there are many different tactics involved in this complex process, it is unclear how they should be put into practice. To improve comprehension of ways to create digital competency in teacher training, methods that can address this complexity are required. Maher (2020) in his study pre-service teachers' digital competencies to support school students' digital literacies, explored how the pre-service teachers' digital competencies affect the digital literacy of their students and found that pre-service teachers were further likely to integrate technology in their courses to increase student engagement when they had higher levels of digital competence. Betaubun (2021) carried out a Survey of Pre-service Teachers ICT's Competencies in Papua. The result shows that the insufficient knowledge of pre-service teachers in fostering a sense of responsibility in utilising ICT as a communication medium and activities involving ICT use indicates the low competence of native students in handling information in the digital environment.

Yang & Alicia's (2022) study "Exploring factors influencing pre-service and in-service teachers' perception of digital competencies in the Chinese region of Anhui" involved 250 pre-service teachers and 248 in-service teachers. The main findings are: (1) participants have good consciousness and attitudes towards using ICT in daily work, but their educational practice is weak; (2) in-service teachers have a digital competence level generally higher than pre-service teachers', which might be their professional practice promote them to reflect on perceptions and attitudes regarding technological education; (3) for in-service teachers, there are significant differences between their digital competence level and age, years of teaching experience, educational background; (4) current ICT courses have no influencing on in-service teachers' digital competence level, implying that current ICT training system may have problems. The study provides insights to improve pre-service teachers' digital competence education in universities and develop well-designed in-service teachers' ICT training courses. Rani & Gandhi (2022) conducted a study to assess the status of Indian teachers' digital competency and discovered there is a lack of knowledge. This paper stresses upon the critical need to improve teachers' digital skills, especially those working in education, so they can perform efficiently and effectively in future classrooms and help young brains develop the capacity to leverage a sustainable future. It draws focus to the many digital competency frameworks which can be included in teacher training programmes.

## *Methodology*

This study used a survey method to collect and analyse data quantitatively. As suggested by Cohen et al. (2002), a survey method is ideal where the researcher wants to explain the characteristics of current situations, establish benchmarks against which current conditions can be compared, or determine the connections between specific events. It offers information that is inferential, descriptive, and explicative.

## *Participant*

The questionnaire was circulated through Google Forms in different Teacher Education Institutes of Delhi-NCR. Out of 74 responses, 14 responses were discarded due to incomplete or repetition of responses. Hence, this study involves 62 pre-service teachers from different universities.

**Table 1:** Sample Distribution

| *Gender* | | *Education* | |
|---|---|---|---|
| *Female* | *Male* | *Bachelors* | *Masters* |
| 42 (67.24%) | 20 (32.26%) | 38 (61.29%) | 24 (38.71%) |

### *Instruments Used*

For assessing the pre-service teacher's digital competence, a questionnaire was adopted from the questionnaire of Çebi & Reisoglu (2020). It has its foundation in the Digcomp framework of the European Commission. The questionnaire has a total of 31 items. "Information and data literacy," "Communication and collaboration," "Digital content production," "Safety," and "Problem-solving" are the five distinct dimensions that comprise digital competence and will further refer as DC1, DC2, DC3, DC4 and DC5 in this study. This constitutes a five-point Likert questionnaire, with the options being 1 for "strongly disagree" and 5 for "strongly agree".

### *Data Analysis*

In the analysis, it was determined whether each sub-group had a normal distribution. For each item, the pre-service teachers' attendance status's mean and standard deviation were computed. Also, the independent t-test was used to see whether there were any differences in the pre-service teacher's perceptions based on their gender and their level of education.

## Results and Findings

**Table 2:** Descriptive Analysis of Pre-service Teachers' Digital Competence

| *Areas of Digital Competence* | *Mean* | *Std. Deviation* |
|---|---|---|
| DC1 | 3 | 2.83 |
| DC2 | 3 | 2.83 |
| DC3 | 2 | 1.4 |
| DC4 | 2 | 1.4 |
| DC5 | 1.5 | .71 |

*Notes: DC1* (Information & Data Literacy), *DC2* (Communication & Collaboration), *DC3* (Digital Content Creation), *DC4* (Safety) and *DC5* (Problem-solving)

The above table summarises all the responses from the survey questions on digital competence for pre-service teachers pertaining to the five dimensions. The responses by the pre-service teachers show that the last three dimensions, those are, DC3, DC4 and DC5 have a relatively lower competence than the first two dimensions, that is, DC1 and DC2.

Following the descriptive analysis, an independent t-test was performed, initially by gender followed by level of education, to find any potentially significant differences. The results of both the t-test are shown in Table 3 and Table 4 respectively.

### *Digital Competence Based on Gender*

**Table 3:** Descriptive Analysis of Pre-service Teachers' Digital Competence Based on Gender

| | *FEMALES* | | *MALES* | | | |
|---|---|---|---|---|---|---|
| | *Mean* | *Std. Deviation* | *Mean* | *Std. Deviation* | *t-value* | *p-value* |
| **DC1** | 3.83 | 0.17 | 4.26 | 0.15 | 4.03 | .002395 |
| **DC2** | 3.92 | 0.17 | 4.13 | 0.20 | 2.7 | .026992 |
| **DC3** | 3.32 | 1.15 | 3.40 | 0.88 | 0.18 | .864698 |
| **DC4** | 3.46 | 4.46 | 3.58 | 5.12 | 0.38 | .707983 |
| **DC5** | 2.29 | 3.14 | 1.49 | 1.84 | -0.16 | .878103 |

As apparent in Table 3, there is a significant difference in the first two dimensions however, there is no significant difference in the last three dimensions statistically. This implies that both female and male teachers have almost similar competence in the last three dimensions, whereas female teachers have a better competence level than male teachers in the first two dimensions.

### *Digital Competence Based on Education*

**Table 4:** Descriptive Analysis of Pre-service Teachers' Digital Competence Based on Education

| | *BACHELORS* | | *MASTERS* | | | |
|---|---|---|---|---|---|---|
| | *Mean* | *Std. Deviation* | *Mean* | *Std. Deviation* | *t-value* | *p-value* |
| **DC1** | 3 | 2.83 | 3 | 2.83 | -3.88 | .00304 |
| **DC2** | 2 | 1.4 | 3 | 2.83 | -2.99 | .017211 |
| **DC3** | 2 | 1.4 | 2.5 | 2.12 | -0.72 | .500734 |
| **DC4** | 2 | 1.4 | 3 | 2.83 | -0.75 | .459543 |
| **DC5** | 1.5 | .71 | 1 | 0 | 0.33 | .746445 |

As noted in Table 4, there is a significant difference in the first two dimensions however, there is no significant difference in the last three dimensions statistically. This implies that both bachelor and master teachers have almost similar competence in the last three dimensions, whereas teachers having master degrees have a better competence level than the teachers having bachelor degrees in the first two dimensions.

## Discussions

The focus of this study was to learn the pre-service teacher's perspectives regarding their digital competence alongside investigating whether or not these perspectives differ depending on the participant's gender. The result shows that pre-service teachers possess a higher degree of competence with regard to communication and collaboration and information and data literacy. The findings coincide with those of Alnasib (2023) and Çebi & Reisoglu (2020). Whereas they have a relatively lower competence in problem-solving, safety and digital content creation dimensions. The result regarding digital content creation is aligned with Alnasib (2023) and Çebi & Reisoglu (2020) and in contrast to the result found by Pozas & Letzel (2021) who discovered that pre-service teachers show an upbeat attitude towards producing and presenting digital content. The outcome of the dimension safety is opposite to what Çebi & Reisoglu (2020) found in their study. The result of problem solving is supported by the result found by Alnasib (2023), Pozas & Letzel (2021) and Çebi & Reisoglu (2020).

The study also shows that there is a significant difference in the digital competence of pre-service teachers in regard to their gender for the first two dimensions whereas there is no significant difference for the last three dimensions. This result was contrasted for the first two dimensions and was in line for the last three dimensions with the studies by Galindo-Domínguez & Bezanilla (2021), Yang & Alicia (2022), Pozas & Letzel (2021) and Çebi & Reisoglu (2020). The studies by these researchers found no significant difference in any of the five dimensions. The findings show that there is a significant difference in the digital competence of pre-service teachers regarding their level of education for the first two dimensions whereas there is no significant difference for the last three dimensions. This result was contrasted for the first two dimensions and was in line for the last three dimensions with the studies by Galindo-Domínguez & Bezanilla (2021) who found no significant difference in any of the five dimensions regarding the level of education of the pre-service teachers.

## Conclusion

After the COVID-19 pandemic, there has been a surge in the adoption of digital technology, resulting in an increase in every individual's digital competence. However, the digital competence of teachers differs from that of other professionals because they are not only expected to instruct students as well as to create digital content to enhance the teaching-learning process. Teachers' digital competency has an undeniable impact on students' digital literacy. For this, teachers need to be highly competent in problem-solving, safety and digital content creation. The school's in-service training is insufficient for developing these competencies. Our pre-service teachers must be trained to develop these competencies (Çebi & Reisoglu, 2020 and Røkenes & Krumsvik, 2016). The teacher education must include training in digital competence in the curriculum. Despite the digital divide, technology is nowadays embedded in every area of the daily life of people including education. Therefore, there is a need to ensure that our pre-service teachers are well equipped with the competence to support the digital competence of young India.

## References

Alnasib, B.N.M. (2023). Digital Competencies: Are Pre-Service Teachers Qualified for Digital Education? *International Journal of Education in Mathematics, Science and Technology*, 11(1), 96–114. https://doi.org/10.46328/ijemst.2842

Betaubun, M. (2021). A Survey of Pre-Service Teachers ICT's Competencies in Papua. *AL-ISHLAH: Journal Pendidikan*, 13(2), 813–820. https://doi.org/10.35445/alishlah.v13i2.651

Çebi, A., & Reisoglu, I. (2020). Digital competence: A study from the perspective of pre-service teachers in Turkey. *Journal of New Approaches in Educational Research*, 9(2), 294–308. https://doi.org/10.7821/naer.2020.7.583

Chen, W., Lim, C., & Tan, A. (2010). Pre-service teachers' ICT experiences and competencies: New generation of teachers in digital age. *Proceedings of the 18th International Conference on Computers in Education: Enhancing and Sustaining New Knowledge Through the Use of Digital Technology in Education, ICCE 2010*, 631–638.

Galindo-Domínguez, H., & Bezanilla, M.J. (2021). Digital competence in the training of pre-service teachers: Perceptions of students in the degrees of early childhood education and primary education. *Journal of Digital Learning in Teacher Education, 37*(4), 262–278. https://doi.org/10.1080/21532974.2021.1934757

Elstad, E., & Christophersen, K.A. (2017). Perceptions of digital competency among student teachers: Contributing to the development of student teachers' instructional self-efficacy in technology-rich classrooms. *Education Sciences*, *7*(1). https://doi.org/10.3390/educsci7010027

Ferrari, A. (2013). Digital Competence in Practice: An Analysis of Frameworks. *Joint Research Centre of the European Commission.*, 91. https://doi.org/10.2791/82116

Hatlevik, O.E., Ottestad, G., & Throndsen, I. (2015). Predictors of digital competence in 7th grade: A multilevel analysis. *Journal of Computer Assisted Learning*, 31(3), 220–231. https://doi.org/10.1111/jcal.12065

Howard, S., Tondeur, J., Ma, J., & Yang, J. (2019). Seeing the wood for the trees: Insights into the complexity of developing pre-service teachers' digital competencies for future teaching. *ASCILITE 2019—Conference Proceedings—36th International Conference of Innovation, Practice and Research in the Use of Educational Technologies in*

*Tertiary Education: Personalised Learning. Diverse Goals. One Heart.*, 441–446. https://doi.org/10.14742/apubs.2019.309

Maher, D. (2020). *Pre-service teachers' digital competencies to support school students' digital literacies.*

Pozas, M., & Letzel, V. (2021). "Do You Think You Have What It Takes?" — Exploring Predictors of Pre-Service Teachers' Prospective ICT Use. *Technology, Knowledge and Learning, 0123456789*. https://doi.org/10.1007/s10758-021-09551-0

Rani, G., & Gandhi, A. (2022). Digital Competence of Teachers: An Urgency For Future Classroom 1Geeta. *International Journal of Multidisciplianary Educational Research, 816*(6), 47–51.

Røkenes, F.M., & Krumsvik, R.J. (2016). Prepared to teach ESL with ICT? A study of digital competence in Norwegian teacher education. *Computers and Education, 97*, 1–20. https://doi.org/10.1016/j.compedu.2016.02.014

Yang, L., & Alicia, F.M. (2022). Exploring factors influencing pre-service and in-service teachers´ perception of digital competencies in the Chinese region of Anhui. *Education and Information Technologies*, 12469–12494. https://doi.org/10.1007/s10639-022-11085-6

# 3

# Unprecedented Walk in the B.Ed. Term-end Examinations during COVID-19 Lockdown in India
## *A Case Study*

Muddam Yochitha Reddy

## Background

Prevalence of coronavirus disease 2019, simply termed COVID-19 pandemic, led to suspension of traditional educational systems in various parts of the world and forced them to adopt different online methods which were inevitable to keep continuity of education across all academia. However, the difficulties involved in sustaining education by adopting online mode has paved the way for blended mode approach to teaching-learning and evaluation. The blended mode is also called hybrid mode which combines online, offline, and face-to-face modes in education.

*COVID-19 lockdowns* did not lead to a cessation of learning, teaching, and assessment; instead, online contingency plans were designed to continue teaching and assessment via a digital interface so that the students can progress with their studies (Rapanta et al., 2020). The emergency response from educational institutions during crises (e.g. pandemics or conflicts) to shift teaching and assessments online is known as Emergency Remote Education (ERE) (Shin and Hickey, 2020).

## Adaptations in Teaching-learning, Examinations and Assessment

Technological advancements have contributed significantly to the changes in teaching-learning, examinations and assessment resulting in various trends which have become more prominent during COVID-19 pandemic situation. The ICT trends in education during the past few decades have shaped the schools and universities to implement the latest technologies in education to improve the teaching-learning, examination, and assessment processes.

An examination is a necessary evil for educational assessment/evaluation. The assessment, however, is done based on different types of examinations such as closed, restricted, and open exams and the specific requirements for them are different. Different types of exams require preparation of different types of questions by the examiners of the university which again require different modes of administering them on the examinees. Each type of exam thus has different considerations and preparation, in addition to knowing the course material. This calls for knowledge of different ways of conducting the examinations which require varying levels/degrees of participation of the examinees and the examiners through diverse modes from different locations at any given time of conducting or organising the examinations. This includes both on campus (or in-person) exams as well as alternative and online exams, or by combining them in diverse ways using different mediating technologies. The COVID-19 pandemic has led to a number of activities previously undertaken on campus becoming online activities, both on and off the campus. These combinations require the examinees and the examiners to attend either in-person on campus or at a study centre, or at any other place through online or virtual participation in the exams, or through blending of the in-person and virtual attendance or participation that meet all the requirements of ensuring a fool-proof conduct of the examination, as can be understood, and appreciated by both the examinees and the examiners.

Different institutions can conduct these examinations in an open and flexible manner in normal conditions and depending upon their relevance and suitability to different situations. Much has been talked about the examination reforms in India for long. Most popular among these talks has been the Open Book Examination. OBE could have been considered as a part of Blended Mode Examination (BME) in the educational system during testing times like COVID-19 lockdown in the country when all teachers and students had been confined to home only. Unfortunately, the country could not gear up to such transformation at national or state level or across all the higher education institutions.

In such context, the initiative of Manav Rachana University to conduct B.Ed. final term-end examinations for its students of 2018-2020 batch was indeed the most welcome step in the country, while all other higher education institutions could not take up on such line. Instead of conducting open book examination in physical mode in a closed classroom of educational institution, conducting the examination by allowing the students to write their examinations while sitting right in their comfortable home environment.

### Blended Learning — An Accepted New Normal

Blended learning is a term applied to the practice of providing instruction and learning experiences through some combination of both face-to-face and technology-mediated learning. During the technology-mediated components of these learning experiences, students are not required to be physically together in one place but may be connected digitally through online communities. For example, one blended learning course could involve students attending a class taught by a teacher in a traditional classroom setting while also completing online components of the course independently, outside of the classroom, on an online learning platform, or vice-versa.

### *Blended Mode Examination (BME) — Yet to become an accepted new normal*

Blended mode can be applied not only to the learning but also to the conduct of examinations, in which case it can be called Blended Mode Examination (BME) and if it is individualised and widely distributed to cater to the individual needs it can be called Distributed Blended Mode Examination (DBME). For example, the students or the examinees can be allowed to take the question paper offline and write the examination online from home, or they can take the question paper online and write the examination offline in individualised exam setting either proctored or un-proctored setting.

### *Manav Rachana University Students—A Case Study*

In conformity with the guidelines of NCTE, different types of programmes are offered by diverse types of teacher training/education institutions at different levels which include Institutes/Departments/Schools of Education in universities. Bachelor of education programme leading to Bachelor of Education (B.Ed.) degree and Four-year Integrated programme leading to B.A.B. Ed/B.Sc.B. Ed (Integrated) degree are the two teacher education programmes offered by Manav Rachana University.

#### *Manav Rachana University's Experience — Pioneering Efforts in Conducting Blended Mode Examinations (BME)*

Manav Rachana University (MRU) is a leading State Private University (established by Haryana State Legislature Act No. 26 of 2014 and under section 2(f) of UGC Act 1956), offering globally relevant education (https://manavrachna.edu.in/university/about/). It is also one of the rare Universities offering both B.Ed. two-year programme and Integrated Teacher Education Programme (ITEP) called Integrated B.Ed. programme.

Manav Rachana University deserves to be counted as one among such institutions particularly in terms of its initiative in conducting final semester examination through Blended Mode for students of B.Ed. Programme (2018-2020 Batch) during COVID-19 pandemic. In such an endeavour, the teachers/faculty concerned, the institutional management including the Dean, the Head of the Department, the Programme Coordinator, and the students had geared up to the pandemic situation and achieved their collective objective of successfully conducting/completing both theory and practical examinations through blended mode. The blended mode model of examination followed or conducted by MRU during the COVID-19 pandemic period for the final semester examination can be called "Distributed Blended Mode Examination" which is described below.

***Distributed Blended Mode Examination (DBME)***: In this model, the students who were already confined to their homes by the COVID-19 pandemic have been facilitated to participate in their theory and practical examinations right from their homes. The students of B.Ed. Programme (2018-2020 Batch) were somehow most fortunate because they had already completed their regular classes and were just waiting to give their examination very shortly through face-to-face mode of examination. That was the time when they were almost expecting their examination schedule to be announced by the university (MRU). It is at that time the Government of India called for a complete lockdown for the next 21 days beginning at midnight on 24 March 2020 and extended periodically up to 31st May, 2020. It is during this long period of lockdown that the Manav Rachana University, conceived and effectively executed the final semester examination for the students through blended mode. It was truly a boon in disguise for the students to have the experience of participating in and successfully completing their final semester through Blended Mode Examination (BME) comfortably sitting in their respective home environment. Hence, the model can be fittingly named as "Distributed Blended Mode Examination (DBME)". This unprecedented endeavour is now being told here as a case study highlights the significance of the paper.

## The Study

### *Review of Related Literature*

Very few related studies could be found, which are as follows.

Hollister and Berenson (2009) highlighted the issues of students' integrity and student performance when online exams are administered in a proctored environment (i.e., in class) versus an un-proctored environment (i.e., offsite). The study reveals that the group taking online exams in the un-proctored environment has significantly more variation in their performance results. In examining potential causes of the greater variation, analyses were performed to assess whether an increased level of possible cheating behaviour could be observed from performance results for students in the un-proctored section. No evidence of cheating behaviour was found. The study throws light on the integrity displayed by students while they participated in the un-proctored examination.

Ardid et al. (2015) conducted a study on use of online exams as part of the evaluation process in the context of blended assessment. In this study, the students' performance under different conditions of application of the blended assessment has been analysed. The online exams have been used in three different situations: in an evaluation-proctored exam, in an evaluation-un-proctored exam and as a training-homework task. The analysis shows that the students' online mark clearly depends on the way the online exam was performed. It has also been proved that the weight of the online exams in the final mark does not affect the results of the online exams, and that the results obtained in the un-proctored environment present a bias towards higher ratings, as well as a greater dispersion of results regarding the case of proctored environment.

Zagouras et al. (2022) attempted to compare the teacher trainees' performance in face-to-face (traditional) teacher training with teacher training through a blended learning approach/model. The findings reveal that the learning outcomes of the blended learning application in this teacher training initiative, overstep those of the "traditional" model in a small scale and with some slight differentiations among teacher specialties.

Ranjan (2020), in an experimental study spread over two years, attempted to compare the effectiveness of the blended learning mode and the online learning modes (including their specific teaching-learning strategies) for a B.Ed. curriculum. The participants were the students of a predominantly face-to-face mode of a B.Ed. course. The researcher found that the average achievement scores of the blended learning mode were higher than the online learning mode. It appears that the interaction of the instructor and the learners was a critical factor for the better performance of blended learning.

Elsalem et al. (2020), in their cross-sectional study, evaluated the students' experience of remote E-exams during the COVID-19 pandemic among medical sciences students in Jordan. A survey of 29 questions was prepared on Google forms and distributed among students at Faculties of Medical Sciences (Medicine, Dentistry, Pharmacy, Nursing and Applied Medical Sciences) at Jordan University of Science and Technology. The questions included students' demographics, stress experience, and factors contributing to stress as well as behavioural changes related to remote E-exams. Among 1019 respondents, 32% reported more stress with remote E-exams. This was associated with academic major and gender. Among students with more stress during remote E-exams, the exam duration, mode of questions, navigation, and technical problems (exam platform and Internet connectivity) appeared as the main factors related to stress in 78%, 76% and >60%, respectively. Other factors include concern regarding the teaching methods, exam environment and students' dishonesty. Remote E-exams had negative impact on students' dietary habits (increase in consumption of caffeine and high energy drinks, high sugar food, fast food), sleep (reduction in sleeping hours, more consumption of insomnia medications), physical activity (less exercises) and smoking habits (increase). Results suggested a negative impact of E-exams on students within medical faculties. Robust exam platform and remote mock E-exams are recommended to reduce students' potential stress. A stress-free environment is very essential to encourage students to adopt remote E-exams, particularly if the pandemic will take longer. Various awareness programs about students' habits related to dietary, sleep quality, physical activity and smoking are highly valuable for students' health benefits. This is of particular importance since the current students at Faculties of Medical Sciences are the future health care providers (https://www.sciencedirect.com/science/article/pii/S2049080120304131).

Above review of studies clearly indicates that there is not a single study conducted for the B.Ed. students of conventional teacher training Department/Institution in distributed blended mode examination (DBME) in India. Hence, the case study of a batch of B.Ed. students of Manav Rachana University (MRU), who appeared in their term-end/final year examinations through blended mode examination (BME) assumes a great significance in the context of COVID-19, as it addressed the most felt-need for the students and the institution in their hardest testing time.

### *Methodology*

The study has used survey research method. The survey has been conducted on all 66 students of 2018-2020 Batch who all have appeared in both theory and practical examinations through blended mode examination, which can be called distributed blended mode examination (DBME). In addition, the Dean, the HOD and 12 faculty members involved in conducting the said examination have also been covered as a case study of particular batch of students of the institution (MRU).

The data has been collected during November 2022 to January 2023 by using three specially prepared questionnaires — one for the students, one for the Dean and the HOD, and the other for the faculty. These questionnaires were administered as Google forms on them. Only 32 students, the Dean and the HOD, and one faculty member have responded to these forms. The data collected have been analysed to arrive at the findings.

## Findings

The findings of the study are presented under the following three headings.

***I. Findings based on the analysis of the students' responses included the following.***

1. *Types of technologies and modes used:* In the blended mode examination (theory and practical exams) the technologies used by the students included: Computer with Internet/Wi-Fi facility (50%), Laptop with Internet facility (81.25%), Mobile Phone (smart phones) with mobile data (87.5%), and/or Wi-Fi (68.75%), Scanners and Printers (18.75%). All the students (100%) used Online synchronous mode (Zoom), and asynchronous modes

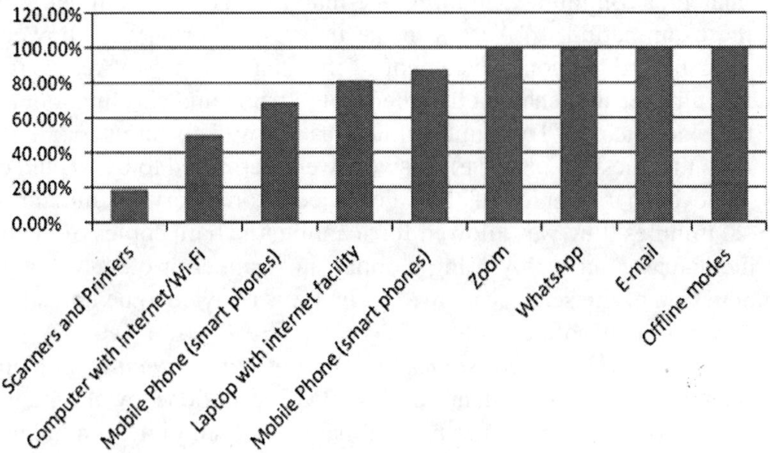


**Figure 1:** Technologies used by the Students during the Blended Mode Examination

(WhatsApp, E-mail), and Offline modes — Individualised, isolated, self-styled physical mode (physical writing of responses on the ruled answer sheets at home) and scanning of written answer scripts.

2. *Students' satisfaction with the timing/schedule and conduct of examination*: All the students (100%) were satisfied with: i) one-month advance announcement of the exam schedule; and ii) actual timing of the sessions of the exams. The majority of students (93.75%) expressed that the exams were conducted as per the announced schedule and sessions whereas 6.25% of them faced slight discomfort.
3. *Technical problems faced by the students during the exams*: 87.5% of the students did not face any technical problem whereas 12.5% of students faced some technical problems while giving the exams. The reasons stated by those who faced the technical problems while giving their exams included Internet or Wi-Fi connectivity issues and the problems related to Zoom connectivity, which they could however overcome.
4. *Role played by the examiner's in dealing with the students' problems: The* examiners played smooth role all through in dealing with the students' problems as expressed by half (50%) of them, whereas it was very facilitative as expressed by 43.75% of them, and highly responsive as felt by 6.25% of them. Not a single student expressed that there was any issue of non-cooperation or non-responsiveness by the examiners in dealing with any problem.
5. *Process/procedure/sequence of steps followed by the institution for conducting the exam:* The sequence of the steps followed in the conduct of the blended mode examination included: a) Instructions were

circulated or communicated through e-mail much before commencement of the examination; b) Access to the university portal was allowed 10 minutes before the commencement of the examination; c) Access to the question paper was enabled by entering the name and enrolment number of the examinee; d) 10 minutes time was allowed for downloading and reading the question paper; e) Answers were permitted to be written only by hand on hard copies of the ruled sheets for theory examination; f) 15-20 minutes time was allowed for scanning the hard copies of the hand written answer scripts by using mobile cam scanner or other scanner; g) Submission of the scanned answer scripts was allowed to be uploaded by the given time deadline.

6. *Flexibility followed in student's identity authentication:* Identity authentication of the students during BME was done by the majority (56.25%) of them by entering the name and enrolment number by themselves in the university portal for enabling access to the University portal; while the remaining did it by sending their names and enrolment numbers to the examiners and by showing their Identity card through video mode.
7. *Students' happiness with the procedure followed in conducting the exam:* Most students (93.75%) felt that the sequence of the steps of BME worked smoothly during the examination, though the remaining expressed some problems for a while.
8. *Students' perception of the duration of the exam:* Most students (62.5%) expressed that the duration of the BME was same as that of face-to-face term-end examination, whereas 37.5% of them expressed that their duration was not the same, due to some technical problems.
9. *Type of questions used in the conduct of the practical exams:* The practical examination was conducted by the examiners by sending questionnaires to all the students as Google forms for some subjects, whereas for some other subjects it was conducted in the form of oral examination or viva-voce only. About the type of questions asked in oral examination (viva-voce), 37.5% of students indicated Objective type questions, 31.25% indicated short answer type questions, 25% indicated long answer type questions whereas the majority (62.5%) expressed that all the above-mentioned variety of questions were used.
10. *The type of questions used in the conduct of the theory exams:* These included — Short answer type questions as expressed by 43.75% of them, long answer type questions (37.5%), Objective type questions (25%), Oral examination (viva-voce) by 6.25%, whereas the majority of them (62.5%) expressed that all the above-mentioned variety of questions were used.

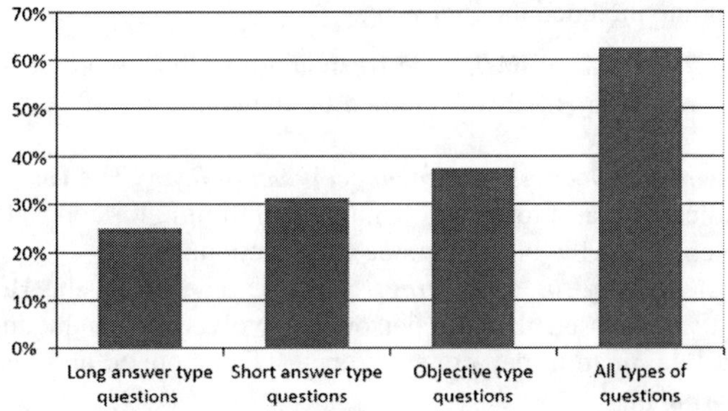


**Figure 2:** Types of questions asked in the practical examination

11. *Students' satisfaction with the conduct of exam, quality of assessment and their own performance in the exam:* All the students (100%) were satisfied with — i) the conduct of BME (theory and practical); ii) quality of assessment/evaluation and declaration of the result; and iii) their own performance in the term-end examinations.
12. *Students' comparison BME with face-to-face examinations*: While one-half (50%) of them felt that the BME was a boon in comparison with face-to-face mode examination, the other half felt that both were equal. The majority (56.25%) of them expressed that their experience in both the examinations was equally comfortable, 37.5% expressed that their experience of giving face-to-face mode examination was better than that of the BME, while 6.25% of them expressed the contrary feeling.
13. *Students' opinion of cost-effectiveness of BME:* While 37.5% of them expressed that both face-to-face and BME were equally economical, 31.25% of them expressed that the face-to-face mode was economical; and remaining 31.25% of them felt that BME was economical.
14. *Students' suggestion about institutionalisation of BME:* The majority i.e. 20 (62.5%) of them suggested continuation of BME to be an institutional practice alternative to face-to-face examinations by the university even in normal situation (i.e. non-COVID situation). Out of these 20 students, 14 students (70%) of them suggested phasing out of the face-to-face examination in lieu of BME, whereas the remaining six students (30%) of them were against phasing out of the face-to-face examination. Rather, they suggested continuation of both the examinations parallelly.

***II. Findings based on the analysis of the responses of the Dean, the HOD and the faculty***

These finding included the following.

1. *Mooting of the idea of BME:* The Dean and the HOD expressed that the idea of conducting BME was mooted by the controller of examinations only.
2. *Time taken for conceptualisation and conduct of BME*: The Dean and the HOD indicated that it took less than one month time for conceptualising and implementing the blended mode examination.
3. *Personnel involved in conducting the BME*: The Dean, the HOD and the faculty expressed that the personnel involved in conducting BME included Examination department/branch, IT personnel, and Faculty of the Department.
4. *Types of technologies considered and used:* The responses of the Dean, the HOD and faculty indicated that the technologies considered and used were almost in conformity with those stated by the students.
5. *Technical issues faced:* The Dean, the HOD and the faculty expressed that because of Internet issues the planned or identified technologies could not be used effectively due to lack of possession of laptops by some students in remote locations, Internet speed and connectivity problems.
6. *Need felt for use of other technologies:* The Dean expressed that the need was felt for using voice-recording technology as an exigent measure, while the HOD and the faculty did not feel such need.
7. *Comparison of face-to-face examinations and BME*: The HOD felt that BME is better alternative to face-to-face examinations while the Dean expressed the contrary view. About the time factor in conducting BME the HOD expressed that is more time taking than face-to-face mode examination, whereas the Dean expressed that both modes of examination consume equal time.
8. *Personnel involved and cooperation in conducting BME:* The Dean, the HOD and the faculty expressed that personnel involved in conducting BME included the Controller of the Examinations, the Dean of the College, the Head of the Department, the Programme Coordinator, the Faculty of Education, Technical staff, among others. The Dean and the HOD expressed that there was good cooperation and coordination between and among all the categories of personnel in the process of conducting BME.
9. *Orientation and training of the personnel:* The faculty felt that conducting BME was definitely very challenging as it involved learning about new tools and technologies and handling them was accomplished through MS Teams who provided rigorous orientation and training to the personnel involved as per their requirement.
10. *Cost-effectiveness of BME:* The Dean, the HOD and the faculty expressed that the conduct of BME is relatively cost-effective in comparison with

face-to-face mode examinations. However, regarding the students' readiness to take or appear in BME, while Dean expressed in affirmative, the HOD expressed in negative for the reasons like the lack of possession of laptops by some students, their remote locations, Internet speed and connectivity.

11. *Students' participation:* While the HOD expressed that all the eligible students appeared in BME, the Dean expressed it otherwise, as it was conducted subsequently for those eligible and missed out students.
12. *Time taken for planning and conducting of BME*: The Dean and the HOD expressed that there was sufficient time in between the notification of BME and its beginning. It took two weeks' time to finalise the whole procedure for conducting BME which included the steps such as finalisation of platform, links, proctoring, etc.
13. *Technical issues and problems faced by students*: The Dean, the HOD and the faculty expressed that there were network and access issues reportedly faced by the students during BME. However, they expressed that timely solutions were adopted to address the problems encountered by the students during the conduct of BME. It also corroborates with the findings based on students' data. Time management, electricity supply and Internet glitches were a few amongst other problems reportedly faced by the students during the conduct of BME.
14. *Evaluation of answer scripts and declaration of results:* The Dean expressed that the evaluation of the answer scripts and the declaration of the results was completed 'within stipulated time'. The HOD stated that evaluation of the answer scripts was got done in 'online' mode. However, the faculty stated that, in comparison with the traditional mode of examination, the evaluation was difficult in the case of BME. It was also stated that the faculty was satisfied with the overall conduct of BME.
15. *Steps in identifying or verifying the authenticity or the veracity of the examinees:* The Dean and the HOD expressed that the procedure followed in this regard involved: examining the identity card shown through video mode, allowing the students to enter their name and enrolment number on the university portal, or obtaining the name and enrolment number of the student through e-mail for enabling the student to access the portal.
16. *Satisfaction in conducting the examination:* The Dean, the HOD and the faculty expressed that they were satisfied with the overall conduct of BME.
17. *Comparison of traditional/face-to-face examination and BME:* Faculty felt that BME was better alternative to traditional/face-to-face examinations. It was also suggested for adoption or institutionalisation of the BME by other higher educational institutions parallelly alongside the traditional/

face-to-face mode examination. However, the BME was suggested for experimentation by all other higher education institutions with suitable modifications.

18. *Considerations and efforts towards institutionalisation of the BME:* The Dean, the HOD and the faculty expressed that the BME has been continued in the subsequent years for those students who missed out the preceding exam and for some other batches of students as well, though it was discontinued later. They suggested adoption or institutionalisation of BME by other higher educational institutions after experimenting BME at the level of the concerned HEIs.

## Conclusion

All the students, the Dean, the HOD and the faculty were satisfied with the conduct of BME, irrespective of the technical issues and problems faced by them. While the duration of the BME was same as that of face-to-face/traditional mode examination, the students were divided about the relative cost-effectiveness of both the types of examinations, as they found in them the relative advantages and disadvantages. Regarding the continuation or otherwise of the BME, most of the students suggested continuation of BME as an institutional practice alternative to face-to-face examinations by the university even in normal situations (i.e. non-COVID situations) as well, and within them, the majority suggested even phasing out of the face-to-face examination in lieu of BME. Although the Dean, the HOD and the faculty expressed that the BME was continued in the subsequent years for those students who missed out the preceding BME and for some other batches of students, it was discontinued later. To conclude, they have, however, suggested adoption or institutionalisation of BME by other higher educational institutions after experimenting it at the level of the concerned HEIs. Further, they were against phasing out the traditional mode examination. Rather, the popular suggestion was for continuation of both the modes of examinations parallelly and their institutionalization accordingly.

## References

Ardid, M., Gómez-Tejedor, J.A., Meseguer-Dueñas, J.M., Riera, J., Vidaurre, A. (2015). Online exams for blended assessment: A Study of different application methodologies, *Computers & Education*, 81, 296-303 (See https://www.researc hgate.net/publication/267573379_Online_exams_for_blended_assessment_Study_of_different_application_methodologies).

Elsalem, L., Al-Azzam, N., Jum'ah, A.A., Obeidat, N., Damer Mahmoud Sindiani, A.M., & Kheirallah, K.A. (2020). Stress And Behavioral Changes with Remote E-Exams

During the Covid-19 Pandemic: A Cross-Sectional Study among Undergraduates of Medical Sciences. *Annals of Medicine and Surgery*, Vol. 60, December, Pp.271-279.

Hollister, K.K., and Berenson, M.L. (January, 2009). Proctored Versus Unproctored Online Exams Studying the Impact of Exam Environment on Student Performance. Decision Sciences, *Journal of Innovative Education*, 7(1), 271 – 294. (See DOI:10.1111/j.1540-4609.2008.00220.x and https://www. researchgate. net/ publication/227820297). https://manavrachna.edu.in/university/about/ - Retrieved on 24.12.2022.

Ranjan, P. (2020). Is Blended Learning Better than Online Learning for B.Ed. Students? *Journal of Learning for Development*, 7(3), 349-366. (See Https://Jl4d.Org/Index.Php/Ejl4d/Article/View/412/528).

Rapanta, C., Botturi, L., Goodyear, P., Guàrdia, L., and Koole, M. (2020). Online university teaching during and after the Covid-19 crisis: refocusing teacher presence and learning activity. *Postdigital Science Education*. 2, 923–945. See doi: 10.1007/s42438-020-00155-y.

Shin, M., and Hickey, K. (2020). Needs a Little TLC: Examining College Students' Emergency Remote Teaching and Learning Experiences during COVID-19, *Journal of Further Higher Education,* 1–14. (See doi:10.1080/0309877X.2020.1847261).

Watermeyer, R., Crick, T., Knight, C., and Goodall, J. (2020). COVID-19 and Digital Disruption in UK Universities: Afflictions and Affordances of Emergency, Online Migration. *Higher Education,* 81, 623–641. (See doi:10.1007/s10734-020-00561-y).

Zagouras, C., Egarchou, D., Skiniotis, P., & Fountana, M. (2022). Face-to-face or Blended Learning? A Case Study of Teacher Training in the Pedagogical Use of ICT. *Education and Information Technologies*, 27, 12939–12967. (See https://Doi.Org/10.1007/S10639-022-11144-Y).

# 4

# Scientific Temperament among Elementary School Teachers
## *Awareness and Application*

Ambrin Khanam
Aerum Khan

### Introduction

Post-independence, then Prime Minister, Pandit Jawaharlal Nehru, emphasised on developing 'scientific temper' in citizens of India. He propounded the thought that scientific temper would play an important role in the developing nation's socio-economic condition. Scientific temper should play a pivotal role in the life of a historian, jurist, sociologist, philosopher, as much as it is pivotal in the life of a zoologist, mathematician, or astronomer. All of them should proceed with their work based on evidence and observation.

After Pandit Nehru, the successive governments continued with their commitment towards science and technology by also introducing constitutional amendments. Pandit Nehru was instrumental in laying foundations for building the infrastructure for science and technology in Indian Universities like Indian Institute of Technology and CSIR labs etc. These became the hardware of science and technology in India, while scientific temper along with scientific thinking among people was the software.

#### *What is Scientific Temperament?*

Thomas Hughes in 1893 defined scientific temperament as a scrupulous outcome of exact science. Pandit Nehru talks about scientific temper as a way along which a man should plan his travel. He explains that scientific temper is the temper of a free man. Despite living in a scientific age, there is little evidence of this temper in people and their leaders. Pandit Nehru argues that a scientific approach is needed, along with a critical temper of science, i.e., a refusal to accept anything without testing and trial. Scientific temper in a person builds the capacity to change previous conclusions when new evidence is found, it develops a temper which relies on observed facts and not preconceived theory — all this is necessary. Pandit Nehru thus explains scientific temper is not only important for application of science but also for everyday life, it can help in solving problems of hunger, poverty, insanitation, illiteracy, superstitions, and the problems of a rich country inhabited by starving people.

Khan A. (2018) describes scientific literacy as an ability in a person to ask questions, determine answers from our everyday experiences; scientific literacy enables a person to seek explanations to the natural phenomena occurring around them, rather than accepting given statements. Kaur and Vadhera (2018) relate the scientific temper of a person to their understanding of the nature of science. They observe that some individuals possess a higher degree of scientific temper, while others relatively have a low scientific temper. The individuals have a different understanding of nature of science, it can be misinterpreted in school science which later develops into misconceptions about science among students and is translated to a low scientific temper later in their lives. A varied thought process is developed among individuals as they have different perceptions about the nature of science.

The very nature of science is tentative, the scientific community worldwide aims on changing laws and ideas on the basis of new evidence and experimentation with dedicated research and

scientific investigation. Scientific temper enables us to change what cannot be verified through experimentation: Saxena A. (2014).

Saxena A. (2014) explains that most people do not correctly understand scientific temperament. The efforts to inculcate scientific temper and rational thinking among common people has been unsuccessful, the reason behind this is the tendency of the society to accept blindly the viewpoints and belief of ancestors, without putting an effort to investigate its relevance.

Scientific temper is an attribute of a person who interacts with the world in rational ways and is guided by evidence in their actions. They tend to have an open mind in considering the issues and have a logical approach in every situation. The attributes of a person with scientific temperament are that they are free from superstition, biasness, rigidness, close-mindedness, irrationality, and indoctrination.

### *Scientific Temperament in the Constitution of India*

India is the first and only country to explicitly adopt scientific temper in its Constitution. In the forty-second amendment in 1976, Article 51 A(h) was added under the Fundamental Duties that states:

> *"It shall be the duty of every citizen of India to develop scientific temper, humanism and spirit of inquiry and reform."*
>
> Article 51 A(h), Constitution of India

There is a close connection between scientific temper and the idea of secularism. Practice of science motivates a change in the society and strengthens the idea of secularism. In India, dogmatic practices and superstitions are popular among citizens so the emphasis on scientific temperament is crucial.

### *Scientific Temperament in Teachers*

Kaur and Vadhera (2018) explain that because of the missing notion of nature of science students often fail to utilise the obtained scientific knowledge. This is related to the failed harmony between scientific methods and process skills in the teaching of science. The science labs in schools are equipped with miniature replicas of experiments, but no time is spent on establishing a harmony between process skills that are required for doing science. Doing science in an abstract way might lead to confusion among young learners. Students are only encouraged to reach a particular conclusion by observing but they are not taught how they can infer from observations; it is important for children to know the background of experiments to move forward with the experiment and build upon it. Till the secondary level of schooling in India the characteristics of science are projected as something which is abstract, difficult, serious, which is not the actual nature of science.

The NCF 2005 states that while deciding on the grading of students in science curriculum, it must be kept in mind that most students who are learning science as a compulsory subject up to class 10th are not going to become professional scientists or technologists later in their career, but it is necessary for the students to become 'scientifically literate'.

Arora B. (2019) argues that any teacher training programme must focus to produce empathetic, dynamic, and creative teachers; the teachers who can be the torchbearers for their students and moreover for the society. Their knowledge should not be rigid and is flexible enough to accommodate new emerging trends in education and society. Teachers need to be prepared for emerging global changes and thus enhancing the learning experiences of students.

The citizens of a country should have a scientific thinking, and science should be a fundamental part of their lives. To take forward the scientific temperament the government needs to make efforts to inculcate scientific thinking in students at a young age. The curriculum should be produced such that it makes scientific thinking a central trait of students. To implement this curriculum the stakeholders of education should also comprehend scientific temperament.

Teachers act as facilitators of students; hence they should be aware of the meaning of scientific temperament and should practise it in the classroom. A teacher's role in fostering scientific temperament in students is to induce a sense of curiosity, questioning and capacity of reasoning. A teacher in the classroom should focus on bringing students out of superstitions by reasoning and creating an environment that fosters open-mindedness. Problem-solving techniques should be used by teachers to develop reasoning among students. The students should be given exposure to science clubs where they know more about scientists, their lives and how they have made huge discoveries. This knowledge among students will help in developing an understanding of science and its application in daily lives; they could use science for the benefit of humankind. Teachers can help in creating a capacity of application in students so that they analyse any phenomena with a divergent thinking.

Every science is guided by curiosity, a passion to explore and understand without misleading or without being misled. Thus, development of scientific temper enables rational thoughts. To nurture scientific temperament in students they should be guided by teachers who have self-internalised scientific temperament. As teachers are the primary source of knowledge and students in every aspect are affected by teachers. So, a teacher's conduct in a classroom is such that it imparts scientific thinking. A teacher must concentrate on creating a democratic environment in the classroom and emphasise holistic learning. The domains of secularism, integrity, democracy, unity, tolerance, communal harmony along with scientific temperament should be the focus of every teacher of the country.

The students may relate to any field of education be it humanities or languages he/she should be internalised with scientific temper. Scientific thinking is not always meant for students who are good at science, the teachers must concentrate on producing scientific minds from every stream of education. We are living in a society with overloaded information. In such a society, one must have a rational bent of mind to choose the right and useful information.

The inculcation of stories of scientists and their discoveries from every era must be a part of science curriculum; students must also be made aware of the stories of some contemporary scientists from India like Satyendra Nath Bose, Homi Bhabha, A.P.J. Abdul Kalam, Meghnad Saha, Vikram Sarabhai. The students get inspired knowing and studying about the scientists. The skill of analysing and evaluating information is very important in the 21st century knowledge economy.

## The Study

### *Objectives*

1. To study the general awareness of scientific temperament in teachers.
2. To study the application of scientific temperament in daily life.

### *Methodology*

This study is descriptive in nature. A self-developed and expert validated questionnaire was used to achieve the objectives of the study. Data were collected directly from the elementary school teachers through the questionnaire. The questionnaire had both open and close ended questions. An online Google form was sent to teachers to record their responses along with a cover letter to explain the purpose of the study.

### Sample

The population consisted of all the elementary school teachers of New Delhi. The sampling technique used was random sampling. The sample were thirty teachers from ten different schools; eight government schools and two private schools of South-East Delhi. The study is delimited to teachers of South Delhi and Central Delhi.

### Background of the Respondents

Teaching Experience in Table 1 and Subjects Taught in Table 2 are given:

**Table 1:** Experience of the Teachers

| *Number of Years of Experience* | *Number of Teachers* |
|---|---|
| 0-5 | 15 |
| 6-10 | 5 |
| 11-15 | 7 |
| 16-20 | 0 |
| 20-25 | 0 |
| 26-30 | 3 |

**Table 2:** Subjects Taught

| *Teaching Subjects* | *Number of Teachers* |
|---|---|
| All subjects | 14 |
| Science (TGT) | 4 |
| Mathematics (PGT) | 4 |
| English (PGT) | 4 |
| Urdu (TGT) | 1 |
| Chemistry (PGT) | 2 |
| Biology (PGT) | 1 |

### General Awareness of Scientific Temperament Among Teachers

Questions related to general awareness were asked to teachers to analyse their knowledge about scientific temperament. This included the meaning of scientific temperament, mention of scientific temperament in the Constitution and attributes of a person with scientific temperament.

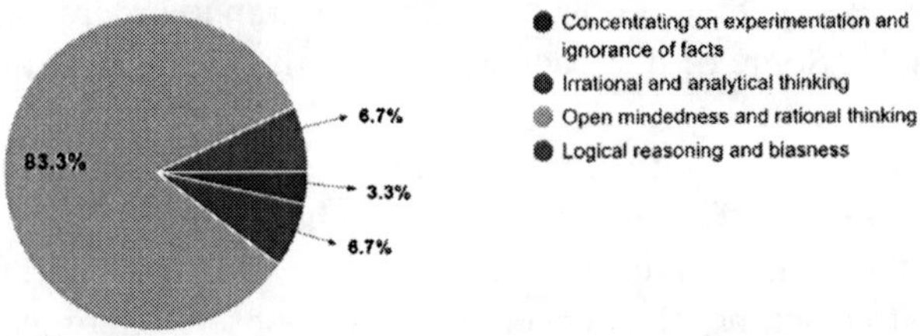


**Figure 1:** Teachers explaining the meaning of scientific temperament

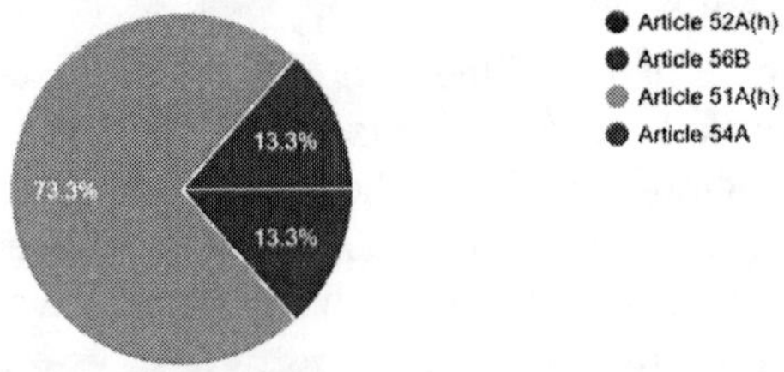


**Figure 2:** Teachers' response to the article of Constitution of India which talks about scientific temper

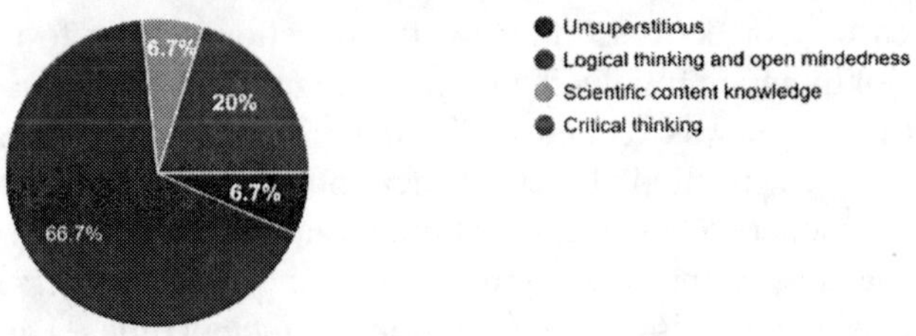


**Figure 3:** Teachers' response to attributes of a person with scientific temperament

## *Application of Scientific Temperament Among Teachers*

All over India it is a popular superstition that if a black cat crosses the path, then we should avoid taking the path. The teachers have rightly mentioned that it is superstition and it is inappropriate to think that black cats bring bad omen. Although there was one response from the participating teachers which stated that they would suggest the child take a round in their place and then go ahead. The teacher is associated with 'children with special needs' and teaches all subjects in a government school. Their response shows that they hold a belief of superstition and consider this situation as bad luck. They lack a sense of scientific reasoning in this situation.

The next question was related to the story that an old woman sits on the moon and stories are framed henceforth. The participating teachers have explained this as a story which is used to scare children in order to make them sleep early at night. Some of the teachers blamed the elders for framing such myths through stories in the minds of children. Majority of the teachers have very well explained they would ask the students to look at the moon and observe other different patterns. A few of the teachers explained that the appearance of the moon from the earth is like this because it has an uneven surface. These teachers pertain to teaching of science. So, we can observe here that teachers pertaining to teaching of science provide a more reasonable answer to the children. One response that was remarkable was that the conditioning of a child may lead to misbelief in them.

It is often seen that people hang chillies and lemons on the entrance of the shops, offices, rickshaws, and trucks. There is a strong belief in the Indian community that chillies and lemons will keep them away from the ill-effects of the evil eye. But the actual reason behind this is that people earlier used this as an insecticide. From the participating teachers, three of them have explained the scientific reason behind this practice.

Nearly 50% of the teachers have given an explanation of why we should not sleep under the trees. They have rightly mentioned that trees produce excess carbon dioxide at night which is harmful for humans. Most of the teachers that have explained the correct reasoning for the question pertain to teaching of science, some of them are involved with primary classes.

The next question was related to the belief of throwing coins in water bodies to get wishes fulfilled. Teachers mentioned in the answer that this is not right, some teachers mentioned this belief as a superstition, and one of the teachers said that they cannot say anything. Only one of the teachers responded with the true reason why this practice was done in ancient times. This is indeed a scientific explanation of why people threw coins in the fountains or lakes. So, we can observe that teachers know that these are traditions and superstitions but only few can explain the reason behind it.

## Findings

It was found that the awareness, understanding and application of scientific temper among teachers pertaining to teaching of non-science subjects was moderate.

1. The general awareness of scientific temper among elementary school teachers is only moderate and some teachers lack the knowledge of facts pertaining to scientific temper.
2. Teachers pertaining to teaching of primary classes lacked a sense of logical reasoning. Teachers' explanation to students about any phenomenon that happens around them is crucial to develop this reasoning.

3. Most of the science teachers have shown a better understanding of scientific temper as compared to non-science teachers; the non-science teachers have given responses which were somehow not scientific in nature.

## Conclusion

From the above findings we concluded that the present study highlighted the awareness of scientific temper among elementary teachers; majority of the teachers presented a positive result i.e., they were aware of the scientific temper related awareness. Although a few of the teachers presented negative results i.e., they were not much aware of scientific temperament related awareness. The study also intended to analyse the application of scientific temperament in daily lives of teachers; results of which show that a lot of teachers lack logical reasoning. The primary school teachers hold beliefs which are superstitious and not logical in nature. Some of the teachers which pertain to teaching in secondary classes are better at providing logical and rational reasons to the students.

Hence, from the findings of the present study it is suggested that teachers from non-science backgrounds need a pre-service training in scientific methods before they start their service. Also, the primary teachers which are found to lack a sense of logical and rational reasoning should also be provided with pre-service training which makes them familiar with scientific methods and scientific temper.

Scientific temper is a crucial element of one's life and it is important for students to internalise this temper at a young age; so, the teachers who are directly involved with the students must also possess a temperament which can differentiate between myth and logic. Teachers are expected to possess a temperament which presents students with logical reasoning and rational judgement of any situation. Teachers are expected to inculcate the same in the students they are teaching and present to them an idea of open mindedness and develop in them a sense of curiosity. Teachers are supposed to make the students aware about their environment and develop into them a sense of protection towards the environment. Through these activities a teacher may facilitate development of scientific temper among her students.

## Educational Implications of the Study

1. The scientific temper is not only related to someone who pursues science as a subject; scientific temperament is a fundamental duty as mentioned in our Constitution. Hence, every citizen must have an internalised scientific temperament.

2. For students to develop a scientific temperament and scientific attitude it is very crucial that the teachers also have an internalised scientific temper.
3. The study indicates that some of the teachers hold myths and superstitions; this could be dangerous when the teachers impart the same in an elementary classroom. Thus, it is very important for teachers to go through a training which enhances their scientific reasoning, and boosts their confidence in applying the scientific methods in their daily lives.
4. The elementary school teachers need proper training before beginning their service. The training should focus on scientific methods, especially the teachers who are not related to science.

## References

Arnold D. (2013). 'Nehruvian Science and Postcolonial India. '*ISIS* Volume 104 number 2. University of Chicago Press Journals.

Abhijeet Bardapurkar A. (2020). 'Teaching Scientific Temper,' Vol. 25, No. 10 *RESONANCE*, October 2020

Arora B. (2019). 'Globalisation and Changing Trends in Science Education in Schools: Implication for Teacher Education Programme,' Vol. 5 No. 2 *Jamia Journal of Education*, March 2019

Basu, Durga Das (1993). *Introduction to the Constitution of India* (15th ed.). New Delhi: Prentice Hall of India.

Bhargava, P.M. and Chakrabarti, C. (2010). *Angels, Devil and Science: A Collection of Articles on Scientific Temper*, National Book Trust, New Delhi, India.

Bharti, Sunanda (11 April 2020). "Spirit of Inquiry and Reform in the Era of Fake News", *Times of India.*

Biswal, A. and Pandey, A. (2021) 'Scientific Temper among Secondary School Students' Journal of Scientific Temper, Vol. 9(3&4), pp. 149-163 July-Dec, 2021

Chacko, Priya (2011). "The search for a scientific temper: nuclear technology and the ambivalence of India's postcolonial modernity", *Review of International Studies.*

Chadha, G. (2005). Towards an Informed Science Criticism: The Debate on Science in Post-Independence India, in *The Making of Identity in Contemporary India*, Ganesh, K. & Thakkar, U. (Eds.), Sage Publications India Pvt. Ltd., New Delhi.

Dewan, H.K. (2018). 'Why a Different Approach to Science Teaching?' *Voices of Teachers and Teacher Educators*, ISSN 2455-1376, Vol. 6, Issue-II, February-2018, pp.7-19, NCERT, New Delhi.

Kaur, N. and Vadhera, R.P. (2018) 'How much Scientifically Tempered we are? A question for introspection', *Online Journal of Multidisciplinary Subjects*, Volume 12 (issue 3) ISSN-2349-266X

Khan, A. (2015). "Scientific Literacy Among Elementary Level Students: An Important Objective of Science Education," *Right to Education: Access and Quality*, Editors: Mohd Rizwan and A.K. Mantry, pp. 34 - 41, Ankur Publication, New Delhi, ISBN 978-81-93165-11-9.

Khan, A. (2015). "Development of Scientific Literacy at Elementary Level," *Awadh International Journal of Information Technology and Education (AIJITE)*, a peer reviewed, refereed journal, Volume 4, Issue 1, pp. 25-31, ISSN: 2277-8985 published by Alfa Publications, New Delhi.

Khan, A. (2018). 'Science, Scientific Literacy and Scientific Temper in the Curricular Documents,' *Voices of Teachers and Teacher Educators*, ISSN 2455-1376, Vol. 6, Issue-II, February-2018, pp.38-49, NCERT, New Delhi.

Keshavamurthy, H.R. (27 February 2014). "Fostering Scientific Temper is Fundamental to Innovation and Progress". Press Information Bureau, India.

Mahanti, Subodh (2013). "A Perspective on Scientific Temper in India". *Journal of Scientific Temper*.

MHRD (2020). *National Education Policy 2020*, Government of India, New Delhi.

Nandy, A. (1982). 'Science for Unafraid, '*Mainstream*, pp. 17-20, New Delhi.

National Policy on Education (1986). In Sharma R.C. (2010), *Modern Science Teaching*, 6th ed., New Delhi: Dhanpat Rai Publishing Company.

Nehru, Jawaharlal (1989). *The Discovery of India* (Centenary ed.). Oxford: University Press. p. 513.

NCERT (1988). National Curriculum Framework for Elementary and Secondary Education. A Framework 1988. New Delhi.

NCERT (2005). National Curriculum Framework for School Education 2005.

Raza, Gauhar; Singh, Surjit (2018). "Politics, Religion, Science and Scientific Temper." *Cultures of Science*.

Saxena A. (2014). 'Understanding Scientific Temper,' *Journal of Scientific Temper*, Vol. 2(1&2), Jan.-April, 2014

Srinivasan, Venkataraghavan (27 May 2020). "Scientific temper: A Nehruvian thought that is much relevant today", *The Federal*.

The Constitution (Forty-second Amendment) Act, 1976, Article 51-A(h). *National Portal of India,* Government of India.

Yadav, K. (2018). Scientific Temper: Need of an Hour, *International Education Journal: Chetana*, Volume-4, pp 73-77.

# 5

# Teachers Perception and Implementation of Constructivist Approach in Teaching Mathematics

Tashnim Ferdaus
Roohi Fatima

## Introduction

Education is a dynamic field that constantly evolves to meet the changing needs of learners. Among the various pedagogical approaches, constructivism stands out as a promising framework for fostering meaningful and engaging learning experiences. Rooted in the belief that learners actively construct their knowledge, constructivism emphasises the importance of hands-on activities, collaborative learning, and student-centred instruction. In the context of mathematics education, constructivism holds particular significance. Constructivist approaches promote a deeper comprehension of mathematical concepts by encouraging students to explore, discover, and apply mathematical principles in meaningful contexts.

The Indian education landscape has undergone significant transformations in recent years, driven by the implementation of the National Curriculum Framework (NCF) 2005 and the National Education Policy (NEP) 2020. These landmark documents have emphasised the need for a shift from traditional rote-based teaching methods to more holistic, experiential, and constructivist approaches to learning. Constructivism, a prominent learning theory that aligns with the principles of NCF 2005 and NEP 2020, emphasises the importance of hands-on activities, collaborative learning, and student-centred instruction. By engaging students in exploration, discovery, and application of concepts, constructivist approaches promote a deeper understanding and appreciation of mathematics. Moreover, constructivist pedagogies foster the development of critical thinking, problem-solving, and communication skills, which are essential for success in the 21st century.

Despite the strong advocacy for constructivism in NCF 2005 and NEP 2020, its effective implementation in Indian classrooms remains a challenge. India's diverse educational landscape, with variations in socio-economic backgrounds, cultural influences, and regional disparities, adds layers of complexity to the adoption of any pedagogical framework. As the country continues to strive for excellence in education, understanding how teachers navigate the challenges and opportunities presented by the constructivist approach becomes crucial.

This research delves into the realm of mathematics education, specifically focusing on teachers' perceptions and implementations of the constructivist approach in the teaching of mathematics.

## The Study

### *Objectives*

1. To study the mathematics teachers' perceptions of constructivist approaches to teaching mathematics.
2. To study the teachers' implementation strategies of constructivist approaches in their mathematics classrooms.
3. The factors that influence the implementation of constructivist approaches in the mathematics classroom.

### *Significance*

The research on teachers' perception and implementation of the constructivist approach in teaching mathematics provides insights into how teachers apply constructivist methods, enhancing teaching strategies that promote critical thinking and problem-solving skills in students. Additionally, it informs professional development for educators, addresses challenges in implementing constructivist methods, and guides curriculum designers in adapting materials to align with India's cultural and educational context.

### *Statement of the Study*

The study explores potential discrepancies between teachers' perceptions and the ideal application of the constructivist approach, identifying factors influencing teachers in implementing the constructivist approach and targeted support in mathematics education. The statement of the study is entitled as "Teachers Perception and Implementation of a Constructivist Approach in Teaching Mathematics."

### *Delimitation*

1. Kamrup district (Metro) is considered the study area for the present study.
2. Only TGT (math) teachers from the government middle school in Kamrup district (metro) were considered.

### *Review of related Literature*

A review of related literature in educational research is the foundation, providing context, identifying existing knowledge, and highlighting gaps in the study. It is a critical analysis of past research, revealing trends, debates, and informing research questions and methodology. The following paragraphs describe various studies related to the present study in detail.

*Mishra, A. (2023)* carried out a study on "A Study on Teachers' Perceptions of the Constructivist Approach to Teaching in Classroom Practices," aimed at exploring teachers' perceptions and experiences regarding the implementation of the constructivist approach, aiming to empower students to take ownership of their learning and foster independent thinking. Using a quantitative research approach with questionnaires and structured observations, the research addressed questions about teachers' views on effectiveness and ways experiences could inform better academic strategies. Most respondents displayed a clear understanding of the constructivist approach, emphasising its creativity, effectiveness, promotion of critical thinking, and facilitation of students in constructing their own knowledge. Concerns were noted about the approach being time-consuming. Teachers generally endorsed the method's effectiveness, highlighting its positive impact on student understanding, active participation, and the development of creative and problem-solving skills. The study concluded with suggestions for teachers to be well-prepared and open to varied learner responses and for students to engage more actively in group discussions and experimental learning. Despite some variations in opinions, the research revealed positive perceptions of constructivist teaching approaches among educators, with teachers expressing confidence in their ability to enhance student learning and promote open expression of thoughts, deeming them crucial for effective education.

*Laskar, A.H., & Bhattacharjee, S. (2022)* had conducted a study on "Teachers' awareness of constructivist approaches in learning: An analytical study," in an attempt to elucidate the constructivist approach as an archetype for teaching and learning. It is also designed to ascertain teachers' awareness of the constructivist approach to learning. The study is limited to the Hailakandi District of Assam, India, with the objective of ascertaining teachers' awareness of the constructivist approach to learning. For the collection of data, a quantitative survey method has been used with a questionnaire consisting of a series of close-ended rating-type questions to gather information from both government and private secondary-level teachers and students in Hailakandi District. The study revealed that both teachers and students in private secondary schools are more aware of the constructivist approach in the teaching-learning process, while in government secondary schools, teachers and students are less aware of the constructivist approach in the teaching-learning process.

## Methodology

The study employed a descriptive research design, utilising questionnaires for data collection. A survey was specifically designed to inquire about teachers' perceptions of the constructivist approach to teaching and learning mathematics.

*Population:* The population of the present study comprises all TGT (math) teachers from government middle schools in the Kamrup district (metro).

*Sample:* For the present study, six government middle schools in Kamrup district (metro) were randomly selected, and 14 TGT (math) teachers participated.

*Source of Data:* The main source of data for this study was TGT (math) teachers from government middle schools in Kamrup district (metro).

*Tool:* For this study, a close-ended questionnaire was used by the researcher.

*Data Collection:* To gather data, the researcher developed a self-made tool in the form of a close-ended questionnaire comprising 13 items. This instrument was administered to TGT (math) teachers of Kamrup district (metro) aiming to comprehend their perceptions on constructivist approach and its implementation in mathematics teaching, additionally, the survey sought to identify the challenges associated with the implementation of this approach.

## Data Analysis and Interpretation

After collecting the responses from 14 TGT (math) teachers of six government middle schools in Kamrup district (metro), we analysed the data to identify patterns and trends in the perceptions of teachers. This involves providing additional training for teachers, modifying instructional materials, or adjusting classroom practices to better align with the approach.

1. How many years of teaching experience do you have?
   It is observed that 43% of teachers have over 10 years of experience, 36% have less than 5 years of experience, and 21% have tenure ranging between 5 and 10 years.
2. Which grade levels do you currently teach mathematics?
   It is observed that, 50% of teachers participated are teaching in Class VIIIth, 31% of teachers participated are teaching in Class VIIth, and 19% of teachers are teaching in Class VIth.
3. What is the average number of students in your classrooms?
   It is observed that 50% of teachers manage classrooms with more than 40 students, 29% of teachers' class sizes range between 25 and 40 students, and 21% of teachers have less than 25 students in their classes.
4. Have you received any pedagogical workshop, training, or professional development on the constructivist teaching approach?
   It is found, 64% of teachers did not receive any kind of pedagogical training on constructivist teaching approach, while only 36% reported having undergone relevant sessions.
5. What do you think about group work? (You can choose more than one option.)

It is observed that that 35% of teachers think that "it is the method where all students get an equal chance to participate in activities", 24% think that "it is a method where students enhance their communicative skills", 23% think that "it is the method where poor students learn from talented students", and 18% think that group work is a way of active learning.

6. Which method of group work do you use in your class when you teach mathematics?
   It shows that 93% of teachers explain the topic first and then divide it into groups to discuss it, and 7% of teachers divide the topic into subparts, assigning each part to a group. Groups then exchange and learn different parts from each other.
7. What kind of resources should be provided to students during group work?
   From the data, it is seen that according to 86% of teachers, for group work, extra and sufficient materials are needed, and for 14% of teachers, there is no need for extra resources.
8. Which teaching approach do you implement in your mathematics teaching? (You can choose more than one option)
   It is observed that, 36% of teachers use collaborative learning, 27% use discovery learning, 20% use peer tutoring, and 17% use lecture-based teaching.
9. How would you describe your involvement with the constructivist teaching approach?
   It is seen that 71% of teachers are highly involved with the constructivist teaching approach, and only 29% have less involvement.
10. What do you consider to be the most significant benefits of implementing a constructivist approach in your classroom?
    It is noted that, for 7% of teachers, it improved students' understanding and retention; for 7%, it arouses active participation, motivation, and self-directed learning; for 7%, it develops critical thinking and problem-solving skills; and 79% of teachers supported all the options.
11. Do you agree with the following statement: "Constructivism is a valid and effective approach to teaching and learning?"
    It is observed that 100% of the teachers agreed with "Constructivism is a valid and effective approach to teaching and learning".
12. What do you consider to be the most significant challenges of implementing a constructivist approach in your classroom?
    It is noted thatfor 45% of teachers, it is time constraints; for 11% and 6% of teachers, it is a lack of instructional materials and support; lack of training and knowledge; and 38% agreed with all of the challenges above.
13. What are your overall thoughts on the constructivist approach in teaching mathematics?

It is observed that 48% of teachers are still learning about the constructivist approach. 42% of teachers believe that the constructivist approach to teaching and learning is valuable and effective. And 10% of teachers do not believe it is an effective approach to teaching and learning.

## Findings

1. How many years of teaching experience do you have?
   a. Less than 5 years
   b. 5-10 years
   c. More than 10 years

   The data indicates that a significant majority (43%) of teachers possess over 10 years of experience, while 36% of teachers have less than five years of professional experience.
2. Which grade levels do you currently teach Mathematics?
   a. VIth grade.
   b. VIIth grade.
   c. VIIIth grade.

   The data indicates that participation is distributed across different grade levels in middle school of Kamrup district (metro). Specifically, the majority (50%) of participating teachers are involved in teaching Class VIIIth, 31% in Class VIIth, and 19% in Class VIth.
3. What is the average number of students in your classrooms?
   a. Less than 25
   b. 25-40
   c. More than 40

   The data reveals that 50% of teachers have classrooms with over 40 students, 29% have class sizes between 25 and 40 students, and 21% have fewer than 25 students. This highlights the diverse range of class sizes teachers manage in their roles.
4. Have you received any pedagogical workshop, training, or professional development on the constructivist teaching approach?
   a. Yes
   b. No

   The data shows that the majority of the teachers, 64%, didn't get any training in constructivist teaching. Only 36% had sessions on it. This suggests teachers need more widespread professional development to learn about and use constructivist teaching.
5. What do you think about group work? (You can choose more than one option.)
   a. Group work is a way of active learning.
   b. It is a method where poor students learn from talent students.

c. It is a method where students enhance their communicative skills.
d. It is a method where all students get an equal chance to participate in activities.

The data reveals how teachers see group work differently. 35% say it gives everyone equal chances. 24% think it boosts communication skills, and 23% believe it helps less proficient students learn from talented peers. Also, 18% view group work as a way of active learning. These different opinions show how teachers see the benefits of using group work in learning.

6. Which method of group work do you use in your class when you teach mathematics?
   a. I divide the topic into subparts and each part is given to a group. After they learnt their part, they exchange in groups and learn other part of the topic from other group members.
   b. I explain the topic and then divide students into groups to discuss what I have explained. Then I ask each group member to answer my question.

   The data indicates that most teachers (93%) explain the topic to the whole class and then divide students into groups for discussion. Only 7% use a different method, breaking the topic into parts and assigning each to a group. With this approach, groups exchange and learn different parts. These findings show how teachers use various methods for group learning.

7. What kind of resources should be provided for students during group work?
   a. No extra resources are needed i.e. what is needed for the lecture is sufficient.
   b. Extra and sufficient materials are needed.

   The data indicates that 86% of teachers believe group work needs extra resources, while 14% think it does not. This shows varying opinions among teachers about the necessity of additional resources for group activities in the classroom.

8. Which teaching approach do you implement in your mathematics teaching? (You can choose more than one option)
   a. Collaborative Learning
   b. Peer Tutoring
   c. Discovery Learning
   d. Lecture-based teaching.

   The data highlights the various instructional approaches employed by teachers. Specifically, 36% of teachers utilize collaborative learning methods; another 27% employ discovery learning; 20% incorporate peer tutoring; and 17% prefer lecture-based teaching. These show the diverse instructional methods implemented by teachers to engage and educate their students.

9. How would you describe your involvement with the constructivist teaching approach?
   a. Highly involved
   b. Less involved
   c. Not involved

   The data reveals that most teachers, 71%, actively use the constructivist teaching approach, whereas only 29% are less involved in this method. These findings show that teachers have different levels of adoption of the constructivist teaching approach.

10. What do you consider to be the most significant benefits of implementing a constructivist approach in your classroom?
   a. Improved student understanding and retention.
   b. Active participation, motivation, and self-directed learning.
   c. Development of critical thinking and problem-solving skills.
   d. All the above.

   The data indicates that 7% of teachers think the constructivist approach helps students understand and remember better. Another 7% believe it makes students more active, motivated, and better at learning on their own. Also, 7% feel it helps develop critical thinking and problem-solving. The majority, 79% of teachers, support all these positive effects, indicating most teachers find value in different aspects of the constructivist teaching approach.

11. Do you agree with the following statement: "Constructivism is a valid and effective approach to teaching and learning?"
   a. Yes
   b. No

   The data reveals that all the teachers, 100% of them, believe that "constructivism is a good and useful way to teach and learn." This means every teacher agrees that using the constructivist approach in teaching is valid and effective.

12. What do you consider to be the most significant challenges of implementing a constructivist approach in your classroom?
   a. Time constraints
   b. Lack of instructional materials and support
   c. Lack of training and knowledge.
   d. All the above.

   According to the data, 45%, 11%, and 6% of teachers respond to the challenge with time constraints, a lack of instructional materials and support, and insufficient training, whereas 38% of teachers face all these challenges. This information shows the various difficulties that teachers encounter, including issues with time, resources, and training.

13. What are your overall thoughts on the constructivist approach in teaching mathematics?
    a. I believe the constructivist approach is a valuable and effective approach to teaching and learning.
    b. I am still learning about the constructivist approach and need more time to evaluate its effectiveness.
    c. I do not believe the constructivist approach is an effective approach to teaching and learning.

    According to the information, 48% of teachers are learning about the constructivist approach. Also, 42% believe it is useful for teaching and learning. However, 10% do not find it effective. This data gives insights into how teachers see and learn about the constructivist teaching approach.

## Suggestions

1. Providing FDP, workshops, seminars, training, etc. on constructivist approach-based teaching in mathematics to all TGT (mathematics) teachers.
2. Providing more resources like instructional materials, manipulative teaching aids, lesson modules, other hands-on learning tools, etc. to every TGT (math) teacher.
3. Create opportunities for teachers to collaborate and demonstrate constructivist practices to each other to ease the planning difficulties. Etc.

## Conclusion

Math blooms from exploration, not lectures. Constructivism empowers math learning by fostering active engagement, deep understanding, and critical thinking, but implementing constructivism requires resources, training, and support for teachers. Teachers are central to enabling the active construction of knowledge, and skilled teachers motivate and structure constructivist math learning. The present research study on teachers' perceptions and implementation of constructivist approaches in teaching mathematics revealed that teachers hold very favourable opinions about the recommended teaching aspects outlined in the study. The data analysis demonstrates that nearly all participants had a positive perception of constructivist teaching approaches. Based on the main findings, most of the teachers did not receive any training or FDP on constructivist teaching approaches. Despite this lack of formal training, the majority of teachers believe that a constructivist approach has significant benefits, including improving student understanding, fostering active participation, self-directed learning, and the development of critical thinking and problem-solving skills. Notably, 100% of the teachers affirmed that "constructivism is a valid and effective approach to teaching and learning". However, the study also identified the challenges faced by teachers in implementing a constructivist approach in their mathematics classrooms. The primary challenge highlighted was time constraints, along with other obstacles such as the lack of instructional materials and support, as well as a deficit in training and knowledge. To overcome the challenges, the Ministry of Education and other concerned bodies should take initiatives and enhance the implementation of the constructivist approach in teaching mathematics.

## References

Arın, E., Tunçer, B.K., & Demir, M.K. (2016). Primary school teachers' views on constructive classroom management, *International Electronic Journal of Elementary Education*, 8(3), 363-378.

Haque, F. (2018). Teachers' perception and practice of constructivist approach of English language teaching at the primary level in Bangladesh. *Society & Change*, *12*(1), 49-68

Laskar, A.H., & Bhattacharjee, S. (2022). Teachers' awareness on constructivist approach in learning: An analytical study, *International Journal of Health Sciences*, 6, 4313-4332.

Melesse, S., & Jirata, E. (2015). Teachers' Perception and Practice of Constructivist Teaching Approach: The Case of Secondary Schools of Kamashi Zone. *Science, Technology and Arts Research Journal*, *4*(4), 194-199.

Mishra, A., A Study on Teachers' Perception on Constructivist Approach of Teaching in Classroom Practices.

Mustapha, Yanti, et al. "Prospect and Challenges of Blended Learning in Malaysia: A Systematic Literature Review." *Asian Journal of Research in Education and Social Sciences* 4.3 (2022): 51-61.

Sattam, P. (2019). A Comparative Study of Teachers' and Students' Perceptions of the Effective English Teacher at Prince Sattam Bin Abdulaziz University

Shahida, N., & Jamal, S. (2021) Constructivism in Teaching and Learning: What Are Teacher Educators' perceptions? Vol 11 / No 2 / Jul-Dec 2021

Shah, R.K. (2019). Implementation of the Constructivist Approach: Primary School Teachers Perceptions and Experiences. Editorial Board, 8(12), 120.

Sthapak, S., & Singh, M.K. (2017). Constructivist approach and attitude of teachers: A study on Bilaspur district, *International Journal of Advanced Research and Development*, 2(5), 107-111.

https://www.bing.com/ck/a?!&&p=5701ef6f9b1016f0JmltdHM9MTcwMzg5NDQwMCZpZ3VpZD0yNDQ2Yjg5Ni1lMmI2LTZmYjctMjFlNC1hYjYxZTM1ZTZlYTYmaW5zaWQ9NTIyMw&ptn=3&ver=2&hsh=3&fclid=2446b896-e2b6-6fb7-21e4-ab61e35e6ea6&psq=nep2020+&u=a1aHR0cHM6Ly9uY2VydC5uaWMuaW4vcGRmL25lcC8vTkVQXzIwMjAucGRm&ntb=1

# 6

# Changing Contexts in Global and Indian Teachers

Shumaila Saif Siddiqui

## Introduction

"शिक्षक सर्वेभ्यो नमः" (Shikshak Sarvebhyo Namah), a revered Sanskrit proverb, encapsulates the profound sentiment that teachers are worthy of utmost respect and gratitude. This age-old proverb serves as a painful reminder of the critical role educators play in influencing the future as we begin our investigation of the shifting context of teacher education in both the Indian and global contexts.

Within the ever-changing context of education, pedagogies, technology, and the global interconnection of learning are all having a transforming effect on the role of teachers. This proverb emphasizes society's shared duty to identify and respond to the evolving demands imposed on educators in addition to acknowledging the respect that is owed to educators.

This introduction sets out to explore the subtleties of the evolving teacher education situation. The core of the proverb — acknowledging the commitment, knowledge, and influence teachers have on moulding the minds that will create the future — resonates as we negotiate the complexities of educational reforms, the incorporation of technology, and the necessity for inclusive practices.

## Concept of Teacher Education

Teacher education is the process and program by which people gain the information, skills, and competencies required to become effective and certified educators. It entails rigorous training of individuals aspiring to become teachers, as well as continual professional development for practising teachers to improve their teaching talents throughout their careers.

The fundamental goals of teacher education are to provide educators with the academic understanding and practical skills necessary for effective teaching. This includes a variety of elements, including:

1. Pedagogical Knowledge: Teachers should have a thorough understanding of teaching methodologies, instructional tactics, and curriculum development. This includes understanding how to effectively prepare and

deliver classes, assess student learning, and tailor teaching methods to diverse learning types.

2. Subject Matter Expertise: Educators must have a thorough mastery of the information they teach, based on the level and subject. This requires an understanding of the subject matter as well as the ability to communicate it understandably to learners.
3. School Management: Teacher education programs generally cover ways to foster a healthy and inclusive school atmosphere. This involves abilities in controlling student behaviour, providing a healthy learning environment, and responding to varied needs within a classroom.
4. Effective Assessment and Evaluation: Teachers must have the ability to evaluate student progress, comprehend various assessment methods, and use data to make informed instructional decisions. This includes formative assessments during teaching and summative assessments to assess overall student learning.
5. Technology Integration: As technology becomes more prevalent in education, teacher education programs may incorporate training on the effective use of tools, online resources, and digital platforms in the classroom.
6. Cultural Competence and Inclusiveness: Teachers must be prepared to work with varied student populations. This entails knowing and accepting cultural differences, tailoring teaching approaches to fit the needs of all students, and encouraging an inclusive learning environment.
7. Reflective Practice: Reflective practice is a key focus in teacher education. Educators are urged to evaluate their teaching methods regularly, reflect on their experiences, and make changes to continuously enhance their classroom performance.

Teacher education can take several forms, including undergraduate and graduate degree programs, teacher certification programs, and professional development courses. The success of teacher education programs is critical for ensuring that educators are well-prepared to fulfil the demands of modern education while also contributing to their student's academic and personal growth.

The National Council for Teacher Education (NCTE) is a governmental authority in India that monitors and governs teacher education. The NCTE is crucial in establishing the criteria and requirements for teacher education programs across the country. According to the NCTE Act of 1993 and later changes, the notion of teacher education, as defined by NCTE, includes many fundamental aspects:

1. Defining Standards: NCTE defines and maintains standards for teacher education programs. These requirements apply to all levels of teacher

education, including pre-service (such as Bachelor of Education — B.Ed. programs) and in-service teacher education.

2. Curriculum Design: NCTE provides guidelines for designing and structuring teacher education courses. This includes defining the curriculum, pedagogical approaches, and practical experiences that should be incorporated into teacher education programs to ensure that educators are well-prepared for their positions.
3. Entry and Exit standards: The NCTE provides the standards for admission to teacher education programs. This includes outlining the academic requirements, qualifying criteria, and entrance examination methods. Furthermore, NCTE specifies the requirements for completing these programs.
4. Quality Assurance: The NCTE strives to maintain and improve teacher education nationwide. It establishes systems for accreditation and quality assurance to ensure that teacher education institutions meet the required requirements and deliver high-quality training to prospective teachers.
5. Professional Development: NCTE emphasizes the value of ongoing professional development for teachers. The council may issue guidelines for in-service training programs, workshops, and other efforts designed to improve the skills and knowledge of practising teachers.
6. Innovations in Teacher Education: NCTE encourages innovation and research in teacher education. It promotes projects that improve teacher training methods, technological integration, and overall program efficacy.
7. Regulatory Functions: NCTE operates as a regulatory authority, ensuring that teacher education institutes follow the council's norms and requirements. To ensure accountability and quality, teacher education programs and institutions are inspected, reviewed, and evaluated regularly.

It is crucial to note that the norms and standards established by NCTE may change, and persons interested in teacher education should consult the most recent NCTE regulations and announcements for up-to-date information. NCTE's overarching purpose is to ensure that teacher education in India meets current educational demands and helps to the development of competent and ethical educators.

## Change in the teacher education context in India since independence

Since Independence, the context of teacher education in India has undergone significant changes, shaped by evolving educational policies, societal demands, and technological advancements. Here is an overview of the changing landscape of teacher education in the Indian scenario over the decades:

1. Early Years Post-independence (1947-1960s): The primary goal was to increase educational access, which resulted in the development of several schools and teacher training institutes. Traditional teacher training approaches survived, focusing on pedagogy and subject knowledge.
2. 1970s-1980s: The Kothari Commission (1964–1966) pushed for qualitative reforms in teacher education. The formation of Regional Colleges of Education was intended to improve the quality of teacher training. Curriculum modifications embraced a more comprehensive view of education, stressing child-centered pedagogy.
3. 1990s-2000s: The 1986 National Policy on Education (NPE) and 1992 Program of Action (POA) placed a fresh emphasis on teacher education changes. District Institutes of Education and Training (DIETs) were founded to decentralize teacher education and respond to local needs. The emphasis switched to in-service teacher training and ongoing professional development.
4. 2000s-2010s: The Right to Education (RTE) Act of 2009 emphasized the need of skilled teachers and established minimum criteria for them. The National Curriculum Framework for Teacher Education (NCFTE) 2009 sought to connect teacher education with the ideas of NCF 2005. The establishment of the two-year Bachelor of Education (B.Ed.) curriculum became the standard.
5. National Education Policy (NEP) 2020 and Recent Developments: NEP 2020 is a ground-breaking strategy that prioritizes interdisciplinary education, a four-year integrated B.Ed. degree, and ongoing professional development. The strategy emphasizes the use of technology in teacher education and takes a comprehensive approach to training educators for a variety of demands.

There is a greater emphasis on research, innovation, and global perspectives in teacher education.

*Challenges and Future Directions*: Despite these good advances, difficulties remain, such as variable quality across teacher education institutions, gaps in in-service training, and the need for effective policy implementation. The future path entails ongoing adaptation to changing educational trends, harnessing technology, supporting research and innovation, and connecting teacher education with the dynamic demands of a worldwide society.

The changing context of teacher education in India reflects a continual effort to enhance the quality and relevance of teacher training programs, ensuring that educators are well-equipped to meet the evolving demands of the education system.

## Changing context of teacher education in the global scenario

Several issues that cross national boundaries impact the changing setting of teacher education in the global scenario.

Several trends and changes influence the landscape of teacher preparation on a global basis.

1. Emphasis on Global Competencies: Teachers must teach more than just subject-specific information, including critical thinking, cultural awareness, and communication skills. Teacher education programs are evolving to guarantee that educators can prepare pupils for a globalised environment.
2. Technology integration: Technology integration in education is a worldwide phenomenon. Teacher education programs throughout the world are embracing training in educational technology, online teaching techniques, and digital literacy to prepare educators for 21st-century classrooms.
3. Inclusive Education and Diversity: Globally, there is a growing emphasis on inclusive education for various student groups. Teacher education programs strive to equip educators to meet the different needs of students, including those with disabilities, while also fostering inclusive and equitable learning environments.
4. Sustainable Development Goals (SDGs): The United Nations Sustainable Development Goals (SDGs) have shifted the worldwide attention to education. Teacher education connects with SDG 4 (Quality Education) by preparing educators to help achieve inclusive, equitable, and high-quality education for everyone.
5. Lifelong Learning and Professional Development: The notion of lifelong learning is gaining popularity among educators internationally. Continuous professional development is regarded as critical for keeping instructor's current on developing educational practices, pedagogies, and research.
6. International Collaboration and Mobility: Teacher education programs are increasingly collaborating globally. Institutions form collaborations and exchanges to share best practices, research discoveries, and new teaching approaches. This promotes a global perspective among instructors.
7. Research-based Practices: The global context highlights the significance of research-based practices in teacher education. Programs attempt to include educational research into curriculum creation, ensuring that instructors are up to date on the newest research results in their sector.
8. Multilingual Education: As multilingualism becomes more recognized, teacher education programs worldwide are tackling the problems and possibilities that come with linguistic variety in the classroom.

9. Quality Assurance and Accreditation: These processes are increasing worldwide. There is an initiative underway to set international standards for teacher education, ensuring that schools throughout the world meet uniform quality norms.
10. Addressing Global Challenges: Teacher education supports attempts to solve global concerns such as climate change, social justice, and health. The programs seek to produce educators who can help to develop a more sustainable and equitable society.

The shifting context of teacher education in the global scenario shows a common commitment to educate educators to manage the complexity of a quickly changing and interconnected world while creating inclusive, creative, and high-quality learning experiences for students all over the world.

Teacher education in the 21st century has been significantly influenced by the challenges and opportunities presented by the globalized world. Here are some key considerations:

### *I. Teacher Education in the 21st Century Globalized world*

In the constantly changing environment of the twenty-first century globalized world, teacher education is at the forefront of transformational change. To negotiate the complexities of a worldwide classroom, educators must now possess a wide range of skills. Cultural competency is essential when instructors interact with pupils from many backgrounds, creating an inclusive and harmonious learning environment. Technological literacy becomes a non-negotiable need, enabling instructors to use digital tools that span boundaries and connect schools around the world. The curriculum must have a global perspective that crosses geographical borders and incorporates insights from many cultures and educational systems. Language ability, not only in one's home tongue but also in many languages, becomes a benefit for efficient communication and comprehension. Locally and internationally, collaborative teaching techniques encourage educators to work together and learn from one another. Continuous professional development is essential for keeping instructors up to date on developing pedagogies, global trends, and creative practices. Furthermore, the curriculum should promote critical thinking, problem-solving abilities, and an understanding of global concerns, equipping teachers to raise knowledgeable and involved global citizens. In summary, teacher education in the twenty-first century is a dynamic process that shapes educators to be adaptive, culturally aware, and technologically competent leaders in a globalized educational environment.

### *II. Globalized Teacher Education and Training Curricula*

In today's worldwide society, teacher education and training curriculum must undergo a radical transition to educate educators for the numerous and interrelated issues of the modern world. The curriculum should incorporate cross-cultural competencies, stressing cultural awareness and encouraging inclusive classroom environments that reflect the worldwide diversity of student populations. Technological competency should be a cornerstone, providing instructors with the ability to use digital technologies for better learning experiences and worldwide cooperation. A global perspective should pervade the curriculum, ensuring that instructors comprehend worldwide educational systems, varied cultural backgrounds, and global challenges. Language ability, both in one's home language and maybe in other languages, is critical for efficient communication and comprehension in today's international educational environment. Collaborative teaching and learning initiatives, such as virtual exchanges and international collaborations, should be used to promote teamwork and interconnection. Professional development activities, with a focus on continuous learning, are critical for keeping educators up to date on changing worldwide trends and teaching innovations. The curriculum should promote critical thinking and problem-solving abilities in teachers, equipping them to face global concerns. Environmental and sustainable education should also play a role in raising awareness of global environmental challenges. Ultimately, adaptation and flexibility should be built into the curriculum, allowing instructors to negotiate the dynamic and ever-changing terrain of global education.

### *III. Models of Teacher Education and Training for the 21st Century*

Teacher education and training paradigms are changing dramatically in the twenty-first century to meet the needs of an interconnected and fast-growing society. One new paradigm stresses a comprehensive approach that includes technology proficiency, cultural competency, and instructional creativity. This approach highlights the value of digital literacy, training teachers to successfully use technology in the classroom and engage with global educational resources. Cultural competency is built into the fabric of this paradigm, ensuring that instructors can navigate different classrooms and create inclusive learning environments. Another model emphasizes real-world classroom experiences and encourages instructors to work in groups. This method not only provides instructors with practical skills, but it also promotes adaptability and teamwork, both of which are essential in today's changing educational scene. Furthermore, a lifetime learning paradigm is gaining traction, stressing ongoing professional growth throughout a teacher's career. This guarantees that instructors keep current on new pedagogies, global trends, and creative teaching techniques. Overall, these approaches represent the diverse nature of teacher education in the twenty-first century, addressing the need for technological knowledge, cultural sensitivity, practical experience, and a commitment to continuous professional development.

### *IV. Globalizing the Teaching Profession*

Globalizing the teaching profession is a critical requirement in the twenty-first century, as education crosses boundaries and becomes more linked. This paradigm change entails teaching teachers to negotiate the difficulties of a globalized environment. Teachers should be cross-culturally competent, able to comprehend and accept various viewpoints in their classes. Technological competency is essential, allowing instructors to use digital technologies to link pupils to a variety of global information. Collaboration becomes a cornerstone as teachers form worldwide connections to enhance mutual learning experiences and prepare students for a global workforce. Language competency, particularly the capacity to teach many languages, improves communication and comprehension in multicultural classrooms.

A globalized teaching profession also entails incorporating global viewpoints into the curriculum, ensuring that students receive knowledge about worldwide concerns and varied cultural contexts. Furthermore, professional development should cross national lines, giving instructors with opportunity to keep current on global educational trends and best practices. Finally, globalizing the teaching profession entails developing educators who can inspire, connect, and educate pupils to flourish in a complex and varied society.

### *V) 21st Century's Teacher Education Program*

The 21st century teacher education program symbolizes a paradigm change, recognizing education's developing demands in a fast-changing world. This unique curriculum is distinguished by its comprehensive approach, which incorporates critical components to prepare educators for the complexity of modern teaching. Technological proficiency is essential, as instructors are prepared to navigate and integrate digital resources, ensuring that they remain effective facilitators of learning in the digital era. Another important aspect is cultural competence, which emphasizes understanding other origins and viewpoints as well as promoting inclusive learning environments. The curriculum promotes experiential learning, giving prospective educators hands-on classroom exposure and collaboration possibilities. Lifelong learning is built into the program's fabric, encouraging instructors to pursue ongoing professional development to stay current on developing pedagogies and global trends. Furthermore, a global perspective is included into the curriculum, exposing instructors to worldwide educational techniques and training them to raise pupils as global citizens. In essence, the 21st century teacher education program is a dynamic, forward-thinking endeavour that not only transmits critical skills but also fosters an adaptable, innovative attitude and a dedication to lifelong learning.

### *V. Twenty-first Century Teacher in India*

The Twenty-first Century Teacher Education Program in India provides a game-changing strategy to prepare educators for today's dynamic problems. Embracing the modern world, the curriculum promotes digital literacy, ensuring that instructors can use technology into their classrooms to improve learning experiences. Cultural awareness is emphasized, considering the different makeup of India's student body. Teachers are trained to manage and celebrate cultural differences, therefore promoting inclusive settings.

The curriculum emphasizes experiential learning, giving prospective educators hands-on teaching experience and allowing them to build practical skills and flexibility. Lifelong learning is a basic premise, with a commitment to ongoing professional development that keeps instructors up to speed on changing pedagogical approaches and worldwide educational trends.

Given India's linguistic variety, language competence is an important factor, and instructors should be fluent in different languages to properly engage with pupils from various linguistic backgrounds. The curriculum also takes a global perspective, exposing instructors to foreign educational best practices and a variety of teaching approaches.

*Teacher Education = Teaching Skills + Pedagogical Theory + Professional skills*

Thus, the Twenty-first Century Teacher Education Program in India is intended to develop educators who are technologically capable, culturally competent, and have the abilities and attitude required to navigate the ever-changing environment of education in the twenty-first century methodologies.

## Conclusion

Finally, the Twenty-first Century Teacher Education Program in India exemplifies a forward-thinking and comprehensive project focused at preparing educators for the challenges of contemporary education. By emphasizing technological literacy, cultural competency, experiential learning, and a commitment to lifelong learning, the curriculum recognizes the diverse and dynamic requirements of both instructors and students in today's educational context. As India continues to change in the global setting, this curriculum guarantees that educators are not only prepared with the essential skills, but also instilled with an adaptable and innovative attitude. By embracing linguistic variety and adopting a global viewpoint, the curriculum equips teachers as positive change agents capable of developing the next generation of informed and internationally conscious citizens. Overall, India's Twenty-first Century Teacher Education Program is an important step in developing an education system that meets the needs of the twenty-first century.

## *References*


Dilanchian, A. (2023, October 19). Book Review: Diversity, Equity, Inclusion, and Belonging Field Guide, *Journal of Experiential Education*. https://doi.org/10.1177/10538259231207063

Martin, R.J. Multicultural Social Reconstructionist education: Design for diversity in teacher education, *Teacher Education Quarterly* 21(3) 77-89, E.J 492(4), 1994.

Loughlin, O.M. Daring the imagination unlocking voices of dissent and possibility in teaching. Theory into Practice 24(2) 170-116 E.J 512860, 1995.

Saravanakumar, A.R., & Subbiah, S. (2011). Teacher Education Programme Through Distance Mode – A Technological Approach, *Indian Journal of Applied Research*, India ISSN: 2249 –555x, 1(3).

Soundararajan, M., Prabakaran B., Padmini Devi K.R., Saravanakumar. A.R., (2022). *Teacher Professionalism and Teacher Education*, Kaav Publications, 1-205 DOI: https://doi.org/10.52458/9789391842598.2022.tb

Subbiah, S., Saravanakumar, A.R., Perumal R., (2012). Multidimensional practices in teacher education (TE) through distance education (DE). *Indian Streams Research Journal*, (1)12, 1-4.

Biswas, S. (2022, October 14). Developmental Context of Teacher Education in the Indian Scenario. Research Gate Education_in_the_Indian_Scenario https://www.researchgate.net/publication/364330115_Developmental_Context_of_Teacher_ (2018, January 1). Past and Present Scenario of Teacher Education in India: Future Prospectn Global Perspective.
https://www.ijcrt.org/papers/IJCRT1705200.pdf.

# 7

# Teacher Education Institutions in Kashmir
## *Recent Developments*

Bashir Ahmad Khan

### Introduction

> "*If you are teaching today what you were teaching five years ago, either the discipline is dead or you are...*" Noam Chomsky

Stating with the above quotation, it is evident that no education system of any country can excel unless it has a strong foundation of teacher education system in the country, we can say that for the successful future of the children as well as the society, we need to make entire education system successful.

The Economic Survey 2006-07 reported that the State of J&K belongs to the lowest social sector in terms of education, public health, sanitation, and social welfare. So, it was seen one among the last four poorest as well as illiterate states in India with the per capita income of Rs. 17,174 against national Rs 25,904 per annum (Dar, 2019).

### Teacher Education in Jammu and Kashmir

The first university established in the state was the University of Jammu and Kashmir in 1948, which was bifurcated into two separate state universities — University of Jammu and University of Kashmir in 1969. The department of education at university was established in the year 1965 prior to its bifurcation. However, first course of teacher education is traced back to 1937 as the first teacher training institution was established as Teacher Training School in the year 1937 which was later promoted into College of Education known as Government College of Education, Srinagar in the year 1968. The college was also promoted and renamed as Institute of Advanced Studies in Education on recommendations of Joint Review Mission commissioned by Department of Higher Education, Government of India. The institute works under the Cluster University Srinagar established under the RUSA Scheme since 2017. During the year 1980-81 there were only three teacher Education Colleges in Jammu and Kashmir with the enrolment around 300 students which led to around 150 colleges in the year 2018 with the enrolment around forty-four thousand (Dar, 2019).

Looking at the scenario of teacher education system in the erstwhile state of Jammu and Kashmir, there are various types of teacher institutions providing trainings such as two Sate and two Central Universities. The two Government Colleges of Education (IASE) working as constituent colleges of Cluster universities of Jammu and Srinagar, Baba Ghulam Shah Badshah University Rajouri, DIETs at each district, recently established SCERT in 2020 and self-financed/ private colleges of education affiliated to University of Jammu and University of Kashmir. Besides it, there is a college of Teacher Education called as MANUU CTE Srinagar, an affiliated college of Maulana Azad National Urdu University, Hyderabad, Telangana.

With the abrogation of article 370 (on 5 August 2019), the implementation of NCTE norms and regulations was automatically extended to J&K (Gazette of India, 2020). The imbalance between the teacher education programme and job opportunities at primary education level from the governmentt as well as the delayed examinations by university and much more theoretical approach has extinguished the interest of the people towards B.Ed. Program (Shah 2019). The privatisation of Higher education especially in teacher education has also put the system into challenges because due to the lack of proper mechanism and monitoring system, the private colleges had become the efficient business hubs for the owners. The mushrooming of secondary teacher education institutions, the unplanned growth, and lack of government willingness to invest in teacher education have affected the quality teacher education very drastically.

## The Study

### *Review of the Literature*

*Rather (2023)* carried out a study to examine the teacher education system in Jammu and Kashmir in terms of the structural as well as functional aspects. The study also examined the physical and digital infrastructure, faculty strength, enrolment among colleges of education in Jammu and Kashmir. The study also aimed to examine the impact of two-year B. Ed. Program on the enrolment level of teacher education institutions. The study found that there is a significant shortage of faculty in training institutions. The private college carried a very low number of qualified teachers and most of them are working on temporary bases as guest faculties.

*Bhattacharya (2021)* studied the developmental changes in teacher education since NEP, 1986 and tried to analyse National Educational Policy 2020. The teacher education was reorganised from time to time in the light of various committees and commissions such as Justice Varma Commission 2012 which led its apex body NCTE to reorient the regulations in teacher education in the year 2014. And in 2018 the new regulations for four-year integrated teacher education program which was adopted by various universities in the country.

*Bhat (2020)* aimed to investigate the historical background of various National Curriculums Frameworks for Teacher Education and compare the various curricular areas of NCFTE 2009 and NCTE Curriculum Framework for Teacher Education 2014. It was found that there were severe variations in weightage in terms of theory and practice portions as well as difference within universities.

*Dar (2019)*. In this study as the growth of teacher education in Jammu and Kashmir, the researcher has given a historical description of the development of teacher education system in the region. The development of teacher education institutions has overwhelmingly increased from the only three colleges in 1980-81 up to 148 till the year 2018. The study found various issues such as poor integration of skills, lack of motivation among teachers and mismatch between demand and supply.

*Shah (2016)* highlighted the root cause of downfall of teacher education system and institutions in the state of Jammu and Kashmir. The researchers found that there has been an acute growth of teacher education institutions, but on the other hand no quality measure or criteria has been followed due to the lack of NCTE regulations because of its exemption being applied into the state. The employability of teacher education courses has witnessed a downfall due to the faulty recruitment policies by government and ministry of education in recruiting teachers in school education department.

*Showkeen (2016)*. The study examined the different problems of teacher education in Jammu and Kashmir State where the researcher found the problem of infrastructure, mass admission without entrance and pupil teacher ratio along with standards which lead to the deficiency of quality in teacher educations. The study showed that there was a high pupil teacher ratio which should be reduced around 1:10. The study also revealed that due to the job criteria at primary level, the interest of aspirants was also decreased.

## Methodology

The study is descriptive in nature; therefore, a survey technique was used in which an institutional survey schedule was used, which is prepared based on the guiding documents from NCTE (N&R) 2014 and NAAC parameters. And some focussed group interviews were also used to collect the necessary narratives from the respondents.

*Population of* the study are the private B.Ed. Colleges of Kashmir Division. For the **sample** twenty colleges are selected through the cluster sampling from the three clusters such as North, Central and South Kashmir comprising six districts such as Kupwara and Bandipora; Srinagar and Ganderbal and Annantnag and Kulgam respectively. The focussed group interviews were also done and the narratives were recorded for the in-depth monitoring of the problem.

*Tools:* Self *constructed* Institutional Survey Schedule; Interview schedule.

## Data Analysis and Findings

Though it is a descriptive survey research, and the data is collected from the institutions through self-constructed institutional survey schedule. Therefore, the analysis is done through the simple frequency and percentage against each item of the survey schedule available in each of the selected college.

### *Institution wise Intake Capacity and Current Enrolment*

From the data it is revealed that only 04 out of total 20 selected colleges have the intake capacity of 50, that is 20 per cent of colleges, while as enrolment upto 50 was seen in six colleges that means only 30 per cent colleges have the enrolment of one unit that is fifty students in a two-year B. Ed. Course. Among 13 colleges, the intake capacity from 50-100 was seen, which forms the percentage of 65, while as the same number of enrolments was found in same number of colleges. The intake capacity from 100-150 was found in three colleges that is the 15 per cent while as the enrolment from 100-150 was only found in one college, which formed the percentage of five out of total selected colleges.

### *Teaching Faculty Strength of the Colleges*

The data reveals that out of total 110 faculty members working in these B. Ed. colleges, 20 (18.18%) were found permanent. These permanent members are either the chairman or the principal of these colleges. "But the full-time faculty members too do not have any future in it as their job is secured within the interest of college chairman as well as the functioning of these colleges." 50 (45.45%) are full time contractual lecturers who are hired for the whole academic year excluding the winter vacations. Though they have not to apply every year. 30 (27.27%) are guest faculties, *but we work in these colleges for few months during any inspection from university* (*one respondent narrate*d). In terms of the faculty strength, 15% that is only three out of total 20 colleges were having the number of faculty members less than five, while as 15 (75%) colleges had the number of faculty members from 05-07. Only two (10%) colleges had the faculty strength from 08-10.

### *Qualification of Faculty Members*

Data reveals that 91 (82.80%) faculty members out of total 110 are having masters in social sciences while 19 (17.20%) faculty members are having masters in science subjects. However, it was also found that 24 (21.82%) colleges have the faculty members having Master's along with M.Ed. degree, while 86 (78.18%) colleges possessed teachers having Masters with B.Ed. only. It was also found that there was no faculty member having Masters in visual arts or computer-based degree working in private B. Ed. Colleges in Kashmir.

### *Institution-wise availability of Administrative and Professional Staff*

Data reveals that the administrative as well as professional staff in selected colleges shows that 20 (100%) colleges were having the adequate library facilities as well as librarians. Three (15%) colleges have one lab assistants as directed by NCTE. All the colleges are having one office cum account assistants. Only 3 (15%) colleges are having the storekeepers while the number of lab attend/ helpers, only 20 (50%) were seen as per the expected umber of 40 as per NCTE.

### *Physical/ Infrastructural facilities*

Data reveals that pertaining to the infrastructural facilities, 15 (75%) colleges were having the number of classrooms up to four only, whereas only 05 (that is 25%) colleges were found with the number of classrooms from 5-8. But it was found that all the 20 (100%) colleges have separate administrative offices and principal's rooms as well as separate staff rooms but common for male and female staff members. However, it was also found that all the colleges had separate washrooms for male and female staff as well as for students. Only 04 (that is 20%) colleges had multipurpose halls as well as ICT Resource centres. No college was found having a curriculum laboratory as well as Health and Physical Education resource.

### *Instructional Facilities*

Data reveals that all the colleges enjoyed magnificent libraries all the 20 (100%) colleges had ample number of books, journals, encyclopaedia available with multiple thousands in number. Only over some instructional facilities the results were disheartening. One (5%) college was having a language resource centre and psychology lab, but the irony was that, there was no trained teacher expert to use it properly to instruct the students. The social science lab was found in 03 (15%) colleges but there too was nothing to excite because only a few geographical and political maps and a globe along with some pictures of rocks, shells and historical monuments were there. Mathematics lab was not found in any college at all.

### *Programme Implementation*

Data shows that regarding the programme implementation, only 08 (40%) colleges were having their academic calendars published in their brochures or on the college website, however the duration, admission procedure, announcement of examination forms and date sheet as well as results are under the discretion of Kashmir University. All the 20 (100%) colleges are having arrangements with the neighbouring schools for IPOTs, but there are two distinct narratives, "*the private schools do not allow the colleges to conduct the practicum in their schools due to strict schedules, while as govt. schools leave everything onto the teacher trainees*". During practice teaching and internship programs in various school in-charge class teachers ask trainees to *"Do practice and teach the lessons which I have not taught so far so that I will not have to teach the same lessons again"* (Respondent replied). Only 06 (30%) colleges are conducting annual day, national education days and other awareness programmes. Eight (40%) colleges were seen which celebrate other important days such as Teacher's Day, Independence day as well as Republic day.

## Recent Developments in Teacher Education

As we know that due to the special provision of Article 370, the state had its own constitution, state flag and state laws. In some of the domains there was partial exemption from implementation of central laws into the state among which the application of NCTE was one of its kind.

As NCTE had published its curriculum framework for teacher education in 2009 called as NCFTE-2009 was not also applied to Jammu and Kashmir, neither its major published regulations called as NCTE Regulations 2014 (Appendix III, IV & V of NCTE Document 2014). But the university of Kashmir had already adopted some of its directions for running the teacher education programmes within its departments at north campus, south campus, and main campus along with Government College of Education, Srinagar as well as across all the affiliated private B.Ed. colleges in Kashmir *(Acad/KU/16)*.

In the year 2009 two Central Universities were established each one at Jammu and Kashmir. Both the universities are providing teacher education courses. In 2013 ministry of higher education appointed a committee called Joint Review committee which stressed upon the reorganisation of teacher education system in Jammu and Kashmir. Overhauling of teacher education program including infrastructure, faculty strength as well as teacher qualification was kept as main minutes of committee. On the recommendations of JRM 2013 the government colleges of Jammu and Kashmir were upgraded and renamed as Institute of Advanced Studies in Education at Srinagar and Jammu.

In 2016 two cluster universities one each at Srinagar and Jammu were established under Srinagar and Jammu Cluster Universities Act, 2016 [Act No. III of 2016]. The government colleges of education Jammu and Srinagar (IASEs) work under respective cluster universities, cluster university of Jammu has its separate school of teacher education besides its affiliated government college of education Jammu.

SIE was promoted into the SCERT Jammu and Srinagar as well as Jammu and Kashmir public university bill was introduced in the year 2022.

## Conclusion

Teacher education system in Jammu and Kashmir with respect to institutions as well as teacher preparations are somehow lagging behind the expected criteria. The institutions are having a good number of buildings as well as land areas as recommended by the NCTE as one of its requirements. The physical and infrastructural as well as instructional facilities are alarming which needs to be rectified. However, the hope is also instilled as the extension of NCTEs application in the teacher education system in Jammu and Kashmir. The admission procedure is already decided by the University of Kashmir and the syllabus, examination procedure, course content, foundational, pedagogical studies as well as practicum are also mentioned by the affiliating Kashmir university, however the students have the choice in selecting their own choice of college, optional papers – one each from language and pedagogical papers (Acad/KU/16).

## References


Rather, R. (2023). "An Objective Based Evaluation of Teacher Education in Jammu and Kashmir." Doctoral thesis, School of Education, Central University of Kashmir.

Bhattacharya, A. (2021). Progress of Teacher Education after NPE, 1986. *International Journal of Research Publication and Review*, 2(7), 740-743. Retrieved from: https://www.ijrpr.com

Bhat, M.A. (2020). "Teacher's effectiveness in relation to their attitude towards teaching, self-esteem and organizational climate in Jammu and Kashmir." Doctoral thesis, Department of Education, Annamalai University Tamil Nadu.

NCTE, 2020 Regional Committees Territorial Jurisdiction, Regulations, (Gazette of India, New Delhi, the 27 January 2020). https://ncte.gov.in/website/regulation.aspx

Dar, R. (2019). "Growth of teacher education in Jammu and Kashmir, A modern perspective, its trends and challenges." *International Journal of Advanced Multidisciplinary Scientific Research* (IJAMSR), 5(*6*), pp.40-50. http://dx.doi.org/10.31426/ijamsr.2019.2.3.1316

Shah, H. (2016). Dismal teacher education in the state of Jammu and Kashmir? Who is responsible? The communications, 24,(1), pp 147-150. Retrieved from http://ddeku.edu.in/Files/2cfa4584-5afe-43ce-aa4b-ad936cc9d3be/Journal/efffc8b8-02d7-40ce-9e2d-3d9e048be746.pdf

Gul, S.B.A; & Ganai, M.Y. (2016). "Teacher Education and Its Present Problems: A Prospective View of Teacher Education of Jammu and Kashmir." *Insight: Journal of Applied Research in Education*, 21, (21), pp 259-264. Retrieved from https://scholar.google.co.in/citations?view_op=view_citation&hl=en&user=SdRjh4QAAAAJ&cstart=20&pagesize=80&citation_for_view=SdRjh4QAAAAJ:nb7KW1ujOQ8C

Sikand, Y. (2008). Chapter 9 Islamist Militancy in Kashmir: The case of the Lashkar-e Taiba. In a. Rao, M. Bollig & M. Böck (ed.), *The practice of war: production, reproduction and communication of armed violence* (pp. 215-238). New York, Oxford: Berghahn books. Https://doi.org/10.1515/9780857450593-013

[Migrator 2018]. State policy on teacher education - Greater Kashmir

***(Acad/KU/16).*** https://ramishtcollege.com/wp-content/uploads/2017/03/BEd_2.pdf

GOI. Press Information Bureau of India 2019. https://www.mha.gov.in/sites/default/files/PressReleaseJ%26KDecisions_06082019.pdf

# 8

# Need of Culturally Responsive and Relevent Teaching Today

Priti Sangray

## Introduction

The concepts of culture and education are intertwined, as culture has the power to shape our frames of reference, our ways of thinking and acting, our beliefs, and even our feelings by moulding the educational content, operational modes, and contexts. In the 21st century, a society is culturally diverse having a mixture of individuals from different communities, linguistic backgrounds, religions and so on which we refer to as multiculturalism. Multiculturalism does not only describe the co-existence of different cultures but also a policy that protects cultural diversity.

Multicultural education emerged in the backdrop of the Civil Rights Movement in the 1960s in the United States demanding the eradication of discrimination in education, employment, housing, and communal accommodation by African Americans (Banks, 2016). The movement had a significant influence in the education sector, allowing all coloured students to play an active role in social issues, also the movement consequences in the reformation of the curriculum which reflects their cultures, histories, and perspectives. NEP 2020 mentioned that "Education is the single greatest tool for achieving social justice and equality" (MHRD, 2020, p. 24). "Multicultural education is a field of study designed to increase educational equity for all students that incorporates, for this purpose, content, concepts, principles, theories, and paradigms from history, social and behavioural sciences, and particularly from ethnic studies and women studies" (p. xii). However, multicultural education encourages critical thinking about power struggles involving gender, class, and ethnicity. It also focuses on preventing racist practices and addressing racial oppression and inequities (Gollnick & Chinn, 2017). Thus, teachers are key players in integrating multicultural education into the classroom because they can modify their methods, to better meet the needs of the students. Additionally, teachers must be capable of self-reflection and can analyse and reflect on their teachings (Gollnick & Chinn, 2017).

## Need of the Study in India

Although the Indian education system and successive government policies have made steady progress toward closing gender and social category gaps at all levels of school education, large disparities still exist, particularly at the secondary level, especially for socio-economically disadvantaged groups that have historically been underrepresented in education. According to the NEP 2020, Socio-economically Disadvantage Groups (SEDGs) can be broadly classified based on gender identities (particularly female and transgender individuals), socio-cultural identities (such as Scheduled Castes, Scheduled Tribes, OBCs, and minorities), geographical identities (such as students from villages, small towns, and aspirational districts), disabilities (including learning disabilities), and socio-economic conditions (such as migrant communities, and low-income housewives) (MHRD, 2020, p.24). Therefore, the NEP 2020 policy mentioned that India's children need to be the primary receivers of the education system, with no child being denied the chance to learn and succeed due to their background or place of birth (MHRD, 2020). About 19.6% of students at the primary level and 17.3% at the higher secondary level are members of Scheduled Castes, according to U-DISE 2016–17 data. The enrolment declines are more noticeable for students from Scheduled Tribes (10.6% to 6.8%) and children with disabilities (1.1% to 0.25%), with even more significant drops for female students in each of these groups. Even more sharply is the enrolment decline in higher education.

The rates of enrolment and retention among the Scheduled Castes have been negatively impacted by a variety of factors, such as poverty, social mores and customs, language barriers, and lack of access to high-quality education. One of the main objectives will continue to be closing these gaps in the learning outcomes, participation, and access of children belonging to Scheduled Castes. Additionally, those classified as members of the Other Backward Classes (OBCs), based on their historical educational and social disadvantages, require special assistance. Due to numerous historical and geographic factors, tribal communities and children from Scheduled Tribes also experience multiple forms of disadvantage. Academically and culturally, children from tribal communities frequently perceive their schooling as alien and unnecessary. Though several programmatic initiatives are in place and will be pursued in the future to improve the lives of children from tribal communities; however, extra precautions must be taken to guarantee that the benefits of these initiatives reach the children who are part of these communities. In school and higher education, minorities are likewise comparatively underrepresented. The Policy recognizes the importance of interventions to promote education for children from all minority communities, particularly those that are educationally underrepresented. The Policy also recognizes the importance of developing enablers to provide Children with Special Needs (CWSN) or Divyang with the same opportunities for a quality education as any other child. Thus, the NEP 2020 "Policy envisions ensuring equitable access to quality education to all students, with an emphasis on SEDGs" (MHRD, 2020, p. 41).

NEP 2020 has mentioned that the future of our country, as well as the future of our children, is genuinely shaped by our teachers. In India, the teacher held the highest regard in society due to their noble profession. Teachers were equipped by society with the knowledge, skills, and ethics they needed to impart to students in the best possible way (MHRD, 2020). The goal of the new school culture according to NEP (2020) is to make sure everyone feels respected and included, and to get rid of unfair beliefs and stereotypes. Also, raising awareness and fostering respect for diversity, would entail a deeper understanding of diverse cultures, religions, languages, gender identities, etc. It is necessary to read the policy initiatives in tandem with those for school education in order to achieve the goals of equity and inclusion in higher education. In addition to being well-versed in the most recent developments in pedagogy and education, teachers need to have a solid foundation in Indian values, languages, knowledge, ethos, and customs, including tribal customs (MHRD, 2020).

According to Gay (2000), culturally responsive teaching is the key component as well as its potential for reversing marginalized students of achievement trends. Also, its main pillars are the concurrent development of ethnically diverse students' academic achievement and cultural identities. Gay (2000) mentioned that "Power Pedagogy through Cultural Responsiveness" (p.21), is an educational approach that prioritizes comprehending and incorporating the diverse cultural backgrounds of students into instructional strategies. In order to create a more inclusive and productive learning environment, it entails identifying the cultural influences that shape students' experiences and applying that knowledge. By appreciating and respecting their cultural identities, students will feel more empowered and find that education has a greater purpose in their lives. This strategy improves the overall educational experience for a diverse student body, fosters equality, and aids in bridging cultural gaps. Furthermore, in a culturally blind teaching environment, instructors may unintentionally neglect to recognize and address the unique needs and perspectives of students from different cultural backgrounds. This lack of awareness can lead to a less inclusive and effective learning experience, as it fails to acknowledge and appreciate the cultural richness that students bring to the educational setting. In contrast, culturally responsive teaching aims to actively recognize, respect, and integrate diverse cultural elements into the educational process for a more meaningful and equitable learning experience. Spring (1995) explains that teachers often tell students to look at them when they are speaking, thinking it shows the students are paying attention. However, in some cultures, like the Apache culture, direct eye contact can be seen as staring, which is considered rude. This is just one example of how cultural differences can affect how people behave in the classroom. Sometimes, teachers might not realize or understand these differences, leading to misunderstandings. It happens because teachers may not be aware of how much culture shapes both their own and their students' attitudes, values, and behaviours. So, teachers need to recognize and appreciate these cultural influences to create a more inclusive and respectful learning environment (as cited in Gay, 2020).

Ladson-Billings (1992) explains that "culturally responsive teachers develop intellectual, social, emotional, and political learning by using cultural referents to impart knowledge, skills, and attitudes" (p. 382). Ladson-Billings (1995) defined Culturally Relevant Teaching as the theoretical model that not only addresses student achievement but also accepts and affirms their cultural identity while developing critical perspectives that challenge inequities that schools perpetuate. Culturally Relevant Pedagogy empowers students socially, intellectually, emotionally, and culturally. Culturally relevant teachers need to acknowledge that inclusion of students of colour and their cultural backgrounds must be integrated into the learning environment. Without knowing the students' identities of race, class, and gender teacher-student relationships cannot be certified (Terry, 2015). The components of Culturally Relevant Teaching are academic success, cultural competence, and sociopolitical consciousness.

Therefore, the rapidly rising diversity in society has expanded the gap between the upper, middle, and lower classes even more. Because in today's globalized age educators face challenges not only to teach the diverse backgrounds the usual subjects but also to prepare them for a future that might have jobs, we have not even heard of yet. So, it is the responsibility of the teacher to give students the right tools and skills for a world that is constantly changing (Gollnick & Chinn, 2017).

## Conclusion

In conclusion, the imperative for culturally responsive teaching and culturally relevant teaching is undeniable in today's diverse educational landscape. As our classrooms become increasingly multicultural, educators need to recognize and embrace the cultural backgrounds of their students. Culturally responsive teaching not only fosters a more inclusive and equitable learning environment but also enhances students' engagement and academic success. By acknowledging and integrating diverse perspectives, educators can create a dynamic and enriching educational experience that prepares students for a globally interconnected world. Ultimately, the adoption of culturally responsive teaching practices is not just a pedagogical choice; it is a commitment to fostering a more equitable and empowering education for all.

## References

Banks, J.A., & Banks, C.A.M. (Eds.). (1995). *Handbook of research on multicultural education*. Macmillan Pub.; Prentice Hall International.

Banks, J.A., & Banks, C.A.M. (Eds.). (2015). *Multicultural education: Issues and perspectives* (Ninth edition). John Wiley & Sons, Inc.

Banks, J.A. (2016). *Cultural diversity and education: Foundations, curriculum, and teaching* (6th ed.). Routledge, Taylor & Francis Group.

Gay, G., & Banks, J.A. (2000). *Culturally responsive teaching: Theory, research, and practice*. Teachers College Press.

Gollnick, D. M., & Chinn, P. C. (2017). *Multicultural education in a pluralistic society* (Tenth Edition). Pearson.

Ladson□Billings, G. (1992). Reading between the lines and beyond the pages: A culturally relevant approach to literacy teaching. *Theory Into Practice*, *31*(4), 312–320. https://doi.org/10.1080/00405849209543558

Ladson-Billings, G. (1995). Toward a theory of culturally relevant pedagogy. *American Educational Research Journal*, *32*(3), 465. https://doi.org/10.2307/1163320

MHRD. (2020). *National Education Policy 2020*. Ministry of Human Resource Development. https://www.education.gov.in/sites/upload_files/mhrd/files/NEP_Final_English_0.pdf

Terry, S.R. (2015). Knowing your who: a qualitative field research on how teachers develop culturally responsive teaching practices in an effort to close the academic achievement gap of students of color.

http://udise.in/Downloads/Publications/Documents/District_Report_Cards-2016-17-Vol-II.pdf

# 9

# Current Trends in TPACK Research in Teacher Education

## *A Systematic Literature Review*

Kaushik Sarkar

### Introduction

In its historical context, the technological pedagogical content knowledge (TPACK) framework, initially introduced as TPCK, traces its roots back to the pedagogical content knowledge (PCK) conceptualized by Shulman in 1986. In response to the ascendancy and swift evolution of information and communication technology (ICT), acknowledged for its efficacy in augmenting students' twenty-first-century skills, the TPACK framework underwent expansion to incorporate technology, as articulated by Mishra and Koehler in 2006.

Notably, since its inception, TPACK has consistently garnered significant attention from educators and evolved into a focal point for teacher professional development. (Chai, Chin, et al., 2013; Voogt et al., 2012, as cited in Irwanto, 2021). Thus, researchers and educators may find it easier to comprehend the state of this field's research and to plan for future studies if they have access to information on research trends and potential directions in TPACK. To achieve this aim, we identified pertinent journal articles published through ERIC. The objective of the present study is to scrutinize the latest developments and offer comprehensive insights into the research on Technological Pedagogical Content Knowledge (TPACK) from 2014 to October 2023 by using a systematic review. Hence, the present study endeavours to offer a thorough and precise perspective in this domain, aiding researchers, and educators globally in their pursuit of TPACK-related research and future paper publications. With the aim of achieving this objective, the study delineates a set of research questions designed to steer the exploration within this field. The ensuing research questions are as follows:

1. What are the annual TPACK publication trends from 2014 to 2023?
2. What are the research approaches in the TPACK researches published from 2014 to 2023?

3. Which countries lead in TPACK research from 2014 to 2023?
4. What are the trends of findings in TPACK research?
5. What are the emerging themes that appear in the reviewed studies from 2014 to 2023?

## Methodology

To fulfil this objective, a manual search of documents was conducted by examining journals associated with TPACK. Initially, we established keywords or a set of key terms to systematically search for literature in electronic databases. The search employed keywords such as "technological pedagogical content knowledge" (TPCK) and "technological pedagogical and content knowledge" (TPACK).

The keywords that were selected were "TPCK" (Technological pedagogical content knowledge) and "TPACK" (Technological pedagogical and content knowledge) and publication periods ranging from 2014 to 2023. Through November 24, 2023, the inquiry was carried out. The initial inquiry on the ERIC database yielded 239 results. Following the elimination of duplicate entries derived from the keyword search across various databases, the total number of distinct articles narrowed down to 136. Subsequently, the researcher meticulously examined each paper, cross-verifying all documents to confirm their alignment with the specified criteria and to eliminate any instances of duplication. The final selection process involved a thorough assessment of titles, followed by scrutiny of abstracts, and ultimately, a comprehensive review of the full text before determining the articles for inclusion in the study. Following this process, a comprehensive total of 110 articles emerged as the final selection for inclusion in the study.

From these sources, we discerned key attributes of the study, encompassing publication years, geographic locations, participant demographics, research methodologies, and emerging trends in findings. Employing a vote counting methodology, we systematically extracted data. The research topics were further scrutinized through coding and categorization based on shared themes.

**Table 1:** Search Equations and Filters

| *Database Search* | *Search Equation* | *Applied Filters* |
|---|---|---|
| ERIC | TPCK<br>TPACK<br>"Technological Pedagogical and Content Knowledge"<br>"Technological Pedagogical Content Knowledge" | Publication status: final.<br>Type of document: article.<br>Open Access:<br>from 2014 to 2023. |

*Source:* Own elaboration

**Table 2:** Inclusion and Exclusion Criteria

| *Inclusion Criteria* | *Exclusion Criteria* |
|---|---|
| The acronym TPACK must be present in the title, abstract or key words. | The acronym TPACK is not present in the title, abstract or keywords. |
| The research had to be developed totally or partially with in-service and high school teachers. | Other type of participants or at another educational level. |
| The studies should be empirical papers. | Systematic review or meta-analysis. |
| Papers published between 2017 and 2022. | Published in another period. |

*Source:* Own elaboration

Thematic considerations were guided by the authors' articulated objectives and emphases evident in the study's purpose. Subsequently, the amassed data were organized into a table using Microsoft Excel. The quantitative analysis involved scrutinizing the percentage distribution within each category. The resultant findings were then elucidated quantitatively, leveraging descriptive percentages to compare and contrast data across different categories.

## Results

In this segment, the outcomes of scrutinizing chosen papers from the ERIC database within the timeframe spanning 2014 to 2023 are delineated. The findings are outlined in five sections, encompassing the yearly TPACK publications, the diverse research approaches and methodologies employed in TPACK studies, the leading countries in TPACK research, the patterns observed in TPACK research findings, and the emerging themes that are apparent in the studies that were reviewed.

### *Annual TPACK publication trends from 2014 to 2023*

Considering the yearly volume of TPACK research, the analysis results suggest variations in the number of papers within this domain. The zenith of publications in TPACK research occurred in the year 2022 (19.09%). The findings of the analysis point to variations in the quantity of papers published in this field when considering the annual volume of TPACK research. The year 2022 marked the pinnacle of TPACK research publications. In both 2014 and 2023, an equal number of scientific articles, specifically five in each year, were published. Among all the years, 2015 documented the smallest quantity (2.23%) of published scientific articles on TPACK, amounting to three. A significant portion, amounting to 79%, of the articles saw publication between the years 2017 and 2022. Among the publications, precisely 56 in number, half of the total were released during the three-year period from 2020 to 2022. Examining the data up to October 2023, it was observed that the number of publications in this field amounted to five papers. The researcher anticipates

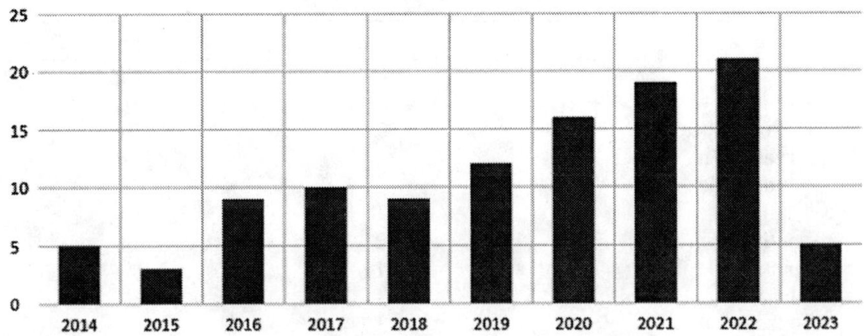


**Figure 1:** Number of Published Papers Relating to TPACK in the Literature

that this subject will persist in garnering attention from researchers globally. Considering the critical need for researchers and educators to incorporate technology into their pedagogical content knowledge, it is foreseeable that there will be an upswing in TPACK publications in the future.

### *Approaches and Methodologies Distribution Across Research*

A predominant 63 out of 111 studies, accounting for 56.75% numerically, opted for a quantitative research approach. Conversely, 29 studies, constituting 26.13% of the total, employed qualitative research approaches, while 15.32% utilized mixed-method research approaches. Within the quantitative domain, 24 studies were characterized by descriptive research, followed by seven employing experimental designs. Additionally, there were seven studies utilizing quasi-experimental methods, three in tools construction, four engaging in correlational studies, two embracing cross-sectional studies, and one each employing cluster analysis, self-report, formative experiment, and casual comparative studies. Among the qualitative studies, a substantial majority, constituting 20 out of 29 studies or 68% in numerical terms, embraced the case study methodology. Following this, two studies employed content analysis, while one each adopted a longitudinal study and a phenomenological study. Additionally, five quantitative studies did not explicitly specify their chosen research methodology. Within the domain of mixed-method approaches, a total of 19 studies were conducted, and notably, embedded mixed-method research emerged as the predominant research method.

### *Leading countries in TPACK research*

The researcher undertook a manual scoring process for each paper, driven by the goal of identifying the most productive countries in the TPACK field as outlined in the third research question. Table 1 outlines the global landscape of TPACK research publications during the period 2014-2023.

**Table 3:** Creating a ranking of the foremost nations in TPACK Research

| *Rank* | *Country* | *No. of papers* | *Percentage (%)* |
|---|---|---|---|
| 1 | Turkey | 73 | 66.36 |
| 2 | Indonesia | 10 | 9.09 |
| 3 | USA | 7 | 6.36 |
| 4 | Kazakhstan | 4 | 3.63 |
| 5 | South Africa | 2 | 1.8 |
| 5 | Thailand | 1 | 0.9 |
| 5 | South Korea | 2 | 1.8 |
| 8 | Spain | 1 | 0.9 |
| 8 | Ghana | 1 | 0.9 |
| 8 | Tanzania | 1 | 0.9 |
| 8 | Malaysia | 1 | 0.9 |
| 8 | India | 1 | 0.9 |
| 8 | Germany | 1 | 0.9 |
| 8 | United Kingdom | 1 | 0.9 |
| 8 | Portugal | 1 | 0.9 |

The analysis indicates that Turkey leads with the highest contribution in this field at 32.08%, followed by Indonesia (11.32%), the USA (6.3%), and Kazakhstan (3.6%). Notably, Table 1 presents three countries with two papers each and eight countries with only one paper. Broadly observed is the fact that, over the ten years, the top four countries have collectively contributed 84.68% of the studies.

## Trends of findings in TPACK research

### *Linkage between TPACK and Supplementary Components in the Integration of Technology*

Technological Pedagogical Content Knowledge (TPACK) is closely entwined with the multiple dimensions of technology integration, particularly converging with the self-efficacy perceptions of teachers in the realms of general technology integration (Sensory & Yildirim, 2018; Wright & Akgunduz, 2018; Simsek & Yazar, 2019; Ormanci et al. 2020; Karaaslan et al. 2022; Yildiz 2022) and self-efficacy beliefs regarding Web 2.0 tools (Kul et al. 2019). Technological Pedagogical Content Knowledge (TPACK) is intricately woven into a tapestry of variables that extend beyond its core components. This interconnection encompasses academic achievements (Ekrem & Recep, 2014), occupational anxiety (Kaya-Uyanik et al. 2019), thinking styles (Canbolat et al., 2016), anxiety related to teaching mathematics (Cetin & Yazlik, 2022; Unveren Bilgic, 2022), social media usage (Setiawan & Phillipson, 2020), technology acceptance of preservice teachers and various personality traits (Thohir et al. 2021) and substantial structural correlation between preservice teachers' adoption of technology and their understanding of web pedagogical content (Akar, 2019). The synergy between Technological Pedagogical Competency

(TPC) and critical thinking (Yildiz, 2017), along with the connection between Techno-pedagogical Skills and Lifelong Learning Tendencies (Sentruk, 2019), can be likened to an energetic partnership that profoundly influences the educational terrain. Furthermore, a complex interrelation exists involving Technological Pedagogical Content Knowledge (TPACK), Web Pedagogic Content Knowledge (WPCK), and the Technology Acceptance of Preservice Teachers, coupled with factors such as facility condition (FC) and the Technological Acceptance Model (TAM) (Thohir et al., 2023).

### *Some strategies for enhancing teachers TPACK*

Various strategies to enhance the Technological Pedagogical Content Knowledge (TPACK) competency of teachers have been identified through an examination of pertinent studies. Among these approaches, digital storytelling stands out as a creative method, enabling educators to weave technology seamlessly into content delivery (Sancer-Tokmak et al., 2014; Ulusoy, 2020; Kukul, 2022). Additionally, the adoption of flipped learning models (Piotrowski & Witte, 2014), blended learning (Qasem & Viswanathappa, 2016), Designing Optical Spreadsheets (Thohir, 2018), Designing Web 2.0 Tools (Arabaci & Orbay, 2022), Technology-based Guided Inquiry (Irdalisa et al., 2020), Creating Technology-Based Mathematics Stories role modelling on integration of technology (Baert, 2014), Astronomy lecture (Sensory & Yildirim, 2018), Reflection (Lu, 2014), purposeful workshops (Ersanli, 2016), teachers training sessions (Can et al., 2017), method course and field experience (Kartal & Cinar, 2018) provide teachers with hands-on experiences, practical insights, and guidance on effective TPACK integration, serving as dynamic platforms for professional development in technology-enhanced teaching methodologies.

Teachers Technological Pedagogical Content Knowledge (TPACK) evolves through the incorporation of various elements, including Information and Communication Technology (ICT) integration (Kihoza et al., 2016). This development extends to adeptly utilizing computer technology (Karakus, 2018), fostering Digital Literacy Skills (Altun, 2019), online case-based learning (Saltan, 2017), Digital Material (Kayaalp, 2022), design activities (Onal & Almdeg, 2018) and effectively leveraging digital resources (Miralles-Martinez et al., 2019), teaching the VuStat Program (Multu et al., 2019) to enhance teaching practices. Moreover, educators enhance their TPACK by incorporating geometric software into instructional methods, demonstrating a nuanced understanding of how technology can amplify the teaching of mathematics concepts (Ozcakir, 2019). Social media platforms like Facebook also play a role (Impeng & Nomnian, 2020), providing avenues for collaborative learning and communication within educational settings. Another facet involves the strategic use of modelling and scaffolding techniques in technology integration (Bergeson & Beschorner, 2020), allowing teachers to guide students progressively in navigating and understanding complex technological tools.

With the introduction of a calculator-based laboratory (Karabuz & Ogan-Bekiroglu, 2020) and graduate programs integrate tools (Love, 2020), we are paving the way for a paradigm shift in education by pioneering technology-infused pedagogy.

Our educational strategy revolves around personalized learning, utilizing online individualized instruction (Kaleli, 2021), to tailor content to each student's needs. The incorporation of the DiKoLAN-Grid Self-Assessment Tool is pivotal (Kotzebue et al., 2021), not only evaluating but actively enhancing teachers' Technological Pedagogical Content Knowledge (TPACK).

Underpinning our educational philosophy is a commitment to project-based learning (Erviana et al., 2022), fostering a dynamic environment where students actively engage with technology. Aemeological competency (Joldanova et al., 2022) is at the forefront, ensuring that learners develop not only technical skills but also a deep understanding of the ethical and societal implications of their technological endeavours.

Consideration of contextual factors (Akyuz, 2023) is integral to our approach, acknowledging that the effectiveness of technology-based teaching is influenced by the unique characteristics of each learning environment. To guide educators in this transformative journey, we advocate for the creation of a robust design framework (Guerra et al., 2017) rooted in the Technological Pedagogical Content Knowledge (TPACK) model. This framework, developed collaboratively by educators, equips teachers with the knowledge and skills needed to seamlessly integrate technology into their pedagogical practices, fostering a holistic and impactful learning experience.

### *Analysing and determining teachers TPACK and its components*

In this study, we discovered that numerous studies utilized diverse methodologies to explore and articulate teachers' Technological Pedagogical Content Knowledge (TPACK). A significant portion of these studies delved into teachers' perspectives (Karaca, 2015; Apeanti, 2016; Turgut, 2017; Ozgen & Narli, 2019; Esposito & Moroney, 2020; Li, 2021; Karatas & Basol, 2021; Tafli, 2021; Strydom et al., 2021; Choi & Park, 2022; Eshelman & Hogue, 2023), opinions (Can et al., 2017; Mailybayeva et al., 2022; Nogerbek et al., 2022; Kazu & Erten, 2014), beliefs (Gunes & Bahcivan, 2016; Adalar, 2021; observation (Kececi & Zengin, 2017), confidence (Rahmadi et al., 2020; Gozum & Demir, 2021; Suzuk & Akinci, 2021), and assessing (Kartal & Afacan, 2017; Atar et al., 2019; Saricoban et al., 2019; Basaran, 2020; Kara, 2021; Kacar, 2022; Kartal, 2022; Saralar-aras & Birgili, 2022; Yildiz & Gokcek, 2017; Ortiz Colon et al., 2021, Uygun et al., 2023), concerning their TPACK levels and the associated sub-dimensions.

### *Applied TPACK: Practical Approaches Employed by Teachers in Classroom Settings*

The implementation of Technological Pedagogical Content Knowledge (TPACK) in the classroom represents a transformative approach to teaching that integrates technology seamlessly with pedagogy and content knowledge. Teachers who embrace TPACK strive to create dynamic learning environments where technology is not just an add-on, but an integral component enhancing the overall teaching and learning experience. Executing TPACK involves examining how pre-service and in-service teachers, put TPACK principles into action within their teaching practices. Like, incorporating TPACK into the classroom setting encompasses the utilization of various technological tools and methodologies. This involves the integration of computer-based instructional materials and micro-teaching techniques (Durdu & Dag, 2017), leveraging the interactive and engaging features of technology to enhance the learning experience. Furthermore, computer-assisted activities play a crucial role in TPACK implementation (Kirikcilar & Yildiz, 2018), providing students with hands-on experiences that bridge theoretical concepts with practical applications. By incorporating real-world contexts into the classroom, web-supported situated learning models (Unal & Yelken, 2020) and website designing technology (West & Malatji, 2021) enable students to apply their knowledge in real-world situations.

Integrating technology into science courses (Felton, 2021) and science teaching (Karakas & Basol, 2021), particularly through flipped classroom (Kusuma, 2022) and flipped learning models (Widyasari, 2022), is instrumental in facilitating the seamless inclusion of Technological Pedagogical Content Knowledge (TPACK) for teachers. The use of observational protocol practices (Rakes et al., 2021) ensures a systematic and evidence-based approach to incorporating technology. The application information and communication technology (ICT)-based courses (Habibi et al., 2022) and innovative activities (Laura et al., 2022) guides pre-service teachers in intentional and strategic TPACK integration. Ethical use of digital resources (Gomez-Trigueros, 2023) emphasizes responsible and principled technology integration. Additionally, gaming activities, coupled with micro-teaching sessions (Acikgul, 2020) and literacy lesson plans (Arya et al., 2020) that incorporate digital texts or tools offer a comprehensive way to embed TPACK seamlessly into the fabric of classroom instruction.

### *Developing and validating tools for TPACK*

Several articles emphasize the creation of instruments; for instance, one article constructs a TPACK self-efficacy scale for pre-service science teachers, aligning with the theoretical framework of TPACK (Kiray, 2016). In a different article, the validation of a TPACK tool for successfully integrating ICT into secondary education was discussed (Nordin & Ariffin, 2016). An additional article concentrated on validating a TPACK tool for efficiently integrating ICT into secondary school instruction (Cetin & Erdogan, 2018). Another article examined the reliability and validity of a technological pedagogical content knowledge scale within the context of Turkish culture (Mustafa, 2021).

### *Emerging themes that appear in the reviewed studies*

The scrutiny of the reviewed studies has revealed a tapestry of emerging themes that encapsulate the current landscape of research in the examined field. Subsequent research endeavours should aim to validate the applicability of our findings across wider domains. The future trajectory of TPACK studies could encompass a variety of methodologies, as suggested by existing research, such as experimental studies (Sancar-Tokmak et al., 2014; Kihoza et al. 2016; Acikgul, 2020; Ulusoy, 2020), qualitative inquiries (Karaca, 2015; Kara, 2021), quantitative analyses (Eshelman & Hogue, 2023), longitudinal investigations (Kartal & Cinar, 2018; Kul et al., 2019; Aksut & Aydin, 2021), case studies (Saltan, 2017), mixed-method research (Ormanci et al., 2020; Jita & Sintema, 2022), and teacher interviews (Ekrem & Recep, 2014). It is also advisable to explore additional variables (Can et al., 2017; Kaya-Uyinik et al., 2019; Saricoban et al., 2019; Torun, 2020; Unveren Bilgic, 2022; Uygun et al., 2023; Yildiz & Gokcek, 2017) and broaden the scope to include a diverse population (Gunes & Bahcivan, 2016; Nordin & Ariffin, 2016; Karatas & Basol, 2021; Thohir et al., 2021; Widyasari, 2022), covering both pre-service and in-service teachers (Oz, 2015). Further avenues for investigation include the exploration of flipped learning methodologies (Piotrowski & Witte, 2016), in-depth and objective assessment strategies (Kececi & Zengin, 2017; Turgut, 2017; Atar et al., 2019; Arya et al., 2020; Felton, 2021), the development and evaluation of computer-based instructional materials (Durdu & Dag, 2017), as well as investigations into technology integration across different cultural backgrounds (Setiawan & Phillipson, 2020). To enhance the comprehensiveness of future studies, varied data collection tools (Kartal & Dilek, 2021; Kartal, 2022; Ortiz Colon et al., 2021) could be employed to capture a more nuanced understanding of the intricate interplay between technology, pedagogy, and content knowledge.

## Conclusion

In summary, the analysis of 110 studies spanning the period from 2014 to 2023 in the realm of Technological Pedagogical Content Knowledge (TPACK) indicates a progressive evolution of research in this domain over the years. Starting from the year 2014, there has been a gradual emergence of literature on Technological Pedagogical Content Knowledge (TPACK) within the ERIC database. Notably, the peak in the number of articles occurred in 2022

(19.09%), with subsequent high publication years in 2020 (16.36%) and 2021 (14.54%). In the last 10 years, TPACK scholars have overwhelmingly favoured specific research methods, with quantitative methods being the most prevalent at 54.54%, followed by qualitative methods at 26.36%, and mixed-method approaches at 16.36%. As of the present moment, research on TPACK is predominantly documented in developed countries, and Turkey holds the leading position among 15 nations, contributing to 66.36% of the reported studies. Following closely, Indonesia accounts for 9.09% and the USA for 6.36% of the documented research in this domain. Secondly, our findings revealed five prominent emerging topics in TPACK research. These include the linkage between TPACK and Supplementary Components in the Integration of Technology, constituting 27.27% of the identified topics. Some strategies for enhancing teachers' TPACK accounted for 36.36%, while analyzing and determining teachers' TPACK and its components constituted 20%. Applied TPACK: Practical Approaches Employed by Teachers in Classroom Settings represented 12.72%, and developing and validating tools for TPACK constituted 3.63% of the observed emerging topics. These studies also offer potential avenues for future trends in TPACK research, indicating a trajectory that may involve exploring flipped learning methodologies, delving into computer-based instruction, mastering the effective use of instructional technology, and investigating the application of diverse tools within varied cultural contexts. TPACK stands as a crucial element for teachers seeking to enhance the quality of education, recognizing that teachers play a pivotal role in translating the intended curriculum into tangible teaching and learning practices within the classroom.

## References

Açikgül, K. (2020). The Effect of Technological Pedagogical Content Knowledge Game Activities Supported Micro-Teaching Practices on Preservice Mathematics Teachers' Self-Efficacy Perception. *Acta Didactica Napocensia*, *13*(2), 157–173. https://doi.org/10.24193/adn.13.2.11

Adalar, H. (2021). Social Studies Teacher Candidates' Self-Efficacy Beliefs for Technological Pedagogical Content Knowledge (TPACK). *International Journal of Education and Literacy Studies*, *9*(3), 169–183. https://doi.org/10.7575/aiac.ijels.v.9n.3p.169

Akman, O., & Guven, C. (2014). TPACK Survey Development Study for Social Sciences Teachers and Teacher Candidates. *International Journal of Research in Education and Science*, *1*(1), 1–10. https://doi.org/10.21890/ijres.97007

Aksut, P., & Aydin, F. (2021). Creating Digital Stories: A Case Study of Turkish Preschool Environmental Education. *I.e.: Inquiry in Education*, *13*(2), 1–18. https://files.eric.ed.gov/fulltext/EJ1338087.pdf

Akyuz, D. (2023). Exploring contextual factors for pre-service teachers teaching with technology through planning, teaching, and reflecting. *International Electronic Journal of Mathematics Education*, *18*(1), 1–14. https://doi.org/10.29333/iejme/12624

Altun, D. (2019). Investigating Pre-Service Early Childhood Education Teachers' Technological Pedagogical Content Knowledge (TPACK) Competencies Regarding Digital Literacy Skills and Their Technology Attitudes and Usage. *Journal of Education and Learning*, *8*(1), 249–263. https://doi.org/10.5539/jel.v8n1p249

Apeanti, W.O. (2015). Contributing Factors to Pre-service Mathematics Teachers' e-readiness for ICT Integration. *International Journal of Research in Education and Science*, *2*(1), 223–238. https://doi.org/10.21890/ijres.29797

Arabaci, A., & Orbay, K. (2022). Impact of Experiencing Event Design with Web 2.0 Tools on Prospective Mathematics Teachers. *Problems of Education in the 21st Century*, *80*(1), 52–68. https://doi.org/10.33225/pec/22.80.52

Arya, P., Christ, T., & Wu, W. (2020). Patterns of Technological Pedagogical and Content Knowledge in Preservice-Teachers' Literacy Lesson Planning. *Journal of Education and Learning*, *9*(5), 1–14. https://doi.org/10.5539/jel.v9n5p1

Atar, C., Aydın, S., & Bağcı, H. (2019). An investigation of pre-service English teachers' level of technopedagogical content knowledge. *Dil ve Dilbilimi Çalışmaları Dergisi*, *15*(3), 794–805. https://doi.org/10.17263/jlls.631517

Baert, H., & Stewart, A. (2014). The Effects of Role Modeling on Technology Integration within Physical Education Teacher Education. *JTRM in Kinesiology*, 1–26. https://files.eric.ed.gov/fulltext/EJ1053415.pdf

Başaran, B. (2020). Examining Preservice Teachers' TPACK-21 Efficacies with Clustering Analysis in Terms of Certain Variables. *Malaysian Online Journal of Educational Technology*, *8*(3), 84–99. https://doi.org/10.17220/mojet.2020.03.005

Bergeson, K., & Beschorner, B. (2020). Modeling and Scaffolding the Technology Integration Planning Cycle for Pre-service Teachers: A Case Study. *International Journal of Education in Mathematics, Science and Technology*, *8*(4), 330–341. https://doi.org/10.46328/ijemst.v8i4.1031

Can, B., Erokten, S., & Bahtiyar*, A. (2017). An Investigation of Pre-Service Science Teachers' Technological Pedagogical Content Knowledge. *European Journal of Educational Research*, *6*(1), 51–57. https://doi.org/10.12973/eu-jer.6.1.51

Can, Ş., Doğru, S., & Bayir, G. (2017). Determination of Pre-service Classroom Teachers' Technological Pedagogical Content Knowledge. *Journal of Education and Training Studies*, *5*(2), 160–166. https://doi.org/10.11114/jets.v5i2.2083

Canbolat, N., Erdogan, A., & Yazlik, D.O. (2016). Examining the Relationship between Thinking Styles and Technological Pedagogical Content Knowledge of the Candidate Mathematics Teachers. *Journal of Education and Training Studies*, *4*(11), 39–48. https://doi.org/10.11114/jets.v4i11.1819

Çetin, İ., & Erdoğan, A. (n.d.). Development, Validity and Reliability Study of Technological Pedagogical Content Knowledge (TPACK) Efficiency Scale for Mathematics Teacher Candidates. *International Journal of Contemporary Educational Research*, *5*(1), 50–62. https://files.eric.ed.gov/fulltext/EJ1207506.pdf

Çetin, İ., & Yazlık, D. Ö. (2022). Examination of the Relationship Between TPACK Competencies and Mathematics Teaching Anxiety: The Mediating Role of Mathematics Anxiety. *International Journal of Modern Education Studies*, *6*(1), 206–235. https://doi.org/10.51383/ijonmes.2022.173

Choi, Y., & Park, N. (2022). The Improvement of Attitudes toward Convergence of Preservice Teachers: Blended Learning versus Online Learning in Science Teaching Method Courses. *Journal of Curriculum and Teaching*, *11*(5), 87–94. https://doi.org/10.5430/jct.v11n5p87

Ekrem, S., & Recep, Ç. (2014). Examining Preservice EFL Teachers' TPACK Competencies in Turkey. *Journal of Educators Online*, *11*(2). https://files.eric.ed.gov/fulltext/EJ1033263.pdf

Ersanli, C.Y. (2016). Improving Technological Pedagogical Content Knowledge (TPACK) of Pre-Service English Language Teachers. *International Education Studies*, *9*(5), 18–27. https://doi.org/10.5539/ies.v9n5p18

Erviana, V.Y., Sintawati, M., Bhattacharyya, E., Habil, H., & Fatmawati, L. (2022). The effect of project-based learning on technological pedagogical content knowledge among elementary school pre-service teacher. *Pegem Journal of Education and Instruction*, *12*(2), 151–156. https://doi.org/10.47750/pegegog.12.02.15

Eshelman, T.C. (2023). Pre-Service Teacher Perceptions on Tpack Instructional Design Micro-Course: A Case Study in the Northeastern United States. *The Turkish Online Journal of Educational Technology*, *22*(1), 161–180. https://files.eric.ed.gov/fulltext/EJ1375570.pdf

Esposito, M., & Moroney, R. (2020). Technology and student-centered learning in higher education: Issues and practices. *Journal of Computing in Higher Education*, *12*(1), 3–30. https://doi.org/10.1007/BF03032712

Fenton, D. (2021). Preparing Elementary Preservice Teachers to Integrate Technology: Examining the Effects of a New Science Course Sequence with Technology Infusion. *International Consortium for Research in Science & Mathematics Education*, *26*(1), 23–32. https://files.eric.ed.gov/fulltext/EJ1344104.pdf

Gómez-Trigueros, I. M. (2023). Digital skills and ethical knowledge of teachers with TPACK in higher education. *Contemporary Educational Technology*, *15*(2), 1–8. https://doi.org/10.30935/cedtech/12874

Gonca, K., & Fikriye, K. Z. (2017). Observing the technological pedagogical and content knowledge levels of science teacher candidates. *Educational Research and Reviews*, *12*(24), 1178–1187. https://doi.org/10.5897/ERR2017.3423

Gozum, A. İ. C., & Demir, Ö. (2021). Technological pedagogical content knowledge self-confidence of prospective pre-school teachers for Science Education during the COVID-19 period: A Structural Equational Modelling. *International Journal of Curriculum and Instruction*, *13*(1), 712–742. https://files.eric.ed.gov/fulltext/EJ1285807.pdf

Guerra, C., Moreira, A., & Vieira, R. (2017). Technological pedagogical content knowledge development: Integrating technology with a Research Teaching Perspective. *Digital Education Review*, *32*, 85–96. https://files.eric.ed.gov/fulltext/EJ1166495.pdf

Gunbas, N. (2020). Pre-service Mathematics Teachers Created Animated Stories to Improve their Technological Pedagogical Content Knowledge. *International Journal of Psychology and Educational Studies*, *7*(3), 209–222. https://doi.org/10.17220/ijpes.2020.03.018

Güneş, E., & Bahçivan, E. (2016). A Multiple Case Study of Preservice Science Teachers' TPACK: Embedded in a Comprehensive Belief System. *International Journal of Environmental & Science Education*, *11*(15), 8040–8054. https://files.eric.ed.gov/fulltext/EJ1118367.pdf

Habibi, A., Razak, R.A., Yusop, F.D., Muhaimin, M., Asrial, A., Mukminin, A., & Jamila, A. (2022). Exploring the factors affecting pre-service science teachers' actual use of technology during teaching practice. *South African Journal of Education*, *42*(1), 1–11. https://doi.org/10.15700/saje.v42n1a1955

Inpeng, S., & Nomnian, S. (2020). The Use of Facebook in a TEFL Program Based on the TPACK Framework. *LEARN Journal: Language Education and Acquisition Research Network Journal*, *13*(2), 369–393. https://files.eric.ed.gov/fulltext/EJ1258789.pdf

Irdalisa, Paidi, & Djukri. (2020). Implementation of Technology-based Guided Inquiry to Improve TPACK among Prospective Biology Teachers. *International Journal of Instruction*, *13*(2), 33–44. https://doi.org/10.29333/iji.2020.1323a

Irwanto, I. (2021). Research Trends in Technological Pedagogical Content Knowledge (TPACK): A Systematic Literature Review from 2010 to 2021. *European Journal of Educational Research*, *10*(4), 2045–2054. https://doi.org/10.12973/eu-jer.10.4.2045

Izgi-Onbasili, U., Avsar-Tuncay, A., Sezginsoy-Seker, B., & Kiray, S. A. (2022). An Examination of Pre-Service Teachers' Experiences in Creating A Scientific Digital Story in The Context of Their Self Confidence in Technological Pedagogical Content Knowledge. *Journal of Baltic Science Education*, *21*(2), 207–223. https://doi.org/10.33225/jbse/22.21.207

Jita, T., & Sintema, E. J. (2022). Pre-service teachers' self-concept and views toward using ICT for teaching science. *Eurasia Journal of Mathematics, Science and Technology Education*, *18*(9), 1–17. https://doi.org/10.29333/ejmste/12396

Joldanova, D., Tleuzhanova, G., Kitibayeva, A., Smanova, G., & Mirza, N. (2022). Formation of TPACK and Acmeological Competency of Future Teachers in Foreign Language Education. *International Journal of Education in Mathematics, Science and Technology*, *10*(4), 935–954. https://doi.org/10.46328/ijemst.2717

Kaçar, I.G. (2022). Pre-Service EFL Teachers as Digital Material Designers: A Case Study into the TPACK Development in the Turkish Context. *Teaching English with Technology*, *22*(3–4), 107–130. https://files.eric.ed.gov/fulltext/EJ1367618.pdf

Kaleli, Y.S. (2021). The Effect of Individualized Online Instruction on TPACK Skills and Achievement in Piano Lessons. *International Journal of Technology in Education*, *4*(3), 399–412. https://doi.org/10.46328/ijte.143

Kara, S. (2021). An Investigation of Technological Pedagogical and Content Knowledge (TPACK) Competencies of Pre-Service Visual Arts Teachers. *International Journal of Technology in Education*, *4*(3), 527–541. https://doi.org/10.46328/ijte.184

Karaaslan, Ö., Akdemir, B., & Yavuz, M. (2022). An investigation of the relationship between technological and pedagogical content knowledge levels and self-efficacy beliefs of special education teacher candidates. *International Journal of Curriculum and Instruction*, *14*(3), 2932–2953. https://files.eric.ed.gov/fulltext/EJ1364576.pdf

Karabuz, O., & Ogan-Bekiroglu, F. (2020). Pre-Service Teachers' Technological Pedagogical Content Knowledge (TPCK) Related to Calculator-Based Laboratory and Contextual Factors Influencing Their TPCK. *Journal of Curriculum and Teaching*, *9*(3), 57–75. https://doi.org/10.5430/jct.v9n3p57

Karaca, F. (2015). An Investigation of Preservice Teachers' Technological Pedagogical Content Knowledge Based on a Variety of Characteristics. *International Journal of Higher Education*, *4*(4), 128–136. https://doi.org/10.5430/ijhe.v4n4p128

Karakus, F. (2018). An Examination of Pre-Service Teachers' Technological Pedagogical Content Knowledge and Beliefs Using Computer Technology in Mathematics Instruction. *Issues in the Undergraduate Mathematics Preparation of School Teachers*, 3., 3. http://files.eric.ed.gov/fulltext/EJ1199683.pdf

Karataş, T.Ö., & Başol, H. Ç. (2021). What Techno-effective Teachers Mean for Preservice Teachers of English: A Socio-Constructivist Study. *PASAA: Journal of Language*

*Teaching and Learning in Thailand*, *62*, 204–235. https://files.eric.ed.gov/fulltext/EJ1334990.pdf

Kartal, B. (2022). Examining Preservice Mathematics Teachers' Technological Pedagogical Content Knowledge Development in The Natural Setting of A Teacher Preparation Program. *I.e.: Inquiry in Education i*, *14*(2), 1–26. https://files.eric.ed.gov/fulltext/EJ1379140.pdf

Kartal, B., & Çinar, C. (2018). Examining Pre-Service Mathematics Teachers' Beliefs of TPACK during a Method Course and Field Experience. *Malaysian Online Journal of Educational Technology*, *6*(3), 11–37. http://dx.doi.org/10.17220/mojet.2018.03.002

Kartal, T., & Afacan, O. (2017). Examining Turkish Pre-service Science Teachers' Technological Pedagogical Content Knowledge (TPACK) Based on Demographic Variables. *Journal of Turkish Science Education.*, *14*(1), 1–22. https://files.eric.ed.gov/fulltext/EJ1344309.pdf

Kartal, T., & DiLek, İ. (2021). Preservice Science Teachers' TPACK Development in a Technology-Enhanced Science Teaching Method Course. *Journal of Education in Science, Environment and Health*, *7*(4), 339–353. https://doi.org/10.21891/jeseh.994458

Kayaalp, F., Gökbulut, B., Meral, E., & Başci Namli, Z. (2022). The Effect of Digital Material Preparation Training on Technological Pedagogical Content Knowledge Self-Confidence of Pre-service Social Studies Teachers. *Kuramsal Eğitimbilim*, *15*(3), 475–503. https://doi.org/10.30831/akukeg.1061527

Kaya-Uyanik, G., Gur-Erdogan, D., & Canan-Gungoren, O. (2019). Examination of the Relationship between Prospective Teachers' Occupational Anxiety and Technological Pedagogical Content Knowledge by Canonical Correlation. *International Journal of Educational Methodology*, *5*(3), 407–420. https://doi.org/10.12973/ijem.5.3.407

Kazu, I.Y., & Erten, P. (2014). Teachers' Technological Pedagogical Content Knowledge Self-Efficacies. *Journal of Education and Training Studies*, *2*(2), 126–144. https://doi.org/10.11114/jets.v2i2.261

Kihoza, P., Zlotnikova, I., Bada, J., & Kalegele, K. (2016). Classroom ICT integration in Tanzania: Opportunities and challenges from the perspectives of TPACK and SAMR models. *International Journal of Education and Development Using Information and Communication Technology*, *12*(1), 107–128. https://files.eric.ed.gov/fulltext/EJ1099588.pdf

Kiray, S.A. (2016). Development of a TPACK Self-efficacy Scale for Preservice Science Teachers. *International Journal of Research in Education and Science*, *2*(2), 527–541. https://doi.org/10.21890/ijres.64750

Kirikçilar, R.G., & Yildiz, A. (2018). Technological Pedagogical Content Knowledge (Tpack) Craft: Utilization of the TPACK when Designing the Geogebra Activities. *Acta Didactica Napocensia*, *11*(1), 101–116. https://doi.org/10.24193/adn.11.1.8

Durdu, L., & Dag, F. (2017). Pre-Service Teachers' TPACK Development and Conceptions through a TPACK-Based Course. *Australian Journal of Teacher Education*, *42*(11), 150–171. https://doi.org/10.14221/ajte.2017v42n11.10

Kotzebue, L.V., Meier, M., Finger, A., Kremser, E., Huwer, J., Thoms, L.-J., Becker, S., Bruckermann, T., & Thyssen, C. (2021). The Framework DiKoLAN (Digital Competencies for Teaching in Science Education) as Basis for the Self-Assessment Tool DiKoLAN-Grid. *Education Sciences*, *11*(12), 1–23. https://doi.org/10.3390/educsci11120775

Kukul, V. (2022). Evaluation of Digital Storytelling in terms of Pre-Service ICT Teachers' Perceived TPACK Levels and Teaching Proficiency Self-Efficacy Levels: A Mixed-Method Study. *International Journal of Technology in Education, 5*(3), 411–422. https://doi.org/10.46328/ijte.240

Kul, U., Aksu, Z., & Birisci, S. (2019). The Relationship between Technological Pedagogical Content Knowledge and Web 2.0 Self-Efficacy Beliefs. *International Online Journal of Educational Sciences, 11*(1), 198–213. https://doi.org/10.15345/iojes.2019.01.014

Kusuma, I. P. I. (2022). How Does a TPACK-related Program Support EFL Pre-service Teachers' Flipped Classrooms? *LEARN Journal: Language Education and Acquisition Research Network, 15*(2), 300–325. https://files.eric.ed.gov/fulltext/EJ1358700.pdf

Laura, T., Akgul, Z., Balazhanova, K., Sholpan, T., Sholpan, S., & Saule, B. (2022). Development of readiness of future teachers of preschool organisations to innovative activity. *Cypriot Journal of Educational Sciences, 17*(6), 1972–1982. https://doi.org/10.18844/cjes.v17i6.7547

Li, L. (2021). Learning Together Online: Insights into Knowledge Construction of Language Teachers in a CSCL Environment. *Iranian Journal of Language Teaching Research, 9*(3), 39–62. https://doi.org/10.30466/ijltr.2021.121075

Love, M. (2020). How EFL Teacher Trainees in a Tesol Graduate Program Integrate Tools and Platforms into Teaching Eap. *Teach\ng Engl\sh W\th Technology, 20*(5), 38–65. https://files.eric.ed.gov/fulltext/EJ1281551.pdf

Lu, L. (2014). Cultivating Reflective Practitioners in Technology Preparation: Constructing TPACK through Reflection. *Education Sciences, 4*(1), 13–35. https://doi.org/10.3390/educsci4010013

Mailybayeva, Z.S., Kurmanbayev, M.R., & Yermentayeva, A.R. (2022). Group psychological and pedagogical technologies for developing the narrative ability in future specialists. *Cypriot Journal of Educational Sciences, 17*(7), 2371–2382. https://doi.org/10.18844/cjes.v17i7.7688

Mazman Akar, S.G. (2019). A Structural Model for Relationship between Web Pedagogic Content Knowledge and Technology Acceptance of Preservice Teachers. *Malaysian Online Journal of Educational Technology, 7*(1), 1–14. https://doi.org/10.17220/mojet.2019.01.001

Miralles-Martínez, P., Gómez-Carrasco, C.J., Arias-González, V.B., & Fontal-Merillas, O. (2019). Digital resources and didactic methodology in the initial training of History teachers. *Comunicar, 27*(61), 45–56. https://doi.org/10.3916/C61-2019-04

Mishra, P., & Koehler, M.J. (2006). Technological Pedagogical Content Knowledge: A Framework for Teacher Knowledge. *Teachers College Record: The Voice of Scholarship in Education, 108*(6), 1017–1054. https://doi.org/10.1111/j.1467-9620.2006.00684.x

Mustafa, A.M., Ulubey, Ö., & Ata, R. (2021). Adaptation of Technological Pedagogical Content Knowledge Scale into Turkish Culture within the Scope of 21st Century Skills. *Psycho-Educational Research Reviews, 10*(1), 77–91. http://files.eric.ed.gov/fulltext/EJ1300203.pdf

Mutlu, Y., Polat, S., & Alan, S. (2019). Development of Preservice Mathematics Teachers' TPACK through Micro Teaching: Teaching the VuStat Program. *International Journal of Technology in Education and Science, 3*(2), 107–118. https://files.eric.ed.gov/fulltext/EJ1227053.pdf

Nogerbek, A., Sumatokhin, S., Maimatayeva, A., Ziyayeva, G., & Childibayev, D. (2022). Future biology teachers' opinions on technological pedagogical content knowledge.

*World Journal on Educational Technology: Current Issues*, *14*(2), 369–379. https://doi.org/10.18844/wjet.v14i2.6971

Nordin, H., & Tengku Ariffin, T.F. (2016). Validation of a Technological Pedagogical Content Knowledge Instrument in a Malaysian Secondary School Context. *Malaysian Journal of Learning and Instruction*, *13*(1), 1–24. https://doi.org/10.32890/mjli2016.13.1.1

Önal, N., & Alemdağ, E. (2018). Educational Website Design Process: Changes in TPACK Competencies and Experiences. *International Journal of Progressive Education*, *14*(1), 88–104. https://doi.org/10.29329/ijpe.2018.129.7

Ormancı, Ü., Kaçar, S., Özcan, E., & Balım, A.G. (2020). The effect of contemporary approaches education on prospective teachers' self efficacy towards science teaching and technological pedagogical content knowledge self confidence. *Uluslararası Eğitim Programları ve Öğretim Çalışmaları Dergisi*, *10*(1), 1–28. https://doi.org/10.31704/ijocis.2020.001

Ortiz Colón, A.M., Izquierdo Rus, T., Rodríguez Moreno, J., & Agreda Montoro, M. (2023). TPACK model as a framework for in-service teacher training. *Contemporary Educational Technology*, *15*(3), 1–12. https://doi.org/10.30935/cedtech/13279

Oz, H. (2015). Assessing Pre-service English as a Foreign Language Teachers' Technological Pedagogical Content Knowledge. *International Education Studies*, *8*(5), 119–130. https://doi.org/10.5539/ies.v8n5p119

Özçakir, B. (2019). Prospective Mathematics Teachers' Technology Usages: A Case for Dynamic Geometry Software. *Acta Didactica Napocensia*, *12*(1), 1–16. https://doi.org/10.24193/adn.12.1.1

Özgen, K., & Narlı, S. (2019). Intelligent Data Analysis of Interactions and Relationships among Technological Pedagogical Content Knowledge Constructs via Rough Set Analysis. *Contemporary Educational Technology*, *11*(1), 77–98. https://doi.org/10.30935/cet.646769

Peng, L. (2020). Practice-Based Technology Teaching Assistantship Program: Preparing Teacher Educators to Support Teacher Candidates' Integration of Technological, Pedagogical, and Content Knowledge. *The Excellence in Education Journal*, *9*(1), 85–103. http://files.eric.ed.gov/fulltext/EJ1246800.pdf

Piotrowski, A., & Witte, S. (2016). Flipped Learning and TPACK Construction in English Education. *Nternational Journal of Technology in Teaching and Learning*, *12*(1), 33–46. https://files.eric.ed.gov/fulltext/EJ1213368.pdf

Qasem, A.A.A., & Viswanathappa, G. (2016). Blended Learning Approach to Develop the Teachers' TPACK. *Contemporary Educational Technology*, *7*(3), 264–276. https://doi.org/10.30935/cedtech/6176

Rahmadi, I.F., Hayati, E., & Nursyifa, A. (2020). Comparing Pre-service Civic Education Teachers' TPACK Confidence Across Course Modes. *Research in Social Sciences and Technology*, *5*(2), 113–133. https://doi.org/10.46303/ressat.05.02.7

Rakes, C.R., Stites, M.L., Ronau, R.N., Bush, S.B., Fisher, M.H., Safi, F., Desai, S., Schmidt, A., Andreasen, J. B., Saderholm, J., Amick, L., Mohr-Schroeder, M. J., & Viera, J. (2022). Teaching Mathematics with Technology: TPACK and Effective Teaching Practices. *Education Sciences*, *12*(2), 1–16. https://doi.org/10.3390/educsci12020133

Saltan, F. (2017). Online Case-based Learning Design for Facilitating Classroom Teachers' Development of Technological, Pedagogical, and Content Knowledge. *European Journal of Contemporary Education*, *6*(2), 308–316. https://doi.org/10.13187/ejced.2017.2.308

Sancar-Tokmak, H., Surmeli, H., & Ozgelen, S. (2014). Preservice Science Teachers' Perceptions of Their TPACK Development after Creating Digital Stories. *International Society of Educational Research*, *9*(3), 247–264. https://files.eric.ed.gov/fulltext/EJ1031448.pdf

Saralar-Aras, İ., & BiRgiLi, B. (2022). An Assessment of Pre-Service Mathematics Teachers' Techno-Pedagogical Content Knowledge regarding Geometry. *International Journal of Psychology and Educational Studies*, *9*(4), 1307–1327. https://doi.org/10.52380/ijpes.2022.9.4.920

Sarıçoban, A., Tosuncuoğlu, İ., & Kırmızı, Ö. (2019). A technological pedagogical content knowledge (TPACK) assessment of pre- service EFL teachers learning to teach English as a foreign language. *Journal of Language and Linguistic Studies*, *15*(3), 1122–1138. https://dergipark.org.tr/en/download/article-file/828141

Sensoy, O., & Ibrahim Yildirim, H. (2018). The Effect of Technological Pedagogical Content Knowledge Based Training Programs Used in Astronomy Classes on the Success Levels of Science Teacher Candidates. *Universal Journal of Educational Research*, *6*(6), 1328–1338. https://doi.org/10.13189/ujer.2018.060624

Sensoy, O., & Yildirim, H. I. (2018). Impact of Technological Pedagogical Content Knowledge Based Education Applications on Prospective Teachers' Self-Efficacy Belief Levels Toward Science Education. *Journal of Education and Training Studies*, *6*(10), 29–38. https://doi.org/10.11114/jets.v6i10.3433

Şentürk, Ş. (2019). Investigation of Pre-service Teachers' Techno-pedagogical Skills and Lifelong Learning Tendencies. *Participatory Educational Research*, *6*(2), 78–92. https://doi.org/10.17275/per.19.14.6.2

Setiawan, H., Phillipson, S., Sudarmin, & Isnaeni, W. (2019). Current trends in TPACK research in science education: a systematic review of literature from 2011 to 2017. *Journal of Physics: Conference Series*, *1317*(1), 1-6. https://doi.org/10.1088/1742-6596/1317/1/012213

Shulman, L. S. (1986). Those who understand: Knowledge growth in teaching. *Educational Researcher*, *15*(2), 4–14. https://doi.org/10.3102/0013189x015002004

Simsek, O., & Yazar, T. (2019). Examining the Self-Efficacy of Prospective Teachers in Technology Integration According to their Subject Areas: The Case of Turkey. *Contemporary Educational Technology*, *10*(3), 289–308. https://doi.org/10.30935/cet.590105

Strydom, S.C., Wessels, H., & Anley, C. (2021). Moving beyond the tools: Pre-service teachers' views on what they value in a digital literacy short course. *South African Journal of Childhood Education*, *11*(1), 2–11. https://doi.org/10.4102/sajce.v11i1.929

Süzük, E., & Akinci, T. (2021). Comparing Pre-Service Teachers' Self-Confidence Levels in Technological Pedagogical Content Knowledge in Terms of Several Variables. *Journal of Education and Learning*, *10*(1), 82–93. https://doi.org/10.5539/jel.v10n1p82

Taflı, T. (2021). A comparative study on TPACK self-efficacy of prospective Biology teachers from the faculties of education & science. *International Journal of Curriculum and Instruction*, *13*(3), 2957–2980. https://files.eric.ed.gov/fulltext/EJ1312866.pdf

Thohir, M.A. (2018). Designing Optical Spreadsheets-Technological Pedagogical Content Knowledge Simulation (S-Tpack): A Case Study of Pre-Service Teachers Course. *The Turkish Online Journal of Educational Technology*, *17*(1), 24–36. https://files.eric.ed.gov/fulltext/EJ1165755.pdf

Thohir, M.A., Ahdhianto, E., Mas'ula, S., April Yanti, F., & Sukarelawan, M.I. (2023). The effects of TPACK and facility condition on preservice teachers' acceptance of virtual reality in science education course. *Contemporary Educational Technology*, *15*(2), 1–15. https://doi.org/10.30935/cedtech/12918

Thohir, M.A., Yuliati, L., Ahdhianto, E., Untari, E., & Yanti, F.A. (2021). Exploring the Relationship Between Personality Traits and TPACK-Web of Pre-service Teacher. *Contemporary Educational Technology*, *13*(4), 1–16. https://doi.org/10.30935/cedtech/11128

Torun, F. (2020). The Effect of a Textbook Preparation Process Supported by Instructional Technology Tools on the TPACK Self-Confidence levels of Prospective Social Studies Teachers. *Review of International Geographical Education Online*, *10*(2), 115–140. https://doi.org/10.33403/rigeo.691943

Ulusoy, M. (2020). Pre-Service Teachers as Creators and Students as Viewers of Children's Literature-Related Digital Stories: A Formative Experiment. *International Journal of Progressive Education*, *16*(6), 365–389. https://doi.org/10.29329/ijpe.2020.280.23

Ünal, K., & Yelken, T.Y. (2020). The Effects of Pre-service English Language Teachers' Making Vocabulary Learning Materials in Web-Supported Situated Learning Environment on Their Vocabulary Learning. *English Language Teaching*, *13*(4), 52–75. https://doi.org/10.5539/elt.v13n4p52

Ünveren BiLgiÇ, E.N. (2022). The relationship between technological pedagogical content knowledge of mathematics teacher candidates and teaching mathematics anxiety. *Journal of Educational Technology and Online Learning*, *5*(3), 619–635. https://doi.org/10.31681/jetol.1115994

Uygun, T., Sendur, A., Dere, R., & Ozcakir, B. (2023). Development of TPACK with Web 2.0 tools: Design-based study. *European Journal of Science and Mathematics Education*, *11*(3), 445–465. https://doi.org/10.30935/scimath/12907

West, J., & Malatji, M.J. (2021). Technology Integration in Higher Education: The use of Website Design Pedagogy to Promote Quality Teaching and Learning. *Electronic Journal of E-Learning*, *19*(6), 629–641. https://doi.org/10.34190/ejel.19.6.2557

Widyasari, F., Masykuri, M., Mahardiani, L., Saputro, S., & Yamtinah, S. (2022). Measuring the Effect of Subject-Specific Pedagogy on TPACK through Flipped Learning in E-Learning Classroom. *International Journal of Instruction*, *15*(3), 1007–1030. https://doi.org/10.29333/iji.2022.15354a

Wright, B., & Akgunduz, D. (2018). The relationship between technological pedagogical content knowledge (TPACK) self-efficacy belief levels and the usage of Web 2.0 applications of pre-service science teachers. *World Journal on Educational Technology: Current Issues*, *10*(1), 52–69. https://doi.org/10.18844/wjet.v10i1.3187

Yildiz, A. (2017). The Factors Affecting Techno-Pedagogical Competencies and Critical Thinking Skills of Preservice Mathematics Teachers. *Malaysian Online Journal of Educational Sciences*, *5*(2), 66–81. https://files.eric.ed.gov/fulltext/EJ1142510.pdf

Yildiz, H., & Gokcek, T. (2017). The Development Process of a Mathematic Teacher's Technological Pedagogical Content Knowledge. *European Journal of Educational Research*, *7*(1), 9–29. https://doi.org/10.12973/eu-jer.7.1.9

Yıldız, T. (2017). A comparison of pre-service, in-service and formation program for teachers perceptions of technological pedagogical content knowledge (TPACK) in English language teaching (ELT). *Educational Research and Reviews*, *12*(22), 1091–1106. https://doi.org/10.5897/ERR2017.3311

Yıldız, Z. (2022). Science Teaching Self-Efficacy Beliefs of Pre-Service Teachers: Context of Technological Pedagogical Content Knowledge and Visual Metaphors. *Journal of Baltic Science Education*, *21*(6), 989–1003. https://doi.org/10.33225/jbse/22.21.989

# 10

# Conceptions of Pre-service Teachers Regarding Science Teaching and Learning

Kothai Nayagi N

## Introduction

Many countries have made substantial reform efforts in science education to develop the student's understanding of science concepts, the nature of science, scientific inquiry, and the role of science and technology in society. In India, the New Education Policy (NEP) 2020 advocates for inquiry, discovery, discussions, and analysis-based teaching and learning methods to promote the overall educational development of students and enhance their scientific literacy. The major objective of the National Curriculum Framework for School Education (NCFSE) 2023 is to develop the student's understanding of basic scientific methods and scientific inquiry skills. Further, NCFSE (2023) highlighted that a science teacher must create a learning environment that promotes natural curiosity, encourages students to ask questions, provides maximum opportunities for hands-on activities, and gives sufficient space to discuss students' ideas. Science teachers should have enough competencies in using different pedagogical strategies and adequate knowledge of science content to provide better science learning experiences to the students. Moreover, the success of science education reform visions depends on how well science teachers understand science teaching since the teachers' teaching strategies are influenced by their conceptions of teaching science (Hewson & Hewson, 1989).

Studies on science teacher education acknowledged that pre-service teachers typically enter their teacher education programme with conceptions of science teaching and learning that mirror their school experiences (Koballa et al., 2000). These conceptions can impact the pre-service teachers' learning of pedagogy and their future teaching strategies (Subramaniam, 2013). Moreover, it can either facilitate or hinder the pre-service teachers' adoption of constructivist teaching practices to teach science (Cansiz & Cansiz, 2020). Bryan and Abell (1999) argued that pre-service teachers' attitudes towards teaching science in terms of their abilities, confidence, desires, and comfort levels depend on their conceptions of teaching science. So, understanding the pre-service teachers' conception of science teaching and learning at the entry-level of the teacher education programme will help to prepare them for inquiry-based science teaching as envisioned in NEP (2020) and NCFSE (2023), which the current study aimed to do.

## Literature Review

Hewson and Hewson (1989) defined conceptions of teaching science as "the set of ideas, understandings, and interpretations of experience concerning the teacher and teaching, the nature and content of science, and the learners and learning that the teacher uses in making decisions about teaching, both in planning and execution" (p.194). The term conceptions of teaching and learning generally seen as beliefs about teaching and learning in the teacher education and science teacher education literature. Chan and Elliott (2004) described the conceptions of teaching and learning as "the beliefs held by teachers about their preferred ways of teaching and learning" (p.819). Many studies categorised the science teachers' beliefs or conceptions of teaching and leaning into teacher-centred or student-centred based on the aspects like meaning of teaching and learning, the roles of teacher and students, teaching strategies, and learning environment (Joy, 2017).

Conceptions of science teaching and learning are considered critical in the planning and implementation stages of teaching instruction (Hewson & Hewson, 1989). This perception was confirmed by the studies conducted with the Indian science teachers. For example, Joy (2016) found a significant relationship between beginning science teachers' beliefs, instructional decisions, and classroom practices. Further, the study revealed that most beginning science teachers have teacher-centred beliefs and practices. Bansal (2017) also found teacher-centred beliefs and practices among science teachers. Bansal (2017) and Joy (2016) explained that as science teachers studied science through teacher-centred methods, they had a strong affinity towards it. Also, science teachers believed teacher-centred methods would help them to complete the syllabus on time for the exams.

Bansal (2017) and Bhoi (2021) found that science teachers viewed inquiry as something scientists and researchers do in the laboratory in controlled environments, which is time-consuming. This incomplete view of the inquiry affected science teachers' confidence and acted as a barrier to implementing inquiry-based teaching (Bhoi, 2021). Furthermore, science teachers primarily rely on explanation and discussion in the classroom and have no experience in the inquiry classroom. Kumar and Panda (2020) also found that secondary pre-service science teachers believed students would easily understand the science concepts through teachers' explanations.

Bansal (2020) conducted a study with the pre-service teachers to understand their conceptualization and enactment of inquiry-based science teaching. The study found that pre-service teachers struggled to plan and implement inquiry-based teaching in the actual classroom due to inadequate training in the teacher education programme and school constraints such as non-cooperation from school administration, in-service teachers and students to practise inquiry during the internship. Moreover, pre-service teachers' beliefs towards didactic teaching prevented them from practising the skills they learned in the teacher education programme (Bansal, 2021). Kumar and Panda (2020) stressed the importance of capturing the pre-service teachers' conceptions of science teaching, which they bring to the teacher education programmes to improve their teaching practices.

However, there has been limited study on the conceptions of science teaching and learning that pre-service teachers bring to the teacher education programme. Therefore, the study aims to explore the secondary pre-service teachers' conceptions of science teaching and learning at their entry level of the teacher education programme. In this study, pre-service teachers' conceptions of science teaching and learning are described as their 'set of ideas about teaching, learning, teaching strategies, and the role of the teacher and student in the science teaching and learning process'.

## Methodology

This study utilised a qualitative methodology (Patton, 2002) to explore the first-year pre-service teachers' conceptions of science teaching and learning. Qualitative methods help to capture the pre-service teachers expressed and enacted conceptions of science teaching and learning in detail (Subramanium, 2013). In a convenient sampling technique, five first-year pre-service teachers in the science pedagogy course of the two-year B.Ed. programme participated in this study. Participants had diverse backgrounds in terms of gender (male-3, female-2), educational qualification (UG-4, PG-1), and subject (Physics -2, Chemistry-1, Biology-2).

Data were collected through semi-structured interviews with the pre-service teachers during the initial few days of their teacher education classes. The average total time spent interviewing each participant was 30 minutes. Then, the interviews were transcribed. The data were analysed through thematic analysis (Creswell, 2012). After reading the data multiple times, initial codes were assigned to it. Then, categories were developed by grouping the relevance codes. The extract of the codes under categories was read carefully and narrowed down into themes. At the end of this process, three themes emerged that describe the participants' conceptions of science teaching and learning.

## Findings

Three themes that emerged from the qualitative data analysis were labelled as: Views of science teaching and learning; Role of the teacher; and Expected students' behaviour — which were common among the pre-service teachers. These themes are discussed in detail below.

### *Views of Science teaching and learning*

At the beginning of the teacher education programme, all the participants had a similar idea about science teaching and learning. They defined science teaching and learning as a two-way interaction between the teacher and student to understand the environment, as stated below,

> *"...Science teaching is like a two-way process, and it should be interactive. First, we (the teachers) should give an overview of the topic and then discuss it with students to make them understand it" (Participant(P)3).*

Further, they mentioned that science teachers must connect the content with learners' real-life experiences through examples and demonstrations. The following extract was typical of such conceptions:

> *"...teacher should connect the science content with the things in their surroundings and give students some direction on how to observe and understand the things" (P4)*

Even though the pre-service teachers knew the importance of the activities in the science teaching and learning process, they stressed that the teacher should carry out activities to help the students observe, think, and learn the science content correctly. For example,

> *"...it is the teachers' responsibility to do the activities in the classroom because the students do not know how to do or observe things, and they will get distracted from the topic..." (P1).*

The above excerpt also represented the participants' perception that the students always need the teacher's direction or help to understand the science concepts. Thus, the pre-service teachers' above responses indicate that they focused more on creating teacher-provided situations in the classroom. They conceived 'teachers' activities as a prime means of science teaching'.

### *Role of the Teacher*

The pre-service teachers defined the role of a science teacher in the teaching process in various ways. One of the participants explained the role of a science teacher as,

> *"...as a science teacher, we should not just focus on the content; we have to focus more on the child's brain development. So, science teachers are responsible for*

*providing the information to develop the students' curiosity to understand how things are happening around us" (P2).*

Other participants mentioned that,

*"...science teachers should present models, animations, and demonstrations and provide some activities to make students learn well" (P1).*

*"...to understand the concept, as a teacher, we should first give an overview of the content and then provide some basic examples from daily life and activities to link the content with the environment" (P3).*

Further, the participants mentioned about the teacher-student relationships in their conceptions of the role of the teacher, as stated below,

*"... teachers should create a friendly environment. The student should not hesitate with the teacher. So, they can express their thoughts on what they observe" (P4).*

*"...the classroom environment should be friendly; the teacher should not be angry with the students if they do not learn. So that everyone can interact out of their fear and not get punishment" (P5).*

Overall, the participants conceptualised 'conveying information', 'providing structured activities' and 'creating a friendly environment' as the main role of the science teacher.

### *Expected Students' Behaviour*

In this theme, the participants described the students' behaviour that they expected during the science teaching and learning process as,

*"...students should be good observer and more attentive towards what teachers taught and how he/she relates the content with real-life examples" (P1).*

Moreover, the pre-service teachers emphasised that students should maintain classroom discipline. For example,

*"...students should sit properly while the teacher is saying something. They should not disturb others" (P5).*

The above responses revealed that the pre-service teachers expected the student to participate in the teaching and learning process 'as a good listener'.

## Discussion and Conclusion

This study aims to explore the secondary pre-service teachers' conceptions of science teaching and learning at their entry level of the teacher education programme. The findings revealed that the pre-service teachers emphasised teachers carrying out activities, models, demonstrations, and teacher provided examples in the science teaching process. Even though the participants mentioned the importance of a learner-friendly environment and interaction with students, they viewed students' science learning need to be under the teacher's guidance. They perceived teachers' major role as 'conveying information' and 'providing structured activities' as an 'instructor', and students' major role as a 'listener' and 'observer'. These views are typical of teacher-centred conceptions of teaching and learning.

These conceptions were similar to the practices of most beginning teachers (Joy, 2016) and experienced teachers (Bansal, 2017; Bhoi, 2021) who primarily relied on teacher-centred methods to teach science. Bansal (2017) and Joy (2016) affirmed that the science teachers' science learning experiences as a student influenced their conceptions/beliefs about teaching and learning. Hence, the participants of this study who are just beginning their educational courses (i.e. pedagogy of science, psychology, philosophy, etc.), their responses tend to rely on their personal science learning experiences as students or mirror their science teachers' practices.

The above discussions inform a need to critically rethink curricular practices of pre-service and continuous professional development (CPD) programmes. Science teacher educators need to acknowledge the pre-service teachers' entry-level conceptions of science teaching and learning and their prior science learning experiences, make them reflect critically on their conceptions, and organise the curricular experiences to strengthen their student-centred practices in their teaching profession.

## References

Bansal, G. (2017). Teachers' perception of inquiry-based science education in Indian primary school. *Indian Educational Review, 55*(1).

Bansal, G. (2020). Indian pre-service teachers' conceptualisations and enactment of inquiry-based science education. *Education 3-13*, doi:10.1080/03004279.2020.1854957

Bansal, G. (2021). Inquiry-based science education in India: prospects and challenges. *Teaching and learning,* 17-19. Retrieved from https://research.acer.edu.au/cgi/viewcontent.cgi?article=1048&context=teacher_india

Bryan, L.A., & Abell, S.K. (1999). Development of professional knowledge in learning to teach elementary science. *Journal of Research in Science Teaching, 36*, 121-139.

Bhoi, S. (2021). *Science teachers' beliefs on inquiry in classroom practices.* Doctoral dissertation, Utkal University, Department of Education.

Cansiz, N., & Cansiz, M. (2020). Profiling preservice science teachers' early experiences, beliefs about teaching, and teaching practices. *Research in Science & Technological Education, 40*(2), 149-167.

Chan, K., & Elliot, R. (2004). Relational analysis of personal epistemology and conceptions about teaching and learning. *Teaching and Teacher Education, 20*(8), 817-831.

Creswell, J.W. (2012). *Education research: Planning, conducting, and evaluating quantitative and qualitative research* (4th ed.). Boston: Pearson Education.

Hewson, P.W., & Hewson, M.G. (1989). Analysis and use of a task for identifying conceptions of teaching science. *Journal of Education for Teaching, 15*, 191-209.

Joy, A. (2016). *Beliefs, practices, and perceptions of beginning teachers: An exploration.* Doctoral dissertation, University of Delhi, Department of Education.

Koballa Jr, T., Graber, W., Coleman, D.C., & Kemp, A.C. (2000). Prospective gymnasium teachers' conceptions of chemistry learning and teaching. *International Journal of Science Education, 22*(2), 209-224.

Kumar, A., & Panda, B.N. (2020). Pedagogical Beliefs of Pre-service Teachers towards Teaching Physical Science at the Secondary Level. Journal of Indian Education, 46(2), 7-21.

MHRD. (2020). *National Education Policy 2020*. Retrieved from https://www.education.gov.in/sites/upload_files/mhrd/files/NEP_Final_English_0.pdf

Ministry of Education, GoI. (2023). *National Curriculum Framework for School Education 2023.* Retrieved from https://ncert.nic.in/pdf/NCFSE-2023-August_2023.pdf

Patton, M.Q. (2002). *Qualitative research and evaluation* (3rd ed.). Thousand Oaks: Sage.

Subramaniam, K. (2013). Minority preservice teachers' conceptions of teaching science: sources of science teaching strategies. *Research in Science Education, 43*, 687-709.

# 11

# Developing Reflective Practitioners in Pre-Service Teachers

Ashu Threja Malhotra

## Introduction

The research asserts that the professionals engaged in reflective practices are the ones who develop in their endeavours. The paradigm shifts with implementation of NCF 2005 and now NEP 2020 and NEP 2020-based NCFSE 2023 in Indian context requires the teachers and teacher educators to reflect on their practices to engage in effective teaching empowering learners to develop the essential competencies related with specific subjects the teachers and teacher educators are professionally equipped for. In this context the researcher in capacity of a Mathematics teacher educator conducts the present study to explore efforts to engage self and the Pre-Service Mathematics teachers in reflective practices using a framework Knowledge Quartet.

## Literature Review

The review of related literature confirms that the Mathematics Teacher educators have engaged in varied practices to help Pre-service Mathematics teachers to critically reflect on their teaching. Artzt (1999) used strategy to make Pre-service Mathematics teachers reflect on different phases of teaching to assess their instructional practices in context of their cognitions and empower them to become reflective Mathematics teacher. Davis (2006) asserts that engaging Pre-service teachers in focused reflections regarding student thinking helps them to relate content and pedagogy. Ball (1988) and Ebby (1999) based on their consistent engagement with Pre-service teachers have asserted that Pre-service Teachers are influenced by the way they have been taught mathematics instead being influenced by the specific needs of teaching and learning Mathematics in correspondence with what Ball (2008) defines as Mathematical content knowledge for teaching. When Pre-Service teachers are engaged in critical reflections, Ma (1999) and Turner (2012) have observed that they realize the need to appreciate content and pedagogical considerations specific to Mathematics. These contributions have led to development of tools and frameworks to facilitate Mathematics Pre-Service Teachers to engage in focused reflections

## Theoretical Framework

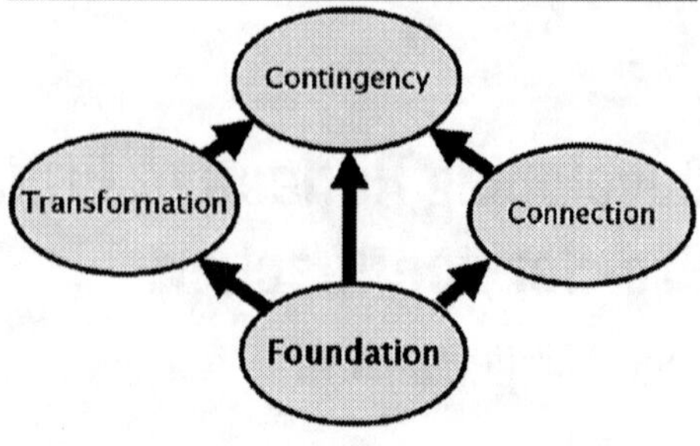


**Figure 1:** The Knowledge Quartet (Image source: http://www.knowledgequartet.org/)

The teachers are empowered to reflect with use of frameworks developed on basis of the research. The Knowledge Quartet is one of them developed to assist Pre-service Teachers engaged in teaching Mathematics across grades to reflect on aspects related with teaching and learning of Mathematics. The Knowledge Quartet (Rowland, Huckstep, & Thwaites, 2005) was developed through the analysis of the classroom observations and videotaped lessons using grounded theory approach. The mathematics lessons across primary and middle grades being executed by Pre-service teachers were observed and analysed. The Quartet suggests four dimensions: foundation, connectedness, transformation and contingency to analyse mathematical content knowledge and pedagogical considerations for teaching of Mathematics.

Foundation relates with teacher's theoretical knowledge related with understanding of mathematics, mathematics pedagogy and beliefs about why and how mathematics is learnt. This knowledge and beliefs have influence on the teacher's classroom practices. The other three dimensions are related with the planning and execution of the plans laid down.

Transformation relates with communicating the mathematical knowledge in class using pedagogical considerations including representations, analogies, examples, illustrations and demonstrations to facilitate construction of concepts and development of the procedures in a Mathematics classroom.

Concepts in mathematics are related with each other within and across the Mathematical themes in school curriculum across different grades and the third-dimension connectedness is concerned with this aspect of conceptual structures in Mathematics. It relates with emphasis on the connectedness in the concepts to be made explicit while planning and execution with due consideration to empower learners to appreciate the relationships amongst the mathematical concepts.

Contingency, the fourth dimension is reflection in action, during teaching, with facilitator's responses to student's unexpected responses/ideas and make deviations from the planned lesson in response to unexpected student teacher interactions.

The participants, in the study, the Pre-service teachers engaged in teaching Mathematics to the middle grade learners are encouraged to reflect on the varied phases of teaching, planning, execution and revisiting the executed plan with perspective of the Knowledge Quartet.

## The Study

### *Objectives*

To explore how the use of the framework Knowledge Quartet facilitates Pre-service teachers to reflect:

1. in action and on action on classroom practices as a Mathematics teacher
2. on use of representations and examples to communicate the abstract Mathematical concepts
3. on connectedness implicit in Mathematical concepts being constructed
4. how to make learners appreciate the implicit connectedness amongst the Mathematical concepts being constructed.

### *Methodology*

The study is a descriptive qualitative study employing the collation of the data through non-participant classroom observations by the researcher of the four student interns of the second year of the 2-year B.Ed. course teaching Mathematics across the middle grades in Govt./Govt-Aided schools as part of School Experience Program. The class observations were followed with debriefing sessions with the student interns. The sessions facilitated the Interns to reflect on their planning, execution, extent their learning objectives were fulfilled and how will they reteach provided an opportunity given to them. The sessions with student interns also provided an opportunity to the researcher to intervene and share with them the dimensions of the Knowledge Quartet and facilitate them to engage in in-depth reflections on aspects peculiar with mathematical content knowledge and pedagogical considerations for teaching Mathematics. The student interns were also asked to write their reflections based on their experience of the corresponding teaching episode and the associated debriefing session with the researcher. The triangulation of the data was done through data collated on basis of classroom observations, debriefing sessions, and written reflections. 08 to 10 lessons were observed and debriefed for each intern across different middle grades and different themes assigned to them.

## Results and Discussions

The researcher takes opportunity to share that the introduction of the Quartet during in-depth debriefing sessions with student interns made them evolve as researchers of their own practice. The interns initially shared their classroom experiences and reflections on the same with a lens of general aspects including challenges in exploring tasks/activities for the plans, classroom management and if they could complete all the tasks planned but gradually the shift was there on varied aspects related with nature of Mathematics and the interns substantiated all the assertions made with evidences from the classroom, and so engaged in evidence-based classroom teaching the most crucial aspect for being a reflective practitioners. The interns were engaged in teaching Fractions and Operations on Fractions across different middle grades.

### *Reflections on exploiting the use of representations, examples, and non-examples to communicate the concepts and facilitate transformation*

Student Intern 2 assigned the theme Multiplication of Fractions for Grade VII learners initially laid down the plans with focus only on learning procedures but during debriefing sessions when made to reflect on emphasis of use of representations and relating concepts and procedures employed use of visual representations to make learners appreciate the multiplication of fractions.

She shared how to develop procedure for multiplication of unit fractions, learners facilitated to represent one of fraction and then considering it as a whole represented the other fraction as part of this whole. Example to find 1/3 of 1/4, the whole divided into three parts and one part shaded and then whole divided into four parts with respect three earlier parts, with 12 parts in all and so requisite fraction as double shaded region representing 1/12, learners could visualize the product and so concept and procedure related. Similarly, use of visual representations for multiplication of fractions (proper fraction with proper fraction) made learners communicating with each other regarding double shaded region (with use of two different colours) representing part of whole to be considered as requisite product and asserting with reasons based on conceptual understanding.

The learners were seen verbalizing amongst each other on representation of the fractions, discerning the whole and procedure was related with concept. The learners accustomed to use only the rule too were motivated to learn with emphasis on concepts.

The intern and student both were reflective of the practices they were engaged in.

Student Intern 3, teaching Division of Whole Number by a fraction, employed representation of whole number by a paper strip. Example, to illustrate 3÷1/2, student teacher employed use of three paper strips of equal size, each divided into two equal parts and making learners visualize how many halves in three. Learners made to do the above task with concrete representation, observe the number of parts and on basis of observed pattern facilitated to generalize rule for dividing whole number by a fraction.

Student Intern 1 teaching fractions to Grade VI, employed use of visual representations to encourage learners to represent the given pairs of like fractions and compare them, it was observed that all learners were representing fractions considering the whole as a collection of objects and then sharing the responses on basis of visuals represented and reasoning for responses.

Student Interns also exploited use of representations based on real life situations to make learners relate Mathematics with daily life.

The use of representations facilitated abstraction of the concepts and also engaged learners in the process of generalization of their observations in their own words on basis of the patterns observed by them.

### *Reflections on making implicit Connectedness in the concepts explicit for the learners*

During the debriefing sessions it was apparent that interns though knew that there are relationships between mathematical concepts within a theme and across the themes but these relationships and their appreciation was not explicit in planning and in classroom teaching, interns when made to reflect on this were observed to make efforts to make learners too appreciate this connectedness.

Student Intern 4 when engaged in teaching multiplication of whole number by a fraction to Grade VII learners, exploited the opportunity to make learners revisit the relationship between multiplication and addition. For example, students to find 3* ¼, added ¼ three times.

Student intern 2 whilst teaching multiplication of Decimal Numbers, made learners appreciate 0.1 and 1/10 are equivalent representations and see how Decimals and Fractional Numbers are connected with each other.

Student intern 3 exploited the task related with comparing 7/2 and 6/2 to make learners observe that how fractions relate to division.

Learners expressed 7/2 as 3 and ½, on dividing 7 by 2, 6/2 as 3, on dividing 6 by 2.

### *Reflection in action and on action by Student Interns as Mathematics Teachers*

The excerpts as shared by interns during the debriefing sessions and written reflections ascertain that they initiated to reflect during the class and after the class on varied aspects characteristic of Maths as a subject.

In words of Student Intern 1

> "*A mistake that I had made in the class was that I used a line "in multiplication there is increment", here I should have told them that this happens in the case of whole numbers. I should have told them the case of proper fractions such as ½ multiplied by ½ gives ¼. Here we can see that ¼ is less than ½ and it is not an increment. In the same way 0.3 multiplied by 0.3 gives 0.09. Here I will help them identify themselves that in case of proper fractions, there is not an increment. I will make them aware of this to avoid any misconceptions.*"

In words of Student Intern 3

> *"Learners facilitated to represent multiplication of fractions, unit fractions visually, but then instead of making them observe the pattern and generalize the procedure on their own, I shared the procedure that when we multiply two fractions, we multiply Numerator with Numerator and Denominator with Denominator ... in subsequent classes...I will emphasize that students verbalize their observations and responses, and generalize the patterns observed."*

In words of Student Intern 3

> *"I will give due emphasis on choice and the sequence of examples to be taken. While facilitating the learners to represent multiplication of unit fractions visually, I initiated with examples as 1/3 of 1/4, 1/7 of 1/8 and then during recapitulation assigned 1/5 of 1/2, I realized as learners had challenges with visual representations, I should have initiated with simple partitions as involved in 1/5 of ½".*

In words of Student Intern 4

> *"I observe the word problems based on multiplication of fractions in the textbook are of same kind related with meaning of multiplication as rate. The variability in questions to be explored by me and learners to have opportunity to meaning of concept exploited in different situations as multiplying factor and cartesian product too..."*

In words of Student Intern 2

> *"As I saw in today's class same questions same answers but the strategies were different.*
>
> *First girl solved 5/100* 450 = 1/20* 450 = 45/2 = 22.5*
>
> *On the other side second girl solved like 5/100*450= (5*45)/10 = 225/10 = 22.5*
>
> *One was using division to simplify and the other was using decimal method to simplify, although both were correct.*
>
> *I missed opportunity to ask learners to verbalize their process.*
>
> *We as teachers, to provide opportunities for employing different strategies and learners appreciate process rather product while engaged in employing procedures."*

All interns reflected that there are lots of conceptual gaps observed and all students to a large extent just emphasize on procedures vis-a-vis conceptual understanding as in words of Student Intern 3.

It was observed while adding fractions when using multiplication as repeated addition to find 3*1/4, learners added ¼ three times and while doing so added numerators and denominators. The response cites how procedures are learnt without relating with concepts.

## Conclusion

The use of the framework empowered Pre-service Teachers to reflect on their mathematical knowledge for teaching and pedagogical considerations to be exploited which involves learner in the process of representation, abstraction, and generalization of concepts in Mathematics class. The Pre-service Interns were explicitly reflecting on classroom interaction based on questions, student's errors and their analysis, use of mathematical language, previous knowledge and content of the curriculum material including textbooks and suggested resources. The discussions and reflections based on varied aspects evolved as internship continued and there was an evident change in planning and execution of plans with emphasis on mathematical content knowledge for teaching, use of varied representations and exploiting opportunities to make connectedness amongst the concepts being realized by the learners. The researcher considers that intervention with use of Knowledge Quartet helped pre-service Mathematics teachers to evolve as reflective practitioners and laid a foundation for their professional development.

## References

Rowland, T., Huckstep, P. & Thwaites, A. (2005). Elementary teachers' mathematics subject knowledge: The Knowledge Quartet and the case of Naomi. *Journal of Mathematics Teacher Education*, *8*(3), 255-281. doi:10.1007/s10857-005-0853-5

Rowland, T., F. Turner, A. Thwaites, and P. Huckstep. 2009. *Developing primary mathematics teaching: Reflecting on practice with the Knowledge Quartet*. London: Sage

Rowland, T. (2014) The Knowledge Quartet: the genesis and application of a framework for analyzing mathematics teaching and deepening teachers' mathematics knowledge. *SISYPHUS Journal of Education*, *1*(3), pp. 15-43

O'Keeffe, L., & White, B. (2022). Supporting Mathematics Pre-Service Teachers Reflection with 360 degree Video and the Knowledge Quartet. *Australian Journal of Teacher Education*, 47(3). http://dx.doi.org/10.14221/ajte.2022v47n3.4

# 12

# Work Life Balance Strategies in Teacher Education

Reena Kumari

> *"Teaching is a very noble profession that shapes the character, calibre, and future of an individual. If the people remember me as a good teacher, that will be the biggest honour."*
>
> *Prof. A.P.J. Abdul Kalam*

## Introduction

Undoubtedly, teaching is a challenging career that is often marked by long hours, attachments, and ever-increasing responsibilities. The various requirements and expectations of the job may have an impact on teacher satisfaction and the achievement of a work life balance. Apart from technology, online learning, and other ever-changing trends in educational institutions, there are other factors that may hinder work life balance and happiness (Owens, 2018). Teachers today have a lot of multiple responsibilities, including employment, kids, volunteering, housework, spousal care, and elderly parental care. Without any question, these roles strain people and cause work life conflicts that affect not only themselves but also their peers, teachers, and the community a healthy work life. In-service teachers may experience a great deal of stress, burnout, and difficulty maintaining balance because of this pressure (Lindqvist et al., 2017). The traditional focus of teacher education programs is on the development of subject matter expertise and pedagogical abilities. But if work life balance is underestimated, which is important, then teachers may not be prepared for the responsibilities of the teaching profession. Achieving work life balance and reducing workplace stress can be facilitated by implementing strategies focused on mentoring and self-care, such as improving physical health, maintaining social connections, and using mindfulness as a cognitive approach (Turner et al., 2012). The purpose of this study is to explore relevant work life balance strategies that might be included in teacher education for preparing future teachers.

## Research Questions

1. What are the specific challenges faced by teachers in maintaining work life balance?
2. Which strategies are most effective in promoting work life balance among in-service teachers?
3. What modifications may be made to teacher education programs to better support for teachers' work life balance?

## Literature Review

Casper, Vaziri, Wayne, DeHauw and Greenhaus (2018) concluded that work life balance is a self-appraisal of how well one blends work and non-work responsibilities based on a thorough literature synthesis on the conceptual definition of work life balance. In the same way, Greenhaus and Allen (2011) characterize life balance as a multimodal strategy that derives from a feeling of efficacy and contentment in a variety of duties. Teachers continue to experience increasing stress and burnout, which can result in anxiety and depression. Teachers who are burned out are at risk for both poor physical and mental health, which can have a negative impact on their health (Agyapong, Donkor, Burback and Wei, 2022). Organizational work cannot be done under pressure as it could be the reason for the low production, disappointment, and bad physical health. Several factors effect on employee's job satisfaction such as overload of work, separation, wide hours worked, harmless work atmosphere, tough affairs between co-workers and role uncertainty, irritation and shortage of chances or inspiration to development in one skill level. New teachers frequently lack the necessary skills and specialty for the academic role. Despite having knowledge and abilities, they lack the necessary preparation for the challenges of teaching, advising, scholarship, and academic citizenship (Richardson and Alsup, 2015). Schools are becoming more conscious of the adverse effects of having overworked teachers (Racho, 2015). One of the factors that has the biggest impact on how well people manage their work and family lives is their working hours. The study emphasizes the need for educational institutions to address staff members' concerns about work life balance, particularly about women (Sunitha, 2020). Considering this, she said that for in-service teachers should achieve the best work life balance by creating work life balance workshops that help them to grasp time management, stress management, change management, technology management, self-management, and leisure management. Some work life balance programs must be included in teachers' training courses to handle stress and otherwise cope more dramatically while other programs help to reduce the absolute stress levels by rebalancing work life (Gardner, 2006). Furthermore (Jacobs and Winslow, 2004) had documented that work life balance programs in education have been demonstrated to have an impact on teachers in terms of their productivity. Evidence supported that increased work life balance contributes to improve in teachers' productivity (Hayman, 2005). The first few years of teaching experience improve productivity, but little else in the way of observed teacher's work life balance seems to matter consistently (Harris and Sass, 2011).

## Difficulties in Realizing Work Life Balance

It extends the period you spend at work in relation to your personal life. It must also speak to how much of your time and attention you devote to teaching in comparison to your life outside of the classroom. It is evident that certain barriers stand in the way of teachers achieving a healthy work life balance.

### *Excessive workload*

Teaching may feel like a hard job at times. Less than half of a teacher's time is spent in the classroom instructing students; the remainder is spent on planning lessons, creating, and organizing resources, printing, and organizing resources, setting up the classroom with displays and basic maintenance, marking assignments, tests, practice questions for exams, essays, and late work, as well as managing students' behaviour with emails, calls home, and detentions. Stress and anxiety might result when individual teachers face these enormous to-do lists and naturally leave them incomplete. Hence devoting even more important time and effort to a teacher's life away from the classroom.

Teachers' training courses can start the way for letting to this unrealistic expectation if they acknowledge that they are not endless. It is possible to rearrange priorities, recognize and celebrate successes, and bring joy back to teaching.

### *The need of perfectionism*

The desire to please and do all works to such a high standard can negatively impact on teachers as well. They never feel like that they have done a good enough job, resulting in them second-guessing their competency. They always feel that there is more that they could have done, leading to a feeling of dissatisfaction. They like things to be done the way that they like it, making it difficult for them to relinquish control or delegate to others. While these seem like well-deserved rewards for doing well in class, they also have unfavourable effects on the larger school community, because they are so proud of what they do, teachers may become unwilling to work together or share resources, which would increase everyone's workload. As they work to prioritize the needs of others over their own, teachers as a group face the risk of burning out. Because of this, professional selfishness and self-care are not encouraged in the school's culture. It is critical that they re-establish their mental boundaries in these scenarios.

### *Dissonance in Thought*

A psychological theory called cognitive dissonance explains the reason in which individuals feel uncomfortable or tense when they have two or more contradicting assumptions, attitudes, or beliefs. Dissonance and dissatisfaction can result from tensions between job demands, perceived control, work environment climate, and work environment culture (Karanika-Murray, Michaelides and Wood, 2017). A growing gap between the expectations of scientists' roles in traditional academic settings and their aspirations to be creative researchers who contribute to industry in a study of 734 academic scientists in the United Kingdom (Lam, 2010). Researchers in business schools have discovered that faculty and administration tension can lead to cognitive dissonance when published school rankings against competitors or national benchmarks and scientific journal rankings for faculty publications are made public (Kodeih and Greenwood, 2013; Malsch and Tessier, 2014).

### *Dissonance in Emotions*

Because of the possibility for long-term attachment in work, jobs requiring a great deal of interpersonal connection, including teaching, may have an adverse impact on the wellbeing of their employees. When linked with other organizational and social factors, such as work overload, deadlines, and role conflicts, emotional dissonance is the thought to be a job requirement that predicts work-related stress (Pace and Sciotto, 2020). The connection between emotional dissonance and interference from work and family is studied by (Cheung and Tang, 2012). They concluded that emotional dissonance and strain-based work-family interference were positively correlated. When the responsibilities of one position infringe on and hinder the performance of another, strain-based work-family interference occurs exhausting personal resources (Nohe, Meier, Sonntag and Michel, 2015).

### *Approaches to Work Life Harmony for Teachers*

When burnout threatens or occurs, it is necessary for in-service teachers to equip themselves with the use techniques to encourage self-care, strengthen resilience, and renew their passion for their work. A multimodal approach to health is a part of life balance. To successfully tackle life's obstacles, one must control their roles, stress, emotions, and cognitive processes. In the same way, resilience is often defined by (Tabibnia and Radecki, 2018) as the capacity to effectively overcome adversity. There are some approaches that assist the teachers to balance the life with work after entering in job:

### *Encourage rest and recreation*

Being a teacher requires a lot of energy and stamina. Take a vigorous power walk or take an easy walk around the community. Give yourself a little sweet time in the hot tub. With a wide range of difficulties teachers come across, it can be difficult to maintain patience and joy. Without a good night's sleep, it is practically impossible. Include a bit of rest in your daily schedule. Set and keep to a bedtime.

### *Physical and mental health support*

Cater to your needs—physical, emotional, mental, and spiritual. Manage the time needs of administrators, parents, and students. Teachers must practise self-care strategies during their teaching courses and maintain their focus on their task. They may use breaks to grow and relax. Many people find that prayer and meditation are beneficial repeatedly. Benefit from the motivational readings found in books on daily meditation. Combine peaceful activities in your personal time.

### *Provide flexible scheduling options*

No matter the age and skill levels of learners, it can be difficult to teach with a positive and compassionate attitude. Though reality frequently differs from even the best-laid plans, preparation is essential. Keep in mind that those around you are impacted by your ups and downs in life. Work, family, health, and other stresses sometimes be too much to handle. Opportunities for couple counselling and shared reflections can be very beneficial in resolving issues that arise in relationships, such as work life balance.

### *Maintain effective communication*

Stress, hopes, and expectations in the classroom may wear down even the most skilled educators. Thus, developing the habit of rising early is necessary. Little things may make your planning, period, or lunchtime too, such a cute tiny gif or emoji and a few words. Feel your face starting to smile. Contact the others during the day.

### *Creating social connections*

According to Pietromonaco and Collins (2017), social support has directly related to a lower incidence of Post Traumatic Stress Disorder, tension, and regret and other stress-related medical problems. Gratitude expression can impact subjective well-being in the long run. This has effects on social reward, empathy, and emotion control. Furthermore, two weeks of daily gratitude improved life satisfaction and decreased anxiety (Kerr, O'Donovan and Pepping, 2015).

### *Cognitive instruction*

Another approach for improving wellbeing and cognitive training is mindfulness. It is frequently defined as the deliberate, judgment-free act of paying attention to the present moment (Crane, Brewer, Feldman and Kabat-Zinn, 2017). Mindfulness techniques have been linked to enhanced attention, good emotions, and a sense of well-being, as well as better relationship quality. The capacity to identify and replace automatic negative ideas with constructive ones is closely linked to resilience (McRae, Ciesielski and Gross, 2012). This refers to reframe or cognitive reappraisal. Positive thoughts can counterbalance negative ones, so teachers can reduce tension and moderate the bad mood that goes along with it. A common instance of this might be considered listening to a podcast during a long traffic block.

### *Trial and error*

Future teachers should be skilled to improve their work life balance and ensure that it is contributing to their happiness by taking time to reflect on the adjustments they have made. Knowledge is always to modify things and facilitate commitment to change. One can always try something out if one is not sure if it will work for them. They might find it useful, or perhaps they would like to make some adjustments.

### *Strategies for the workplace*

The ability of teachers to learn and develop at work is important for the quality of their performance and their well-being (Caspersen, 2015). Teachers at different stages of their career believe that continued professional development activities are necessary because these are the "means of recharging their batteries" and an investment in their careers (Day et al. 2007). Informal, unplanned collaboration with colleagues and former peers, as well as participation in traditional forms of formal induction programs and mentoring, are significant for novice teachers› professional learning (McCormack et al. 2006). Teacher's professional development initiatives have the greatest chance of success when there is obvious administrative support, a lengthy and consistent duration, teacher ownership of the initiatives, and peer mentoring (Klingner, 2004). Fostering a supportive and collaborative atmosphere in the academic setting is essential to reduce the rate of burnout (Stupnisky, Weaver-Hightower and Kartoshkina, 2015). It is possible that teachers may lack the necessary preparation for in-person or virtual training, as well as knowledge of instructional or pedagogical strategies (Clinefelter, 2012). An orientation to the institution that clearly outlines the requirements for teaching, service, and scholarship should be a part of teachers' development.

## Conclusion

After incorporating each of these aspects, it is reasonable to draw the conclusion that contemporary organizations, particularly educational ones, should address work life balance-related issues among the teachers and adopt a comprehensive plan for implementing policies that support the teaching staff in managing their work life balance, which will improve staff performance. Incorporation into the institutional atmosphere and culture, mentoring into the role, and substantial support with instructing and learning techniques are all necessary for teachers. Hence, we can say that this issue must be resolved since in-service teachers who implement appropriate work life balancing techniques have a higher chance of being successful and happy teachers.

## References

Agyapong, B., Obuobi-Donkor, G., Burback, L., & Wei, Y. (2022). Stress, burnout, anxiety, and depression among teachers: A scoping review. *International Jjournal of Environmental Research and Public Health, 19*(17), 10706.

Casper, W., Vaziri, H., Wayne, J., DeHauw, S., & Greenhaus, J. (2018). The jingle-jangle of work–nonwork balance: A comprehensive and meta-analytic review of its meaning and measurement. *Journal of Applied Psychology, 103*(2), 182-214. https://doi.org/10.1037/apl0000259.

Caspersen, J. (2015). Teachers' learning activities in the workplace: how does teacher education matter? *Creative Education, 6*(1), 46-63.

Cheung, F.Y., & Tang, C. S. (2012). The effect of emotional dissonance and emotional intelligence on work-family interference. *Canadian Journal of Behavioral Science, 44*(1), 50-58. https://doi.org/10.1037/a0025798.

Clinefelter, D. (2012). Best practices for online faculty development. Retrieved from https://www.learninghouse.com/wpcontent/uploads/2017/09/Best-Practices-for-Online-Faculty-Development_Web_Final.pdf.

Crane, R.S., Brewer, J., Feldman, C., & Kabat-Zinn, J. (2017). What defines mindfulness-based programs? The warp and the weft. *Psychological Medicine*, *47*(6), 990-999. https://doi.org/10.1017/S0033291716003317.

Day, C., Sammons, P., Stobart, G., Kington, A., & Gu, Q. (2007). *Teachers Matter: Connecting Work, Lives and Effectiveness*. Maidenhead: Open University Press.

Gardner, S. (2006). Stress among prospective teachers: A review of the literature. *Australian Journal of Teacher Education, 36*(1), 18-28. doi: 10.14221/ajte.2010v35n8.2

Greenhaus, J.H., & Allen, T.D. (2011). Work–family balance: A review and extension of the literature. In J.C. Quick, & L.E. Tetrick (Eds.), *Handbook of occupational health psychology* (2nd ed). Washington, DC: American Psychological Association.

Hayman, J. (2005). Psychometric assessment of an instrument designed to measure work life balance. *Research and Practice in Human Resource Management, 13*(1), 85-91. Retrieved from https://espace.curtin.edu.au/handle/20.500.11937/46385.

Jacobs, J.A., & Winslow, S.E. (2004). The academic life course, time pressures and gender inequality. *Community, Work & Family, 7*(2), 143-161.

Karanika-Murray, M., Michaelides, G., & Wood, S.J. (2017). Job demands, job control, psychological climate, and job satisfaction: A cognitive dissonance perspective. *Journal of Organizational Effectiveness: People and Performance*, *4*(3), 238-255. https://doi.org/10.1108/JOEPP-02-2017-0012.

Kerr, S.L., O'Donovan, A., & Pepping, C.A., (2015). Can gratitude and kindness interventions enhance well-being in a clinical sample? *Journal of Happiness Studies, 16*(1), 17-36. https://doi.org/10.1007/s10902-013-9492-1

Klingner, J.K. (2004). The Science of Professional Development. *Journal of Learning Disabilities, 37*, 248-255.

Kodeih, F., & Greenwood, R. (2013). Responding to institutional complexity: The role of identity. *Organization Studies, 35*(1), 7-39. https://doi.org/10.1177/0170840613495333.

Kerr, S. L., O'Donovan, A., & Pepping, C. A., (2015). Can gratitude and kindness interventions enhance well-being in a clinical sample? *Journal of Happiness Studies, 16*(1), 17-36. https://doi.org/10.1007/s10902-013-9492-1

Lindqvist, H., Weurlander, M., Wernerson, A., and Thornberg, R. (2017). Resolving Feelings of Professional Inadequacy: Student Teachers' Coping with Distressful Situations. *Teach. Education. 64*, 270–279. doi:10.1016/j.tate.2017.02.019.

Malsch, B., & Tessier, S. (2014). Journal ranking effects on junior academics: Identity fragmentation and politicization. *Critical Perspectives on Accounting, 26*(2) 84-98. https://doi.org/10.1016/j.cpa.2014.02.006

McCormack, A., Gore, J., & Thomas, K. (2006). Early Career Teacher Professional Learning. *Asia-Pacific Journal of Teacher Education, 34*, 95-113.

McRae, K., Ciesielski B., & Gross J. J. (2012). Unpacking cognitive reappraisal: Goals, tactics, and outcomes. *Emotion, 12*(2), 250-255. https://doi.org/10.1037/a0026351.

Nohe, C., Meier, L., Sonntag, K., & Michel, A. (2015). The chicken or the egg? A meta-analysis of panel studies of the relationship between work–family conflict and strain. *Journal of Applied Psychology, 100*(2), 522-536. https://doi.org/10.1037/a0038012.

Owens, E. (2023). Building Healthy Academic Communities Journal. Reviews: *The Journal of Journal Reviews, 2*(2).

Pace, F., & Sciotto, G. (2021). The effect of emotional dissonance and mental load on need for recovery and work engagement among Italian fixed-term researchers. *International Journal of Environmental Research and Public Health, 18*(1), 1–18. https://doi.org/10.3390/ijerph18010099

Pietromonaco, P.R., & Collins, N.L. (2017). Interpersonal mechanisms linking close relationships to health. *American Psychologist, 72*(6), 531-542. https://doi.org/10.1037/amp0000129.

Racho, L.L.B. (2015). Administrators' Quality of Work in Relation to Teachers' Productivity. Unpublished Dissertation. Jose Rizal Memorial State University, Main Campus, Dapitan City.

Richardson, J.C., & Alsup, J. (2015). From the classroom to the keyboard: How seven teachers created their online teacher identities. *International Review of Open and Distributed Learning, 16*(1), 142-167. https://doi.org/10.19173/irrodl.v16i1.1814.

Stupnisky, R.H., Weaver-Hightower, M.B., & Kartoshkina, Y. (2015). Exploring and testing the predictors of new faculty success: A mixed methods study. *Studies in Higher Education*: *40*(2), 368-390.

Tabibnia, G., & Radecki, D. (2018). Resilience training that can change the brain. Consulting Psychology Journal: *Practice and Research, 70*(1), 59-88. https://doi.org/10.1037/cpb0000110.

Turner, S., Zanker, N., and Braine, M. (2012). An Investigation into Teacher Wellbeing During the Teacher Training Year. Des. *Technology Education. 17* (2), 21–34.

# 13

# Self-efficacy of Higher Secondary School Teachers
## *Study of Chandel and Senapati Districts of Manipur*

Vandana Laishram

### Introduction

Self-efficacy is a person`s optimistic self-belief. It is the belief that a person can develop the skills to perform new or difficult task to cope with changes in health and functioning. It is believing that we have in our own abilities, specifically our ability to meet the challenges ahead of us and complete a task successful (Akhtar, 2008). General self-efficacy refers to our overall belief in our ability to succeed, but there are many more specific forms of self-efficacy like academic, parenting, sports as well. Psychologist Albert Bandura has defined self-efficacy as one's ability to succeed in specific situations or accomplish a task. One's sense of self-efficacy can play a major role in how one approaches goals, tasks, and challenges. The theory of self-efficacy lies at the centre of Bandura's social cognitive theory, which emphasizes the role of observational learning and social experience in the development of personality. Self-efficacy is typically task-specific, which means an individual may feel competent at a task depending on prior experiences and beliefs. It affects learning and motivation, and it plays a significant role in individual behaviour modification. It can be especially helpful in analysing human interaction with their surroundings and past experiences.

#### *Teacher self-efficacy*

Teacher self-efficacy is defined by Bandura (1977) as the teacher's ability to attain desirable student engagement and learning outcomes, irrespective of their intelligence and level of motivation. It is individual teachers' self-belief in their capacity to design, organise, and execute the tasks necessary to achieve educational objectives (Skaalvik and Skaalvik, 2007). A common interpretation of teacher self-efficacy is that it describes how a teacher feels and views about their capacity to give a powerful impact on overall outcomes of students and the educational settings as a whole (e.g., Soodak & Podell, 1996; Wheatley,

2005). The success of educators and the schools in which they work depends on teacher's efficacy which covers a variety of academic topics, fields, and global educational contexts (Martin & Mulvihill, 2019). Self-efficacy affects teachers' psychological well-being and classroom executions and classroom management skills is one of such classroom executions.

According to Bandura's theory, high teacher self-efficacy is developed from these sources which are: (a) mastery learning experiences, (b) vicarious experiences, (c) social persuasion, and (d) physiological/emotional states. Mastery experience is when a person performs his duty or complete the task successfully. The teachers provide examples of their own successful classroom instruction proving their capability and competency. One of the most important factors influencing the development of teachers' self-efficacy is mastery experiences (Pfitzner-Eden, 2016). Vicarious experience is learning from observation — teachers observe and imitate other successful teachers, teacher educators, parents, and administrators, which leads to building their own self-efficacy. Social persuasion involves feedback and encouragement from others. Self-efficacy of teachers grows from such emotional support from others. The final source is physiological/emotional indexes. These bodily reactions can indicate our sense of competence making them one of the important sources of self-efficacy. Teachers with high self-efficacy know are more capable when they find that they are not stressed out in instructional and other related tasks.

### *Importance of teacher's self-efficacy*

In the 1970s, psychologist Albert Bandura developed the framework of self-efficacy, and it has been widely used in the field of education over the past three decades. He argued that people with high self-efficacy will apply effort, persevere, and demonstrate resilience when faced with challenging tasks, while those with low self-efficacy tend to hold back during difficult tasks, expect mediocre results, and give up easily. According to Tschannen-Moran and Woolfolk Hoy (2001), teacher self-efficacy is a teacher's assessment of their own ability to bring desired student learning outcomes engagement, even in challenging situations and difficult students. One can conclude from this definition that teacher with a high self-efficacy would effectively handle problems related to classroom, student, and management efficiently. Geijsel et al. (2009) indicated that teachers' professional learning is connected to their teaching practices and is influenced by their self-efficacy. A study by Temiz and Topcu (2013) showed that constructive teaching methods are more common among teachers with high self-efficacy. Dixon et al. (2014) found a direct and positive correlation between teachers' self-efficacy and their willingness to modify instructional practices in the classroom. Self-efficacy affects people's performance on a certain set of tasks which led to an increase or decrease in the level of their performance and effectiveness of those tasks. It impacts people's cognitive processes, persistence, and motivation. Self-efficacy has significant implications for motivation because people's belief in their ability to complete tasks or achieve goals strongly influences goal setting, aspirational levels, their effort for the same, and to persist or tendency to give up when faced with any problems and difficulty (Bandura, 1997). The concern for professional development, openness to implement innovative teaching techniques, work engagement, stress tolerance, and observations of high-quality education in the classroom have all been positively related with teachers' self-efficacy (Klassen & Chiu, 2011; Klassen & Tze, 2014; Lauermann & Konig, 2016; Schwarzer & Hallum, 2008; Tschannen-Moran & McMaster, 2009; Zee & Koomen, 2016). Teachers' self-efficacy shapes occupational wellbeing and also generates a positive educational outcome (Schwarzer & Hallum, 2008). Thus, the goals, effort, and general teaching performance of the teachers are considered to be significantly dependent on their level of self-efficacy.

## The Study

### *Objectives*

1. To study self-efficacy of higher secondary school teachers in Chandel and Senapati districts of Manipur.
2. To determine self-efficacy of higher secondary school teachers with reference to their gender variations.
3. To analyse the level of self-efficacy of the higher secondary school teachers according to their marital status.
4. To study the level of self-efficacy of higher secondary school teachers based on their level of teacher training.
5. To study the level of self-efficacy of higher secondary school teachers according to their years of teaching experiences.

### *Hypotheses*

1. High level of self-efficacy exists among the Higher Secondary School teachers in Chandel and Senapati districts of Manipur.
2. There exists no significant difference on the level of self-efficacy among the higher secondary school teachers with reference to their gender variations.
3. There exists no significant difference on the level of self-efficacy among the higher secondary school teachers according to their marital status.
4. There exists no significant difference on the level of self-efficacy among the higher secondary school teachers based on their level of teacher training.
5. There exists no significant difference on the level of self-efficacy of higher secondary school teachers according to their years of teaching experiences.

### *Research method and sampling*

For the present study, the investigator has adopted descriptive method of research. Simple random sampling will be employed for the study. Eighty higher secondary school teachers have been randomly selected from eight schools of Chandel and Senapati districts of Manipur.

**Table 1:** Sample of the study

| *Sl. No.* | *School* | *Female* | *Male* | *Total* |
|---|---|---|---|---|
| 1. | Asufii Christian Higher Secondary School, Mao, Senapati | 2 | 6 | 8 |
| 2. | Bethany Higher Secondary School, Senapati | 3 | 5 | 8 |
| 3. | Brook Dale Higher Secondary School, Senapati | 5 | 3 | 8 |
| 4. | Lao Radiant Higher Secondary School, Senapati | 5 | 4 | 9 |
| 5. | Don Bosco Higher Secondary School, Maram Khunou, Senapati | 3 | 4 | 7 |
| 6. | Anallon Christian Institute, Chandel | 7 | 4 | 11 |
| 7. | Maha Union Higher Secondary School, Chandel | 9 | 10 | 19 |
| 8. | St. Peter Higher Secondary School, Chandel | 5 | 5 | 10 |
| Total | | 39 | 41 | 80 |

### *Tools*

In the present study, the researcher used a standardised scale Teachers' Self-efficacy Scale (TSES-SVSS) developed by Vishal Sood and Sapna Sen (2016). The scale has 56 positive items.

For the present study, the researcher used Mean, Standard Deviation, t-Test, ANOVA for data analysis.

## Analysis and Interpretation of data

### *Objective 1: To study self-efficacy of higher secondary school teachers*

**Table 1:** Overall level of self-efficacy of the teachers in Chandel and Senapati districts of Manipur

| *Variable* | *N* | *Mean* | *SD* | *Z Score Mean* | *Z Score SD* |
|---|---|---|---|---|---|
| Teachers' Self-efficacy | 80 | 215.1625 | 25.37239 | 0.000 | 1.00 |

*Interpretation:* The above table indicates the overall level of self-efficacy of the teachers in Chandel and Senapati districts of Manipur. The mean and SD are 215.1625 and 25.37239, respectively. The Z Score Mean and Z Score SD are 0.000 and 1.00 respectively. Hence, there exists an average or moderate positive level of self-efficacy among the teachers. So, the hypothesis 1 is rejected.

### *Objective 2: To determine self-efficacy of higher secondary school teachers with reference to their gender variations.*

**Table 2:** Level of self-efficacy of higher secondary school teachers with reference to their gender variations.

| *Variable* | *N* | *Mean* | *SD* | *Df* | *SED* | *t-value* | *P* | *Result* |
|---|---|---|---|---|---|---|---|---|
| Male | 37 | 0.1022472 | 0.94583744 | 78 | 0.22464097 | 0.847 | 0.576 | NS |
| Female | 43 | -0.0879802 | 1.04738265 | | | | | |

*Interpretation*: The above table reveals the level of self-efficacy of higher secondary school teachers concerning their gender. The mean of the male and female teachers is 0.1022472 and -0.0879802, and the standard deviation of the male and female teachers is 0.94583744 and 1.04738265 respectively. The calculated t value of male and female teachers is 0.847 with a degree of freedom of 78 and significance at 0.576, greater than the 0.05 level. Hence, there is no significant difference on the level of self-efficacy among the higher secondary school teachers with reference to their gender variations. So, the hypothesis 2 is accepted.

### *Objective 3: To analyse the level of self-efficacy of the higher secondary school teachers according to their marital status.*

**Table 3:** Level of self-efficacy of higher secondary school teachers according to their marital status

| *Variable* | *N* | *Mean* | *SD* | *Df* | *SED* | *t-value* | *P* | *Result* |
|---|---|---|---|---|---|---|---|---|
| Married | 28 | 0.2891923 | 1.06916511 | 78 | 0.23045978 | 1.931 | 0.372 | NS |
| Unmarried | 52 | -0.1557189 | 0.93445279 | | | | | |

*Interpretation*: The above table reveals the level of self-efficacy of higher secondary school teachers in the Chandel and Senapati districts concerning their marital status. The mean of the married and unmarried teachers is 0.2891923 and -0.1557189, and the standard deviation of the married and unmarried teachers is 1.06916511 and 0.93445279, respectively. The calculated t value of married and unmarried teachers is 1.931 with a degree of freedom of 78 and significance at 0.372, greater than the 0.05 level. Hence, there exists no significant difference in the level of self-efficacy among the higher secondary school teachers with regard to their marital status. So, the hypothesis 3 is accepted.

### *Objective 4: To study the level of self-efficacy of higher secondary school teachers based on their level of teacher training.*

**Table 4:** Level of self-efficacy of trained and untrained teachers

| *Variable* | *N* | *Mean* | *SD* | *Df* | *SED* | *t-value* | *P* | *Result* |
|---|---|---|---|---|---|---|---|---|
| *Trained* | *50* | *-0.1033604* | *0.82597326* | *78* | *0.23031090* | *-1.197* | *0.013* | *S* |
| *Untrained* | *30* | *0.1722673* | *1.23380811* | | | | | |

*Interpretation*: The above table reveals the level of self-efficacy of trained and untrained teachers in the Chandel and Senapati districts. The mean of the trained and untrained teachers is -0.1033604 and 0.1722673, and the standard deviation of the married and unmarried teachers is 0.82597326 and 1.23380811, respectively. The calculated t value of trained and untrained is -1.197 a degree of freedom of 78 and significance at 0.013, greater than the 0.05 level. There exists significant different on the level of self-efficacy among the higher secondary school teachers concerning their training for teaching. Hence, the hypothesis 4 is rejected.

### *Objective 5: To study the level of self-efficacy of higher secondary school teachers according to their years of teaching experiences.*

**Table 5:** Descriptive table of teachers according to their years of teaching experiences.

| *Variables* | *N* | *Mean* | *Std. Deviation* |
|---|---|---|---|
| Below 5 years | 37 | -0.0958826 | 0.96647194 |
| 5 years and above | 31 | 0.0063092 | 0.94412325 |
| 10 years and above | 12 | 0.2793391 | 1.25606651 |
| Total | 80 | 0.0000000 | 1.00000000 |

*Interpretation*: The above table reveals Mean and Standard Deviation of teachers regarding their teaching experiences. The Mean and Standard Deviation of below 5 years are -0.0958826 and 0.96647194, 5 years and above are 0.0063092 and 0.94412325 and 10 years and above teaching experience are 0.2793391 and 1.25606651 respectively.

**Table 6:** Descriptive table of Teaching Experience.

| *Variables* | *Sum of Squares* | *df* | *Mean Square* | *F* | *Sig.* | *Result* |
|---|---|---|---|---|---|---|
| Between Groups | 1.278 | 2 | 0.639 | 0.633 | 0.534 | NS |
| Within Groups | 77.722 | 77 | 1.009 | | | |
| Total | 79.000 | 79 | | | | |

*Interpretation*: The above table reveals the level of self-efficacy among the secondary school teachers with regard to their teaching experience. The total sum of the square for between groups is 1.278 and within groups is 77.722, with the degree of freedom 2 (between groups) and 77 (within groups), the F-value is 1.063 and the significance at 0.534, which is greater than 0.05 significant level. Hence, no significant difference exists in the level of self-efficacy of higher secondary school teachers according to their years of teaching experiences in Chandel and Senapati districts of Manipur. So, hypothesis 5 is accepted.

## Main Findings

On the basis of the analysis and interpretation of the collected data, here are the main findings:

1. There exist an average positive self-efficacy among the teachers of selected higher secondary schools in the Chandel and Senapati districts, Manipur.
2. There is no significant difference in self-efficacy among male and female teachers.
3. There is no significant difference in self-efficacy among the married and unmarried teachers.
4. There exists significant difference on the level of self-efficacy concerning their training for teaching.
5. There exists no significant difference in the level of self-efficacy according to years of their teaching experiences.

## Conclusion and Discussion

The study of teacher self-efficacy has provided significant understandings into the relation between teachers' perceptions of their ability to affect student learning outcomes and the ever-changing educational environment and its needs. It has also emphasized the mutual correlation between teacher self-efficacy and student achievement, that teachers play in influencing how their students learn. Acknowledging and addressing the diverse sources of teacher self-efficacy can empower educators by providing them the required support.

Also, teacher training plays a fundamental part in developing self-efficacy in teachers by enhancing their confidence and efficiency in the classroom (Bruna et al., 2023). Some reasons on why teacher training is essential for development self-efficacy includes skill development, pedagogical knowledge, feedback, classroom management, professional development. Skills can be developed by teacher training programmes by providing them opportunities to acquire and enhance their teaching skills, contributing to teacher's sense of competence and efficacy which impact positive student learning outcomes (Bruna et al, 2023). Pedagogical Knowledge are developed in training programs introducing teachers to the latest and most effective teaching methods. Teacher training often incorporates opportunities for feedback and reflective practice. Through this process, teachers can refine their instructional practices and develop a deeper understanding of their capabilities, contributing to a heightened sense of self-efficacy (Redmon, R.J., 2007). Opportunities for feedback are also frequently included in teacher training programs, thereby gaining awareness of their own practices and capabilities through this process, which will increase their sense of self-efficacy (Shajaad & Naureen, 2017). As teachers gain expertise in managing student behaviour and fostering a positive classroom culture, they feel more in control of their teaching environment, enhancing their self-efficacy. One of the most important aspects of good teaching is effective classroom management. Teachers' self-efficacy increases as they become more effective in regulating students in the classroom and creating a healthy learning environment. Ongoing professional development opportunities are integral to sustaining and enhancing teacher self-efficacy. This commitment to lifelong learning reinforces a sense of efficacy as teachers see themselves as capable and evolving professionals.

In conclusion, we can say that providing teachers with the information, skills, and resources they need to successfully handle the demands of the classroom, teacher training acts as an agent for the development of self-efficacy in teachers. Educational institutions can contribute to the building of competent and empowered teachers by providing them best updated training which will eventually lead to a better learning outcome for students. It is equally important for educational stakeholders to realize the significance of developing and maintaining teacher self-efficacy as a facilitator for successful educational outcomes.

## Suggestions

Some suggestions for the further studies are:

1. The same study can be carried out in other schools.
2. The same study can also be conducted in different levels like high school, college, or university.
3. The same study can also be conducted in other districts.

## References

Bandura, A. (1977). Self-efficacy: Toward a unifying theory of behavioural change. *Psychological Review, 84*(2), 191–215. https://doi.org/10.1037/0033-295X.84.2.191

Bandura, A. (1997). *Self-efficacy: The exercise of control.* W H Freeman/Times Books/ Henry Holt & Co.

Bruna, D., Pérez, M.V., Bustos, C., & Villarroel, V. (2023). The impact of a university teacher training program promoting self-regulated learning on teacher knowledge, self-efficacy, and practices. *Frontiers in Education, 8*, 1007137. https://doi.org/10.3389/feduc.2023.1007137

Dixon, F.A., Yssel, N., McConnell, J.M., & Hardin, T. (2014). Differentiated Instruction, Professional Development, and Teacher Efficacy. *Journal for the Education of the Gifted, 37,* 111-127. https://doi.org/10.1177/0162353214529042

Franziska Pfitzner-Eden (2016). I feel less confident so I quit? Do true changes in teacher self-efficacy predict changes in preservice teachers' intention to quit their teaching degree? *Teaching and Teacher Education (55),* 240-254. https://doi.org/10.1016/j.tate.2016.01.018.

Klassen, R., & Chiu, M.M. (2011). The Occupational Commitment and Intention to Quit of Practicing and Pre-Service Teachers: Influence of Self-Efficacy, Job Stress, and Teaching Context. *Contemporary Educational Psychology, 36,* 114- 129. http://dx.doi.org/10.1016/j.cedpsych.2011.01.002

Lauermann, F., & König, J. (2016). Teachers' professional competence and wellbeing: Understanding the links between general pedagogical knowledge, self-efficacy, and burnout. *Learning and Instruction, 45,* 9–19. https://doi.org/10.1016/j.learninstruc.2016.06.006

Linda E. Martin & Thalia M. Mulvihill (2019) Voices in Education: Teacher Self-Efficacy in Education, The Teacher Educator, 54:3, 195-205, DOI: 10.1080/08878730.2019.1615030

Mark Sherer, James E Maddux, Blaise Mercandante, Steven Prentice-dunn, Beth Jacobs & Ronald W. Rogers (1982). The Self-Efficacy Scale: Construction and Validation. *Psychological reports, 51(2),*663-671. DOI:10.2466/pr0.1982.51.2.663

Robert M. Klassen & Virginia M.C. Tze Teachers' self-efficacy, personality, and teaching effectiveness: A meta-analysis. *Educational Research Review(12),* June 2014, Pages 59-76. https://doi.org/10.1016/j.edurev.2014.06.001

Schwarzer, R., & Hallum, S. (2008). Perceived Teacher Self-Efficacy as a Predictor of Job Stress and Burnout: Mediation Analysis. *Applied Psychology, 57,* 152-171. http://dx.doi.org/10.1111/j.1464-0597.2008.00359.x

Skaalvik, E.M., & Skaalvik, S. (2007). Dimensions of teacher self-efficacy and relations with strain factors, perceived collective teacher efficacy, and teacher burnout. *Journal of Educational Psychology, 99*(3), 611–625. https://doi.org/10.1037/0022-0663.99.3.611

Soodak, L.C., & Podell, D.M. (1996). Teacher efficacy: Toward the understanding of a multi-faceted construct. *Teaching and Teacher Education, 12*(4), 401–411. https://doi.org/10.1016/0742-051X(95)00047-N

Tschannen-Moran, M., & McMaster, P. (2009). Sources of self-efficacy: Four professional development formats and their relationship to self-efficacy and implementation of a new teaching strategy. *The Elementary School Journal, 110*(2), 228–245. https://doi.org/10.1086/605771

Tschannen-Moran, M., & Woolfolk Hoy, A. (2001). Teacher Efficacy: Capturing an Elusive Construct. *Teaching and Teacher Education, 17,* 783-805. http://dx.doi.org/10.1016/S0742-051X(01)00036-1

Tugma Temiz & Mustafa Sami Topcu (2013) Preservice teachers' teacher efficacy beliefs and constructivist-based teaching practice European Journal of Psychology of Education 28(4) DOI:10.1007/s10212-013-0174-5

Wheatley, K.F. (2005). The case for reconceptualizing teacher efficacy research. *Teaching and Teacher Education, 21*(7), 747–766. https://doi.org/10.1016/j.tate.2005.05.009

Zee, M. & Koomen, H.M.Y. (2016). Teacher self-efficacy and its effects on classroom processes, student academic adjustment, and teacher well-being: A synthesis of 40 years of research. *Review of Educational Research, 86*(4), 981–1015. https://doi.org/10.3102/0034654315626801

# 14

# Popularising Science and Fighting Superstition

## *Exploring Student Mindset by Using Writeup and Diagram Approach*

Pradeep Gusain

### Introduction

Indian Knowledge System has a very vast potential to guide not only the Indian society but also the international society. Indian knowledge system has always been the driving force for Indian society since ancient times. Indian Knowledge system has been the guiding light for the National Education Policy (NEP) 2020. The ultimate aim of the Indian knowledge system was not only the driving force for preparation for life but also the guiding force for self-actualization.

According to NEP 2020, the Indian Knowledge System engaging course will also be available to secondary school students as an elective. Indian Knowledge System has rich potential, which can be utilized in fighting the superstition prevailing in the society (Fig. 1). The efforts to popularising science education must begin with the early stage of the education system, through which the students can build a strong foundation for the development of the scientific temper in them. Also, by imparting the Indian Knowledge system to the students at the early stage, the fight against superstitions can be taken to a much greater extent.

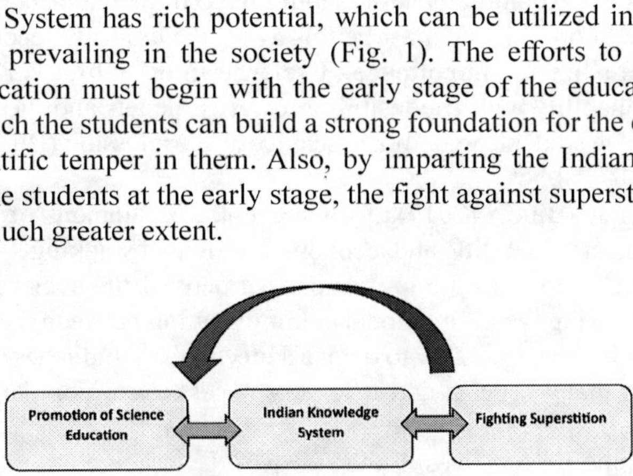


**Figure 1:** Indian Knowledge System — Promotion of Science Education and Fighting Superstition

The learner must develop an understanding of the social forces that are responsible for the growth as well as the birth of all kinds of superstition. The learner must be aware of the circumstances as well as conditions that foster the growth of superstitions in society. The factors that favour the formation of the superstitions must be identified as well as must be worked upon for their demolition from the present state as prevailing in society.

School teacher plays a very important role in fostering the development of the scientific temper among school students, from the very initial state of the school education. Besides the teacher at school, the parents also play a very important role in the development of the personality of the students at home. Hence the child must be kept in a positive environment both at the school as well at home, so ensure the development of scientific inquiry among the school students. Besides the role of the teacher at the school and the parents at the home, the child must be watched to have a positive environment in his/her social circle and this can be ensured through careful and supportive observation of the students. Once the scientific temper is developed in the child, the fight with the superstitions will become easier.

## Literature Review

According to Dr. Kalam (2011 as cited in Masih, 2012), the bandwidth of communication does not limit the role of science communication but does limit the imagination power of the scientists. According to Dr. Kalam, experts engaging in science communication should have three major concerns, first the excitement about science must be felt by all the citizens, secondly all the citizens must realize the importance of science in daily life with sensitivity towards sustainability and responsibility towards planets and the third is the motivation of the students to embrace science as a profession (Bhattacharyya, 2013).

According to Binoy (2017), to achieve the attainment of social and environmental sustainability and economic growth by taking the fruits of science and technology to the lowermost segment of the social pyramid as well as by increasing the bidirectional communication between the public and the scientist, it is very necessary to devise a mechanism. India has a vast range of diversity in many aspects and it is very necessary to popularize science communication.

Human being indeed lives in the real world, but there are a lot of many beliefs that are not logical but are based on illogic. In one of the studies, conducted on two hundred and fifty students, it was enquired whether there exists any relationship between superstition and locus of control. It was found that there is a significant relationship between external sources of control and superstitious beliefs (Kashiha, 2015).

According to a study conducted by Chakraborty (2017), it was found that there exists a significant difference between distance learners and on-campus students (caste-wise, locality-wise, and gender-wise) concerning superstitious beliefs. It was also found that a girl's score is less for superstitious beliefs than a man's.

## The Study

### *Research Methodology*

The present study utilizes the Descriptive Research Design where both qualitative and quantitative approaches are used.

***Sampling*:** Convenience sampling is used, in which two sections of Class IX were assigned an assignment that needed to be submitted in the assigned time period. The participant strength was 58 in each, however only 36 and 43 students participated in the assignment and the Google questionnaires respectively.

#### *Research Tool*

1. An assignment was assigned to the Class IX in both sections to make a write-up as well as make a diagram about "Popularizing science education and combating Superstition vis-à-vis Indian Knowledge System".
2. A questionnaire based on a 5-point Likert Scale, consisting of 10 items about the Indian Knowledge System and Superstitions (5 items each)- https://forms.gle/KsdtNxddjLVL6g839

#### *Scoring Key*

1. Content Analysis of the write-up and analysis of the diagrams.
2. Google Questionnaire scoring key.

**Table 1:** Scoring of items

| *Items* | *Item Numbers* | *Strongly Agree* | *Agree* | *Neutral* | *Disagree* | *Strongly Disagree* |
|---|---|---|---|---|---|---|
| Positive Items | 1,2,3,5,6,7,8,10 | 5 | 4 | 3 | 2 | 1 |
| Negative Items | 4.9 | 1 | 2 | 3 | 4 | 5 |

#### *Participant Coding*

Coding of the Participant — The participant is coded as follows:

**Table 2:** Coding of the Participant

| *S. N* | *Male Participant* | *S. N* | *Female Participant* |
|---|---|---|---|
| 1 to 20 | IXM1* to IXM20 | 1 to 15 | IXF1* to IXF15 |

*IXM1 and IXF1 stands for the Nineth Class Male Participant Number-1 & Nineth Class Female Participant Number-1 respectively, similarly rest are defined accordingly.

## Result and Data Analysis

### *A. Writeup and Diagram*

*Participant Details* — Out of total 43 participants, Female were 17, whereas Male were 26

*Objective 1:* Using a Diagram Approach to Explore the Student Mindset for Popularizing Science and Fighting Superstition
Diagrams submitted by the participant were analysed and some of them are in Table 1.

**Table 1:** Diagrams — Female and Male Participant

| *S. No.* | *Participant Code* | *Diagram* | *Features* |
|---|---|---|---|
| 1 | IXF2 | 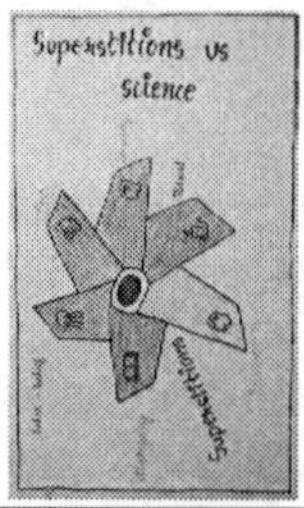  | The connection between superstitions and cause is explored |
| 2 | IXF3 | 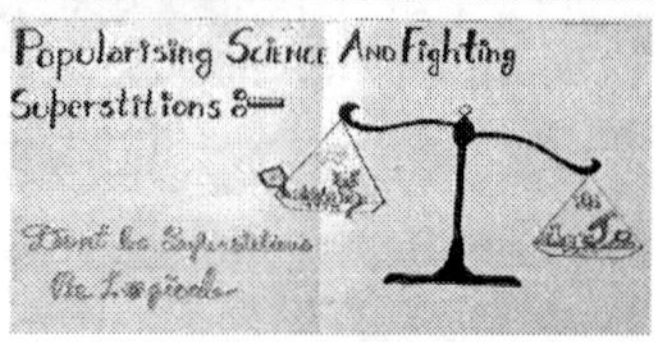  | Myths and facts are compared |
| 3 | IXF4 | 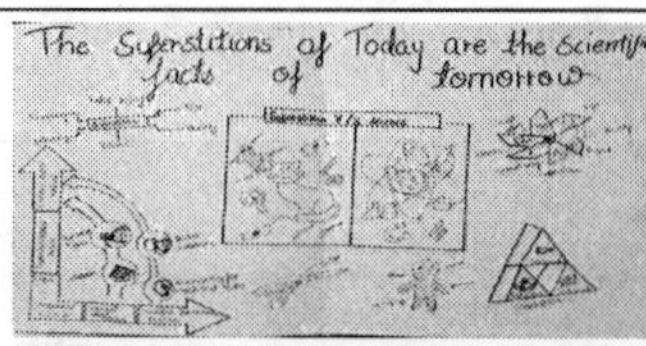  | Traditional practices and traditional herbal practices, causes of superstition are explored |
| 4 | IXF5 |   | Superstition and science are explored |
| 5 | IXF12 |   | Science is more powerful than superstition, as is shown through a weighing balance |

| *S. No.* | *Participant Code* | *Diagram* | *Features* |
|---|---|---|---|
| 6 | IXF14 | 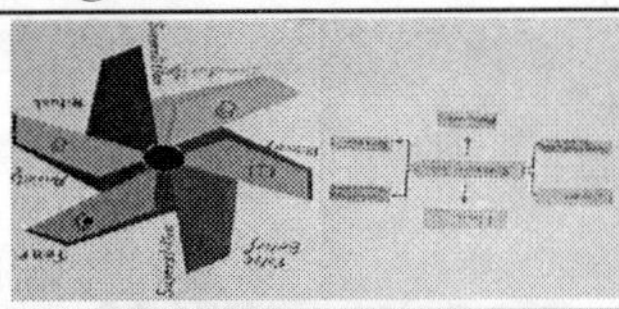 | Cause of superstition is explored |
| 7 | IXF15 | 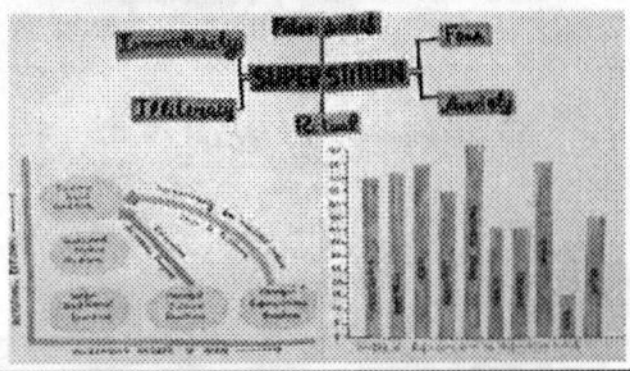 | A plot of increasing efficiency and increasing degree of harm is shown and a graphical representation of superstition belief is also drawn |
| 8. | IXM5 | 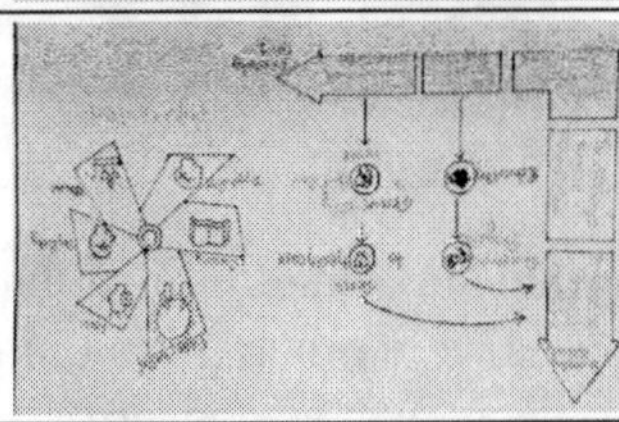 | Increasing harm and increasing efficacy and factors of superstition are explored |
| 9. | IXM6 |  | Simple representation of science and religion |
| 10. | IXM7 |  | Sign of superstition is shown |
| 11 | IXM10 |  | Sign of superstition is shown |
| 12 | IXM12 |  | Sign of superstition is shown |

| *S. No.* | *Participant Code* | *Diagram* | *Features* |
|---|---|---|---|
| 13 | IXM17 |  | ISRO, PSLV, SERB POWER, CAWAE, scientific publication, WHO, super computer, lunar brick, |
| 14 | IXM18 | 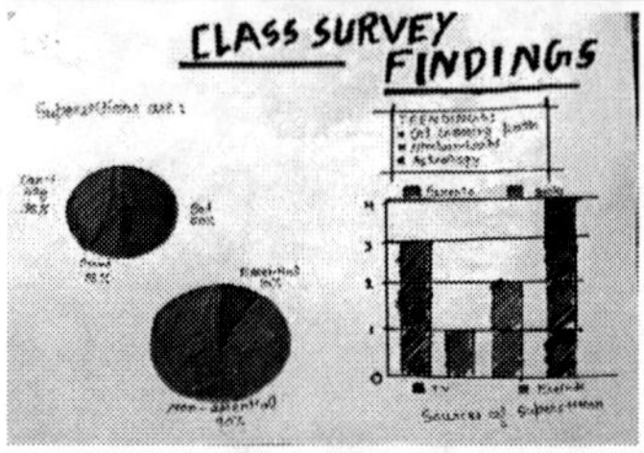 | Class survey findings of superstitions, essential or not, good, or bad, trending superstitions are mentioned |

After exploring the diagram submitted by the students it was found that the female participant responses were much more unique and showed a good understanding level of the topic as well as concern, as compared to the boys' responses. However, one boy's IXM18 responses included the class survey finding which was unique and innovative.

*Objective 2: Using Writeup to Explore Student Mindset for Popularizing Science and Fighting Superstition*

On analysing the responses from female as well as male participants, it was found that the responses were very fascinating, innovative, mature, optimistic, encouraging, effective, efficient, and with a lot of other valuable quality-driven parameters. One of the participants IXF2- categorized the writeup under three main headings, namely (1) Embracing Cultural Sensitivity by Integration of traditional and scientific knowledge and by community engagement, (2) Media and Communication by Science communication and Debunking myths, and (3) Policy and Institutional Support by support for research and incorporating science in policy. One of the participants IXF13 provides the association between certain superstitions and the science behind them. Participant IXF14, advocates the way of popularizing science through: (a) Promotion of Scientific Education, (b) Science Communication Initiatives, and (c) Digital Platform for Dissemination. Participant IXF15 responded that "measures that we can take to fight against superstition are: Cognitive Behavioural Therapy and Exposure Therapy…". She also responded that "The Indian Knowledge System consists of Jan, Vignan, and Jeevan Darshan that have evolved out of the experience, observation, experimentation, and rigorous analysis."

As per the response from IXFM1 participant "To promote science, there is a need to intervene the Indian Knowledge System with the cultural fabric demonstrating that scientific understanding is not at odds with traditional wisdom but complements it."

Another participant IXFM6 emphasized (1) The integration of traditional and scientific knowledge, (2) Education and Awareness Programme, (3) Promoting a scientific temper, (4) Leveraging Digital Platforms, and (4) Justification for fighting superstitions.

As per the response obtained from participant IXM18:

> "Popularizing science and dispelling superstitions in the context of the Indian knowledge system requires a multifaceted approach. By blending traditional wisdom with modern scientific understanding, fostering accessible education, engaging in effective communication, and respecting cultural sensitivities, India can create a scientific narrative."

Participant IXM19 provides valuable inputs for popularising Science by (i) Education reforms, (ii) Community outreach programme, (iii) Media and Technology, (iv) Role models and Mentorship and provides various concerns about the justification for combating superstition as (i) Misguided Practices, (ii) Social Progress, (iii) Health and Wellbeing and (iv) Global competitiveness.

Besides this participants also emphasized preserving cultural heritage, community involvement, encouraging curiosity, and critical thinking, public awareness programme, a collaboration between scientists, educators, and influencers, use of social media platforms, books, magazines, podcasts, videos, blogs, organizing and participating in science events such as fairs, festivals, exhibitions, competitions or workshops, supporting and collaborating with science institutions such as museums, centres, clubs or societies. Besides this, the participant also responded about the reason for fighting superstitions to develop modern societies.

### B. Questionnaire Responses

*Participant Details* — Out of total 43 participants, Female were 17, whereas Male were 26

Objective 3: To Explore Student Mindset for Popularizing Science and Fighting Superstition

**(I)** *Indian Knowledge System (IKS) Concern*: The average score of the respondent is as follows (Figure 2):

Q.1 The Knowledge system is very essential to the new age of fast life.

Q.2 Our society is still guided today through the ancient knowledge system.

Q.3 The Indian knowledge system has the vast knowledge base to combat the wrong practices prevailing in society today.

Q.4 Indian knowledge system does not have enough power to guide the world in spiritual, and philosophical aspects (Negative Item).

Q.5 Steps need to be taken to popularize the ancient knowledge system.

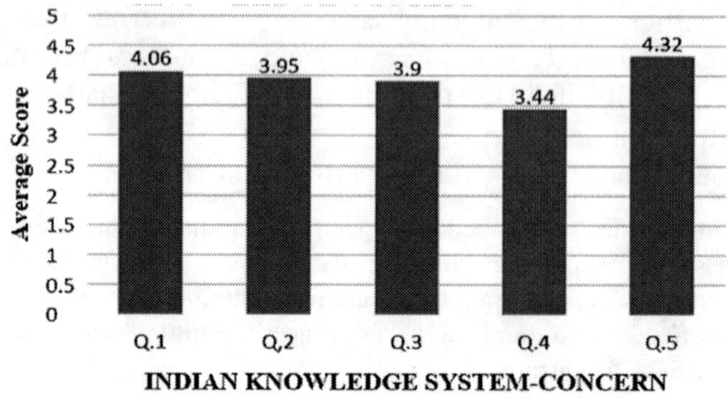


**Figure 2:** Average score of the Participant — Indian Knowledge System

Thus, based on the responses obtained, it can be inferred that the students have more than neutral responses and approach nearly to agree (positive item) and disagree (negative item) concerns.

***(II)*** *Superstition Concern Score:* The average score is shown in the given Figure 3:

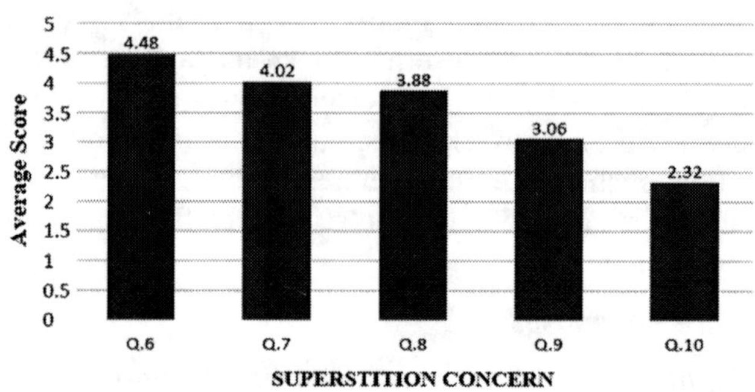


**Figure 3:** Average Score of the Participant for Superstition Concern

Q.6 It is very essential to popularize science education to fight superstitions.

Q.7 Due to lack of good education, people get trapped in superstitions.

Q.8 Superstitions put hurdles in the development of society.

Q.9 Superstitions do not lead to oneself negative growth (Negative Item).

Q.10 I believe in superstitions.

From Figure 3, it can be inferred that for questions 6 and 7 the average score corresponds to more than agree concern whereas for question 8, it is more than neutral concern. For question 9 the average score corresponds to a more than neutral approach whereas for question 10 the average score corresponds to below neutral approach to disagree concern.

## Conclusion and Discussion

To popularize science and fight superstitions, a lot of efforts need to be put at the individual, societal, and government levels. First of all, the benefit of science education must be realized to the masses through various rigorous initiatives at all levels. The rich Indian Knowledge System must be aligned with modern science and rich cultural practices need to be redefined in the light of modern science and demands of the modern society in a harmonious manner. The questionnaire also provides valuable insight, in which participants' average score value confirms that for the superstition beliefs they have either neutral concern or disagree concern. Most of the average score provides positive insights into the Indian Knowledge System as well as into superstition beliefs.

From the questionnaire, it can be inferred that the student's perception of the Indian Knowledge System for today's day's requirements is more than agree on concern and moves towards strongly agreeing on the concern. Thus, it can be inferred that the Indian Knowledge System has a very strong demand in terms of its relevance for enlightening the Indian Society in a sphere of life. Secondly, the questionnaire also led to the conclusion that there is a need for the popularization of science education to combat the superstitions prevailing in Indian Societies. The outcome of the study also laid strong emphasis on popularizing the Indian Knowledge System. By popularizing the Indian Knowledge System, every section of society gets benefits in all spheres of life. The outcome of the study also emphasized that education is necessary for people so that they can develop rational thinking and act in resonance for the development of a better society and nation.

The present has the following delimitation:

1. The study is confined to IX class only,
2. The study utilizes less sample size, that too from one school only,
3. The study is confined to responses from students only and not from teachers.

## Suggestions for Future Research

Some of the future research domains are as follows:

1. Various class students ranging from VIth to XIIth can be taken,
2. The large sample size can be explored,
3. The responses from Teachers and other stakeholders can be taken in future research,
4. Another observational tool can be utilized in recording the responses.

## References

Abdul Kalam, A.P.J. (2011), 'Powerful Science Communication is an Asset to the Transformation of Societies: Science Leads to Borderless World', Patairiya, M.K., Nogueira, M.I. (eds.), *Sharing Science*, chapter 1, pp. 1-5. Errata: book Sharing Science.

Binoy, V.V. (2017). Introduction: When Science Meets the Public — Bridging the Gap. *Bridging the Communication Gap in Science and Technology: Lessons from India*, 1-9.

Bhattacharyya, K.K. (2013). Science communication as a tool for development. *Global Media Journal–Indian Edition, 4*(1).

Chakraborty, Sudipta (2017). A comparative analysis of superstitious beliefs existing among college students. *International Journal of Educational Science and Research, 7*(6), 57-66.

Kashiha, S. (2015). On the relationship between adolescents' tendency to superstition and the source of control. *International Journal of Academic Research in Business and Social Sciences, 5*(4), 134-145.

Masih, W. (2012). Efforts towards popularisation and public understanding of science: a literature review of 30 publications. *International Journal of Scientific & Engineering Research, 3*(9), 1-7.

# 15

# Social and Emotional Learning through Work Education in D.El.Ed. Curriculum

Mridula Bhardwaj
Raisa Khan

## Introduction

Social-emotional learning (SEL) skills are robust competencies as they have been demonstrated to (a) enhance the learning process, (b) cultivate emotional resilience, (c) encourage prosocial behaviour, and (d) foster pluralistic thinking. Pre-service teacher preparation pertains to the educational and training experiences undergone by individuals aspiring to become teachers before they officially enter the profession. The question is how can we effectively equip teachers to instruct students from diverse backgrounds and establish conditions conducive to optimal teaching and learning? This is a crucial concern for policymakers, educational leaders, and researchers revolves around the extent to which pre-service teacher education equips future educators with the essential information, coursework, and experiences needed to effectively handle aspects related to social-emotional learning (SEL). This includes coverage of theories and research on social and emotional development, as well as the knowledge and skills required to establish well-managed classroom learning environments that foster both academic growth and the mental well-being of students. In schools nowadays, there is a focus on helping students develop skills like understanding their own emotions, being aware of others, managing themselves well, building healthy relationships, and making responsible decisions. However, educators indicate a lack of sufficient training and confidence when it comes to addressing the behavioural requirements of students and subsequently fostering their social-emotional learning (SEL) and development.

## Conceptual understanding of Social-emotional Learning (SEL)

Social-emotional Learning (SEL) refers to the journey of individuals to gain and employ the knowledge, attitudes, and skills essential for comprehending and handling emotions, accomplishing positive goals, demonstrating empathy toward others, fostering, and sustaining positive relationships, and making responsible decisions. SEL is crucial for personal development, interpersonal relationships, and overall well-being. The key characteristics associated with social-emotional learning includes:

i. *Self-awareness:* Understanding one's own emotions, strengths, weaknesses, values, and beliefs.
ii. *Self-management:* Developing the ability to regulate and control one's emotions, thoughts, and behaviours. Cultivating resilience and coping mechanisms.
iii. *Social Awareness:* Recognizing and understanding the emotions, perspectives, and needs of others. Demonstrating empathy and compassion.
iv. *Relationship Skill:* Building and maintaining positive relationships. Communicating effectively, resolving conflicts, and cooperating with others.
v. *Responsible Decision-making:* Making ethical and constructive choices. Considering the well-being of oneself and others when making decisions.

The above-mentioned attributes recognize the importance of addressing the social and emotional aspects of a person alongside academic development. It equips individuals with essential life skills that contribute to success in various aspects of life, including school, work, and relationships. So overall the SEL is required to:

i. Prevent Negative Behaviours such as aggression, substance abuse, and bullying.
ii. Establish Positive School Climate and fostering a supportive and conducive environment for learning.
iii. Boosting long-term success involves enhancing academic achievements, improving social skills, and developing increased resilience when confronting challenges.
iv. Fostering cultural competence entails encouraging an understanding and appreciation of diverse perspectives and cultural differences, nurturing a heightened level of cultural proficiency.

## Literature Review

Next, we examine existing researches to assess the extent to which this phenomenon is presently taking place. Our emphasis is on recent studies that investigate the content and regularity of coursework within teacher preparation programs, specifically addressing themes related to fostering students' social-emotional learning (SEL) and development (Corcoran & O'Flaherty, 2022). The research findings suggest that the social and emotional competence of teachers has had an impact on the recruitment, training, and retention of teacher candidates. Over a four-year period, there were notable changes in the six sub-domains: autonomy significantly increased, while environmental mastery, positive relations with others, and purpose in life, all significantly decreased. Meanwhile, self-acceptance and personal growth experienced non-significant decreases. The study emphasizes the necessity for evidence-based teacher preparation programs to cultivate academic, social, and emotional learning in pre-service teachers.

Wajid et al., (2013) studied the implementation of social-emotional learning (SEL) initiatives in schools and classrooms and found that the effectiveness of these programs is significantly shaped by teachers' own social-emotional competence and well-being, which, in turn, has a profound impact on their students. Environments characterized by strong teacher-child relationships foster deep learning and contribute to positive social and emotional development in students.

Ee et al., (2014) researched on social-emotional learning (SEL) integration in classrooms, focuses on teachers' explicit incorporation of SEL. A three-day training program equipped teachers with skills to infuse SEL into their curriculum. Analyzing 29 lessons from 15 primary and 47 lessons from 26 secondary teachers, the study assessed five domains. Results showed greater success in integrating SEL into Character Education and English compared to Math and Science. Teachers emphasized self-awareness and social awareness over relationship and self-management. The study suggests refining instructional scaffolding and addressing spontaneous responses for effective SEL integration.

Van den Beemt & Vrieling, (2016) researched the significance of comprehending the role and influence of informal social networks on the professional growth of teachers. The research questions of the case study are twofold: 1) How can the DSL-framework bring the group configuration into focus?, 2) Which social configuration, based on dimensions and indicators, supports the role of student teachers within a group alongside teachers and educators? These questions are addressed through video recordings of group activities, reflective notes, the use of an online learning environment, and semi-structured interviews. The research outcomes reveal that teacher groups can assess the social configuration of the learning group by creating an image with the DSL-framework. It empowers educators to assess whether the composition of their group aligns with its learning goals or necessitates adjustments. It enriches professional development within teacher learning groups by examining strategies to optimize the involvement of student teachers in a group led by experienced educators.

Durlak et al., (2011) present the results of a meta-analysis encompassing 213 school-based, universal social-emotional learning (SEL) initiatives involving 270,034 students from kindergarten to high school. In comparison to control groups, participants in SEL programs exhibited noteworthy enhancements in social and emotional skills, attitudes, behaviour, and academic performance, reflecting an 11-percentile-point advancement in achievement. School teaching staff demonstrated successful execution of Social-emotional Learning (SEL) programs. Program outcomes were influenced by the use of four recommended practices for skill development and the occurrence of implementation issues. These findings contribute to the growing body of empirical evidence highlighting the positive impact of SEL programs.

K. Schonert-Reichl et al., (2015) addressed three main sections in their research: (1) Social- Emotional Competence (SEC) of Teachers, covering pre-service teachers fostering their own SEL competencies; (2) Social-Emotional learning (SEL) of Students, involving pre-service teachers in developing their students' SEL skills; and (3) the Learning Context, focusing on environments like classrooms, schools, and communities that promote students' SEL skills. The first two categories were further divided into the five SEL dimensions (Self-awareness, Social Awareness, Self-management, Relationship Skills, Responsible Decision-making). The third classification, Learning Context, was further divided into 13 subcategories: Classroom Context, Facilitating Schoolwide Coordination, Cultivating School-family Partnerships, and Establishing School-Community Partnerships. These dimensions aimed to evaluate how pre-service teachers learn to create an optimal environment for fostering SEL and collaborate with others to enhance students' SEL skills.

State et al., (2011) discussed in their study the social, emotional, and behavioural issues among youth w.r.t individuals and society. Teachers, being in an optimal position to identify symptoms of these problems and facilitate or access appropriate services, underscore the requirement for a thorough examination of the training provided to pre-service teachers. The curriculum requirements for certification in randomly selected college/university elementary teacher training programs was assessed in this study. Analysis of course syllabi aimed to determine the extent and nature of the training imparted to future elementary teachers concerning social, emotional, and behavioural problems. The results reflected a limited exposure to such information. The implications of the findings are discussed in relation to college/university teacher preparation programs, potential impacts on student outcomes, and recommendations for future research.

While only a limited number of studies have explored but they consistently reveal that these programs often lack emphasis on providing teachers with the necessary knowledge and skills. Examinations of educational curricula affirm that programs designed to train future teachers are insufficiently equipping them to handle issues related to students' social, emotional, and behavioural challenges. This deficiency hinders teachers from effectively fostering their students' social-emotional competence and establishing positive classroom environments conducive to student success. In more recent investigations, researchers are exploring the social-emotional skills and competencies that teachers require to effectively promote students' social-emotional learning (SEL).

## Importance of Social-emotional Learning

In the past few years, there has been a growing focus in both theory and practical research on enhancing the social and emotional skills of students within the school environment. This heightened interest is driven by the collective efforts of educators, parents, and policymakers to address current challenges like diminishing academic motivation and performance, rising dropout rates and the surge in incidents of school bullying and aggression. Approximately 80% of children facing issues related to social, emotional, and behavioural problems do not access the necessary support services (U.S. Public Health Service, 2000). Educators serve as the driving force behind the implementation of social-emotional learning (SEL) initiatives in schools and classrooms. The effectiveness of these programs is significantly shaped by teachers' own social-emotional competence and well-being, which, in turn, has a profound impact on their students. Positive and nurturing teacher-child relationships in classrooms foster profound learning and contribute to the positive social and emotional development of students (K.A. Schonert-Reichl, 2017). In educational institutions globally, educators are incorporating Social-emotional Learning (SEL) to provide youngsters with crucial life abilities, including handling emotions, attaining objectives, expressing empathy, fostering connections, and making prudent decisions. This comprehensive method not only readies pupils for academic success but also empowers them with indispensable life skills to confront the numerous intricate challenges awaiting them beyond their school years. This paper examines how topics pertaining to social-emotional learning (SEL), such as understanding students' social and emotional development, evaluating teachers' social and emotional proficiency, and establishing nurturing and secure classroom settings that are effectively organized, engaging, and secure, are integrated into pre-service teacher training.

## Curriculum Analysis in Special Reference to Work Education

Curriculum refers to the set of courses and content that make up an educational program. It encompasses the subjects, topics, and learning objectives designed to be covered within a specific academic or training period. Curriculum delineates the knowledge, comprehension, and skills that students or learners are anticipated to acquire by the conclusion of a program. It functions as a roadmap for educators, specifying the order of lessons, instructional approaches, and evaluations to be employed during the educational journey. Teacher Education involves the preparation and training of individuals aspiring to become educators. This process equips prospective teachers with the knowledge, skills, and strategies necessary to effectively teach and manage a classroom. Teacher education programs typically include a combination of coursework, practical teaching experiences, and pedagogical training. These programs aim to develop not only subject-specific expertise but also the ability to create a positive and inclusive learning environment, understand diverse student needs, and employ effective teaching methods. The teacher education curriculum is the structured plan of study that aspiring educators follow during their teacher preparation programs. It encompasses a range of subjects and experiences designed to equip future teachers with the tools they need to be successful in the classroom. Key components of a teacher education curriculum include educational theory, teaching methods, classroom management, assessment strategies, and field experiences. The curriculum is designed to ensure that prospective teachers acquire a deep understanding of their subject matter, develop effective pedagogical skills, and cultivate a professional and ethical approach to education. It often integrates both theoretical knowledge and practical application to prepare teachers for the complexities of the teaching profession.

The components outlined in the D.El.Ed. Work Education Curriculum syllabus theory as well as practical part reflects a comprehensive integration of Social-emotional Learning (SEL) principles. Here is an analysis of how each unit incorporates SEL components:

**Table 1:** Name of units and Components of SEL in each unit

| *Work Education Curriculum (Theory)* | *Components of SEL* |
|---|---|
| *Unit 1: Pedagogical Processes of Work Education* | |
| Weekly, Monthly, Yearly Plan with Focus on Local Relevance | Emphasizing local relevance promotes cultural awareness and understanding, fostering social awareness and empathy among students. |
| Learning Format: Activity Plan (Lesson Plan) | The activity plans encourage collaborative learning, communication skills, and adaptability, all essential SEL competencies. |
| Organization of Work Education Activities | Aligning activities with national educational policies demonstrates a commitment to holistic student development, encompassing both academic and social-emotional aspects. |
| Work Education Activities for Children with Special Education Needs | This component addresses inclusivity, empathy, and understanding, fostering a positive and supportive environment for all students. |

| *Work Education Curriculum (Theory)* | *Components of SEL* |
|---|---|
| *Unit 2: Planning, Organising, and Management of Work Education Activities* | |
| Importance of Knowledge, Understanding, and Application in Skill Development | Skill development involves self-awareness, self-management, and interpersonal skills—all integral to SEL. |
| Criteria for Selection and Planning of Activities | The criteria likely include considerations for teamwork, communication, and problem-solving, aligning with SEL principles. |
| Management and Costing | Understanding resource management and collaboration in planning activities contribute to SEL competencies like responsible decision-making and relationship skills. |
| *Unit 3: Work Education and Community* | |
| Orientation of Parents and Community Members Towards the Importance of Work Education | Involving parents and the community promotes social awareness, cooperation, and shared responsibility for students' holistic development. |
| Role of School and Community in Work Education | Collaborative efforts emphasize relationship skills, social responsibility, and community engagement. |
| *Unit 4: Assessment and Evaluation of Work Education* | |
| Continuous and Comprehensive Evaluation (CCE) | CCE aligns with SEL principles, emphasizing continuous improvement, self-awareness, and adaptation. |
| Tools and Techniques of Evaluation and Processes | Various tools, such as observation schedules and attitude scales, can measure SEL competencies like communication, empathy, and teamwork. |
| Self-evaluation, Peer Evaluation, and Community-based Evaluation | These evaluation methods promote self-awareness, collaboration, and community engagement—core SEL skills. |
| *Unit 5: Integrating Work Education with Other Subjects* | |
| Integration of Work Education in Teaching Other Pedagogical Subjects | Integrated learning experiences foster collaboration, effective communication, and critical thinking — key SEL competencies. |
| **Work Education Curriculum (Practical Components)** | |
| Cleanliness and Beautification | Fosters a sense of responsibility, civic duty, and environmental awareness. Teamwork and collaboration are essential for maintaining and beautifying shared spaces. |

| *Work Education Curriculum (Theory)* | *Components of SEL* |
|---|---|
| Community Services — Preservation and Protection | Encourages social responsibility, empathy, and an understanding of one's role in preserving public spaces. |
| Gardening | Cultivates patience, responsibility, and environmental consciousness. Working with nature promotes emotional well-being. |
| Environmental Care and Protection | Emphasizes sustainable practices, reducing waste, and reusing materials, instilling a sense of responsibility toward the environment. |
| Individual Portfolio | Encourages self-reflection, self-awareness, and personal growth as students maintain a record of their activities. |
| Products from Waste | Promotes creativity, problem-solving, and a sense of accomplishment through repurposing materials. |
| Utility Articles, Food and Nutrition, Paper Craft, Cloth Craft, Wood Craft, Clay Modelling, Photography, etc | Enhances creativity, teamwork, and self-expression, fostering emotional intelligence and interpersonal skills. |
| Visit to Old Age Home/Orphanage/ Cultural Heritage Places | Encourages empathy, understanding, and communication skills. Students learn to appreciate diverse perspectives and cultures. |
| Practical File on Optional Activities | Documentation promotes organization, responsibility, and self-evaluation. Understanding the benefits of activities contributes to holistic learning experiences. |

Thus, it is reflected that the D.El.Ed. Work Education Curriculum effectively integrates SEL components across its units, and through the practicum from community service to creative projects and experiential visits, students engage in activities that promote social awareness, responsibility, teamwork, creativity, and self-reflection, all of which are fundamental to Social- emotional learning promoting a holistic approach to education that encompasses both academic and social-emotional development. SEL should not be treated merely as a subject confined to the classroom, to be studied, tested, and then disregarded. Instead, it should be cultivated through a blend of academic instruction and practical application in real-life situations and challenges.

## Conclusion

Social-emotional Learning (SEL) is indispensable not just for academic achievement but also for navigating the challenges of daily life and excelling across various domains, contributing to a life characterized by peace, happiness, and contentment. It emphasizes the importance of emotional intelligence, interpersonal skills, and responsible decision-making in navigating the complexities of life. Research on the inclusion of direct information and/or training in social-emotional learning (SEL) within pre-service teacher education is currently in its early stages. Nevertheless, insights from a few recent studies offer a glimpse into the incorporation of foundational factors for fostering students' SEL in classrooms and schools in teacher preparation programs. The D.El.Ed Work Education curriculum caters to theoretical as well as practical aspects of SEL. The ultimate objective of this educational approach is to transform qualities such as empathy, compassion, and emotional resilience from mere competencies into inherent traits, integral aspects of an individual rather than acquired skills pursued for instrumental reasons. These endeavours should be grounded in robust conceptual models and well-founded researches, as the promotion of social and emotional competencies is integral to the educational mission.

## References

Corcoran, R.P., & O'Flaherty, J. (2022). Social-emotional learning in teacher preparation: Pre-service teacher well-being. *Teaching and Teacher Education*, *110*, 103563. https://doi.org/10.1016/j.tate.2021.103563

Durlak, J.A., Weissberg, R.P., Dymnicki, A.B., Taylor, R.D., & Schellinger, K.B. (2011). The Impact of Enhancing Students' Social-emotional learning: A Meta-Analysis of School-Based Universal Interventions. *Child Development*, *82*(1), 405–432. https://doi.org/10.1111/j.1467-8624.2010.01564.x

Ee, J., Zhou, M., & Wong, I. (2014). Teachers' Infusion of Social Emotional Learning. *Journal of Teaching and Teacher Education*, *02*(01). https://doi.org/10.12785/jtte/020103

Ludvik, M.B. (n.d.). *How Mindful Compassion Practices can Cultivate Social- emotional learning.*

Schonert-Reichl, K.A. (2017). Social-emotional learning and Teachers. *The Future of Children*, *27*(1), 137–155. https://doi.org/10.1353/foc.2017.0007

Schonert-Reichl, K., Hanson-Peterson, J., & Hymel, S. (2015). *Social-emotional learning and pre-service teacher education.*

State, T., Kern, L., Starosta, K., & Mukherjee, A. (2011). Elementary Pre-service Teacher Preparation in the Area of Social, Emotional, and Behavioural Problems. *School Mental Health*, *3*, 13–23. https://doi.org/10.1007/s12310-010-9044-3

U.S. Public Health Service. (2000). *Report of the Surgeon General's Conference on Children's Mental Health: A National Action Agenda.* Washington, DC: Department of Health and Human Services.

Van den beemt, A., & Vrieling, E. (2016, May 1). *Dimensions of social learning in teacher education: An exemplary case study.*

Wajid, B., Garner, P.W., & Owen, J.E. (2013). Infusing Social Emotional Learning into the Teacher Education Curriculum. *International Journal of Emotional Education*, *5*(2), 31–48.

D.El.Ed Curriculum

# 16

# How do Teachers Perceive their School Heads

Shadma Absar

## Introduction

School education in India has grown considerably in recent years. With the successful implementation of programmes for Sarva Shiksha Abhiyan and the Right to Education Act (2009) for achieving the Universalisation of elementary education, the demand for secondary education has increased manifold. Also, programmes like Rashtriya Madhyamik Shiksha Abhiyan (RMSA) is a flagship scheme of the Government of India, launched in March 2009, to enhance access to secondary education and improve its quality. RMSA aims at universalizing secondary education by focusing on three major areas i.e. improving physical facilities, through quality and equity interventions. One of the focus areas under quality interventions includes the governance of schools, which emphasized the teacher management and leadership development of school heads and other functionaries in the educational system. The recent programme on Samagra shiksha also emphasised capacity building of school heads.

School is an institutional space for learning, to achieve school effectiveness school leadership is critical. School leadership has occupied a central position in the deliberations for achieving quality education. School leadership has been recognised as a key factor in transforming schools as learning organisations both internationally (Leithwood et al., 2006; Bush, 2008; Harris, 2008; Robinson, 2009; Barber, Whelan & Clark, 2010; Day et al., 2010) and in the Indian context (Mukhopadhyay, 2001 & 2012; Chaudhuri, 2002; Govinda, 2002 & 2016; Diwan, 2011; Panda, 2013).

School leadership is second only to classroom teaching as an influence on student learning (Leithwood et al., 2006; Leithwood and Jantzi, 2006; Robinson, 2009; Day et al., 2010). School leaders influence staff motivation, commitment, and working conditions, (Leithwood and Jantzi, 2006; Barber et al., 2010) develop conducive climate and prevent emotional exhaustion by nurturing trustworthy relationships in schools (Van Maele & Van Houtte, 2015)) and have direct impact on the teachers' performance, their expectations, the way they think, standards they follow and planning and implementing of their teaching-learning activities (Leithwood et al., 2006; Day et al., 2010).

## Review of Literature

Leadership theories have traversed a long journey over the years from Trait-based approach including great man theories to style-based approach which mainly focuses on assessing the leadership styles and putting the leaders into certain prototypes, like democratic, autocratic, *laissez-faire*, transactional transformational etc. School leadership in the present context is moving from the heroic or person-centric forms of leadership to distributed leadership (Elmore, 2002; Gronn, 2002; Spillane, 2006; Harris, 2009; Hulpia, 2009, Robinson, 2009) wherein teachers work along with school leaders in complementary ways to achieve school goals (Andrews & Lewis, 2004, Elmore, 2002) and spreads decision-making process throughout the school thereby creating a flatter structure of governance as opposed to top-down approach (Harris, 2009).

Distributed leadership is an evolving concept (Hulpia & Devos, 2010; Hulpia, 2009; Harris, 2008, Spillane, 2006, Gronn, 2002) and has originated from the critiques of transformational and charismatic theories (Camburn, Rowan & Taylor, 2003; Gronn, 2002; Yukl, 1999) who pointed out that these theories focussed on individual behaviours of the leaders and overlooked the process by which followers were influenced by the leaders. Distributed leadership reconceptualises leadership in terms of the "many rather than few" (Harris and Lambert, 2003). Distributed leadership is different from delegated and other forms of leadership, delegated leadership is restricted to division of labour and allocation of responsibilities for completing a task among members of the group, it is solely initiated from the top of the organisation wherein functions are given away to the subordinates and delegation is something done by an individual to others. In contrast, distributed leadership is more concerned with developing leadership capabilities of all, sharing mutual responsibility whereby distribution does not depend only on the school head (Oduro, 2004).

Distributed leadership consists of two elements; the leader plus and the practice aspect. The leader plus focussed on having multiple leaders in the schools, the leader plus other individuals. The practice aspect emphasises on the interaction among leaders, followers, and their situation. It implies a social distribution of leadership wherein leadership functions are stretched over the work of multiple leaders, and the tasks are accomplished through their interaction (Spillane, 2006). Distributed leadership spreads decision-making throughout the school, creating a decentralised and more representative governance structure (Barry, 1991; Bennett et al., 2003; Andrews and Lewis, 2004). As a result, everyone gets more opportunities to contribute to improving teaching and learning and the overall organizational effectiveness of the schools.

Leithwood et al. (2006) conceptualised Distributed leadership as a pattern. They elaborated four patterns of distributed leadership which were Planful Alignment, Spontaneous Alignment, Spontaneous Misalignment and Anarchic

Alignment. They found that planful and spontaneous contribute to short term organisational productivity, whereas only planful alignment contributed significantly than other patterns to long term organisational productivity. Spillane (2006) espoused that distributed leadership consisted of two elements, the leaders plus and practice aspect. Hulpia (2009) claimed that distributed leadership is existence of multiple leaders in the system and interactions between those leaders are important to achieve school goals. She explored the relationship between distributed leadership practices, participative decision-making, job satisfaction and organisational commitment. Distributed leadership has been conceptualised based on the work of Leithwood et al. (2006), Spillane (2006) and Hulpia (2009). In the Present study distributed leadership of school heads was studied through pattern of leadership distribution, distribution of leadership practices and participative decision-making.

Hulpia, Devos, & Van Keer (2009) studied the impact of cooperation of leadership team, distribution of leadership support and supervision and participative decision-making on the organisational commitment of teachers. Findings of their study revealed that distribution of supportive leadership functions and participative decision-making has a significant positive impact on the organisational commitment of teachers. Distributed leadership influences teachers' behaviours by building morale, developing belongingness to the school, providing greater opportunities for teachers to exercise initiative and responsibility, encouraging environment, professional development of teachers, and improved students' outcomes (Whitby, 2006), mutual trustworthy relationships among school heads and teachers (Angelle, 2010; Day et al., 2010; Beycioglu, Ozer & Ugurlu, 2012), satisfaction with the work environment (Mullick, Sharma & Deppeler, 2013), academic optimism (Mascall et al., 2008), self-efficacy, organisational commitment (Hulpia, 2009: Park & Yu, 2019), job satisfaction, innovative behaviour (Angelle, 2010; Jain, 2016), improvement in teaching learning (Botha & Triegaardt, 2016) and ultimately leads to organisational change and school improvement (Harris, 2011).

Recent researches on distributed leadership are mainly focussed on the conceptualisation of distributed leadership in various contexts and exploring the empirical evidences of linkages between distributed leadership and school improvement. This study aimed at exploring the distributed leadership of school heads in the Indian context and its impact on their teachers' work behaviour.

## Operational Definition

Distributed Leadership is defined as existence of multiple leaders (both formal and informal) in the schools and their interaction, coordination, planning and cooperation to accomplish various tasks. It involves the distribution of leadership practices, participative decision-making and task divisions among various members and their mutual relationship to achieve the school goals. In the present study, distributed leadership is explored through pattern of leadership distribution in schools, distribution of leadership practices and participative decision-making across school managements and teachers' designation.

Work behaviour refers to the responses displayed in the workplace. They are attitudes/feelings towards work. These behaviours are goal directed and purposive and ensure organisational effectiveness (Suar & Khuntia, 2010: Suar, Tewari & Chaturbedi, 2006). They include range of behaviours including motivation, Organisational commitment, Organisational citizenship behaviour, job satisfaction, interpersonal relationship, stress effect etc. In the present study work behaviour is studied through teachers' organisational citizenship behaviour.

### *Organisational Citizenship Behaviour*

'Individual behaviour that is discretionary, not directly or explicitly recognised by the formal reward system, and in the aggregate promotes the efficient and effective functioning of the Organisation' (Organ et al., 2006).

## The Study

### *Objectives*

1. To study the perception of teachers on distributed leadership of school heads
2. To study the work behaviour of teachers
3. To study the impact of distributed leadership of school heads on the work behaviour of teachers.

### *Hypothesis*

1. There will be differences in the perception of teachers on distributed leadership of school heads across school managements
2. There will be differences in the work behaviour of teachers across school managements
3. There will be impact of teacher's perception on distributed leadership of school heads on their work behaviour.

### *Methodology*

Data was collected from 240 teachers across thirty senior secondary schools from two public funded school managements, i.e. central government, and state government schools. Schools from these managements were selected using stratified random sampling technique. Teachers' perceptions on distributed leadership of school heads were explored using a self-constructed distributed leadership scale. Teachers' work behaviour which included organisational citizenship behaviour was assessed using standardised rating scales. Quantitative techniques like Analysis of variance (ANOVA) and step-wise multiple regression were used to assess the impact of distributed leadership of school heads on teachers' work behaviour.

## *Sampling*

Data was collected from 30 schools which were selected from two school managements using a stratified random sampling technique. Eight teachers (4 PGTs and 4 TGTs) from each school were selected using equal-sized stratified random sampling technique. In total, 240 teachers were the final sample for the study as shown in Table 1.

**Table 1:** Sample Distribution

| | | *Central Government (15 Schools)* | *State Government (15 Schools)* | *Total (30 Schools)* |
|---|---|---|---|---|
| Teachers N=240 | TGTs | 60 | 60 | 120 |
| | PGTs | 60 | 60 | 120 |

## *Tools Used*

*a) Distributed Leadership Scales for Teachers and School Heads (Self Constructed)*

The scales were bilingual both in English and in Hindi. Details of dimensions of distributed leadership scale is represented in Table 2. Reliability coefficient Cronbach's alpha of the distributed leadership scale was computed using SPSS version 19. The reliability of Section A was found to be 0.672, Section B had reliability of 0.93 and lastly Section C's reliability was 0.823 for Distributed Leadership Scale for Teachers.

**Table 2:** Dimensions of Distributed Leadership Scale

| Dimension |
|---|
| Support |
| Individual Consideration |
| Mentoring |
| Fairness |
| Problem Solving |
| Instructional Supervision |
| Punctuality |
| Professional Development |
| Participative Decision-making |

*b) Teachers Organizational Citizenship Behaviour Scale*

Organizational Citizenship Behaviour Scale (OCBS) for Teachers developed by Kuldeep Kumar & Aarti Bakhshi (2009) was adapted for the study. It is five-point Likert scale consisted of five dimensions; Conscientiousness, Courtesy, Sportsmanship, Helping co-worker and Group Activity Participation. In the present study the researcher used only four dimensions of the scale and Group activity participation was dropped. The OCBS used in the study consisted of 26 items. The reliability of the scale was found to be 0.839.

## Findings and Discussion

Teachers' perceptions on distributed leadership of their school heads were found to be moderate. They perceived their school heads as distributed leaders to some extent. Teachers agreed that their school heads demonstrate distributed leadership in their schools. This finding corroborated with the findings of earlier researches (Hulpia, 2009; Hulpia et al., 2009). Teachers had very strongly agreed that their school heads provided support to teachers, act as mentors for them, considered teachers as an individual, help them in solving their problems, expect them to be punctual, provide opportunities for professional development, supervise their teaching and were fair in dealing with them. In this section teachers had to express their perceptions for both principal and vice principal (formal heads) separately. Teachers had higher perceptions for principals in comparison to vice principals, this indicated that as per teachers' perceptions principals were more active in supporting, mentoring, providing professional development opportunities, problem solving, supervising their teaching learning and being fair in dealing with teachers in comparison to Vice principals. Teacher perceptions was highest on punctuality dimension, followed by support, individual consideration, professional development, instructional supervision, mentoring, and problem solving. Teachers' perception on participative decision-making (Section C of DLS) was found to be moderate, this finding was in line with Hulpia (2009). This finding implied that teachers were moderately or involved to some extent in decision-making process in the schools.

Teachers from central government schools and state government schools perceived the distributed leadership practices and its dimensions for principals differently. The teachers from Central government schools had higher perceptions on distributed leadership practices of school heads and all its dimensions as compared to teachers from state government school. This implied that Central government school teachers emphasized that their principals were better in distributing the leadership practices, they provided facilities in schools, encouraged teachers, respected them, inspired teachers' towards higher levels of performance, helped new teachers, helped teachers to develop their strengths, created friendly atmosphere in school, maintained friendly working relationships, listened to teachers' problems and acted in their best interest, complemented them on completing tasks, were fair with teachers, trusted them, provided feedback, responded favourably to the suggestions made by teachers, encouraged teachers to contribute their best effort for school's success, guided teachers in solving teaching and administrative problems, expected teachers to be punctual, collaborated with colleagues and promoted leadership development etc. as compared to state government school principals. Also, teachers of central government schools perceived that their vice principals were instrumental in improving facilities in school, managing school staff well, encouraging teachers to use innovative methods, encouraging teachers for their professional learning, listening to their problems, respecting, and trusting them as well as complimenting teachers in comparison to state government school teachers. These findings were in line with the findings of Harris (2008) and Day et al. (2010) where they emphasised that school management had significant influence on leadership practices. Whereas these findings contradicted with the findings of Mullick, Sharma & Deppler (2013) who pointed out that school management did not have any significant influence on teachers' perception on leadership practices.-

Since there were differences in the perception of teachers on distributed leadership of school heads across school managements (central government schools/state government schools), the hypothesis framed was accepted.

Teachers agreed that they displayed OCBs at their schools very frequently. This finding had been substantiated by prior researches (Polat, 2009; Ozsaker et al., 2012). Out of the four dimensions of OCB, teachers agreed to display conscientiousness and courtesy more frequently followed by sportsmanship and Helping Co-workers. This indicated that teachers worked beyond their minimum role requirement more frequently by taking extra responsibilities. They also made efforts to maintain harmonious relationships and avoid work-related problems with others, tolerate less than ideal conditions and circumstances and willingly help their colleagues at their schools.

Teachers of central government schools display OCBs more frequently in comparison to teachers of state government schools. This finding corroborated with the findings of Somech & Oplatka (2014) and Absar (2016). Teachers of central govt. schools were found to differ significantly from state govt. school teachers on OCB, helping co-workers, conscientiousness, and courtesy. The higher means of central government school teachers indicated that they displayed OCBs more frequently than state govt. school teachers. This finding implied that teachers of central government schools had higher perceptions on helping colleagues in solving work-related problems and in non-work related matters as well, assisting new teachers to adjust to work and adapting to the new environment, engaging themselves in self-study to enhance quality of teaching, by taking extra responsibilities, obeying rules and regulations, maintaining harmonious relationships and mitigating conflicts, avoid creating problems for other teachers and avoid taking actions that hurt others, when compared to state govt. school teachers.

Since there were differences in teachers' work behaviour across school management, therefore the hypothesis that there will be differences in the work behaviour of teachers across school management is accepted.

***Impact of distributed leadership of school heads on the work behaviour of teachers***

Work *planned in Advance, Participative Decision-making* in schools, *Mentoring and Professional Development* by school heads ($R^2 = 16.9\%$) had significant impact on the organisational citizenship behaviour of teachers. Pattern of leadership distribution in schools predicted a variance of 8.3% in organisational citizenship behaviour. It is one dimension *Planned in advance* significantly predicted teachers' organisational citizenship behaviour. This finding was in confirmation with the findings of Mascall et al., (2008). In Section B, *Instructional Supervision, Professional Development* and *Mentoring* together explained variance of 9.8% in organisational citizenship behaviour. These findings corroborated with the findings of Oplatka, (2006), Ross & Gray (2006), Somech & Oplatka (2014). *Participative Decision-making* was also found to have an impact on the teachers' organisational citizenship behaviour. This finding corroborated with the findings of (Bogler & Somech, 2002, Somech, 2012).

Teachers' perception on distributed leadership of school heads was found to have significant impact on their work behaviour, therefore the hypothesis framed is accepted.

## Conclusion

The present study is an important contribution in the field of school leadership at a time when it is being considered as an important vehicle to empower and drive critical education reform in the country. School leadership is considered as an important means to achieve quality in school education system. The study attempted to fill the gap in existing literature by bringing in the Indian context in school leadership, development of a contextualised rating scale on school leadership and understanding leadership practices in the senior secondary schools. The study implicates that distributed leadership should be included in the curriculum frameworks for capacity building of school heads, thereby enhancing the potential of school heads, motivating them, and training them how to develop the leadership capacities and empower the teachers in their schools. The study also pointed out that mentoring and support from school heads, working in a planned way and participative decision-making are the key indicators which influences teachers' behaviour at work place. So, the school heads must be trained in all these areas to enhance teachers' performance. The study also explored the differences and similarities between teachers' perceptions on distributed leadership of school heads in the schools managed by central and state government. Findings of the study pointed out that there were significant differences between the two school managements in teachers' perception on distributed leadership of school heads. Therefore, the study suggested that distributed leadership should be institutionalised in the system through professional support. These differences across two public funded school management structures could be attributed to the differences in their management structure, governance policies, work culture, accountability measures, monitoring practices, strict performance appraisal, transfer policy, administrative policies, work environment, working conditions, leadership practices, physical infrastructure, fringe benefits and other support systems available to the teachers in the central government and state government funded schools.

## References


Andrews, D. & Lewis, M. (2004) Building sustainable futures, Improving Schools, 7(2), 129-150

Angelle, P.S. (2010). An Organizational Perspective of Distributed Leadership: A Portrait of a Middle School. Research in Middle Level Education Online, 33 (5), 1-16.

Barber, M., Whelan, F., & Clark, M. (2010). *Capturing the leadership premium: How the world's top school systems are building leadership capacity for the future.* McKinsey and Company.

Barry, D. (1991), *Managing the Bossless team: Lessons in distributed leadership Organizational Dynamics*, Volume 20(1), 31-47

Bennett, N., Wise, C., Woods, P. & Harvey, J.A. (2003), Distributed Leadership: A review of Literature, National College for School Leadership. www.ncsl.or.uk

Beycioglu, K., Ozer, N., & Ugurlu, C.T. (2012). Distributed leadership and organizational trust: the case of elementary schools. Procedia-Social and Behavioral Sciences, 46, 3316-3319.

Botha, R.J.N., & Triegaardt, P.K.P. (2016). The Perceptions of South African Classroom Teachers with Regard to the Role of Distributed Leadership in School Improvement. *International Journal of Educational Science*, 14(3), 242–250.

Bush, T. (2008). *Theories of Educational Leadership and Management.* London. Sage publications.

Camburn, E., Rowan, B., & Taylor, J.E. (2003). Distributed Leadership in Schools: The Case of Elementary Schools Adopting Comprehensive School Reforms Models. *Educational Evaluation and Policy Analysis*, 25 (4), 347-373.

Chadha, N.K. (2009). *Applied psychometry*, New Delhi: SAGE Publications Ltd.

Chaudhuri, S.H. (2002). Role of Headteachers in school Management: A synthesis of state experiences. In R. Govinda, *Role of Headteachers School Management in India*. New Delhi: ANTRIEP, NUEPA.

Day, C., Sammons, P., Hopkins, D., Harris, A., Leithwood, K., Gu, Q., & Brown., E. (2010). 10 strong claims about successful school leadership.

Day, C., Sammons, P., Hopkins, D., Harris, A., Leithwood, K., Gu, Q., … Kington, A. (2007). The impact of school leadership on pupil outcomes: Interim report.

DeVellis, R.F. (2003). *Scale Development: Theory and Applications* (Applied Social Research Methods Series Vol 26) (2nd Edn).

Diwan, R. (2011). School Leadership in the Wake of RTE Act 2009 Mapping Changes and Challenges. *Journal of Indian Education*, XXXVII (1), 97-110

Elmore, R. (2000), Building a new structure for School Leadership, The Albert Shankar Institute, Winter retrieved from http://www.shankerinstitute.org/Downloads/building.pdf

Govinda, R. (2002), Role of Headteachers in School Management in India: Case studies from six states, ANTRIEP

Govinda, R. (2016). Transforming Indian School Education: Policy concerns and Priorities. *Yojana*, (January).

Gronn, P. (2002). Distributed Leadership. In K. Leithwood, & P. Hallinger (Eds.), Second International Handbook of Educational leadership and Administration (pp. 653-696). Dordrecht, The Netherlands: Kluwer.

Harris, A. & Lambert, L. (2003) *Building leadership Capacity for School Improvement*, Milton Keynes Open University Press

Harris, A. (2014). *Distributed leadership Matters perspectives, Practicalities and Potential*. Corwin.

Harris, A. (Ed.). (2009). *Distributed Leadership: Different perspectives*. Springer.

Harris, A. (2008). *Distributed School Leadership*. UK: Routledge.

Hulpia, H. (2009). Distributed Leadership and Organisational Outcomes in secondary school. Ghent University, Belgium.

Jain. A.K. (2016). The mediating role of job satisfaction in the relationship of vertical trust and distributed leadership in health care context. *Journal of Modelling Management*, 11(2).

Leithwood, K. & Jantzi, D. (2006). Transformational leadership for large-scale reform: Effects on Students, teachers and their classroom practices. School Effectiveness and School Improvement, 17(2), 201-227

Leithwood, K., Day, C., Sammons, P., Harris, A., & Hopkins, D. (2006). Seven strong claims about successful school leadership.

Liljenberg, M. (2015). Distributing leadership to establish developing and learning organisations in Swedish context. Educational Management Administration {&} Leadership, 43(1), 152–170.

Mascall, B., Leithwood, K., Strauss, T., & Sacks, R. (2008). The relationship between Distributed Leadership and Teachers' Academic Optimism. *Journal of Educational Administration*, 46 (2), 214-228.

Mukhopadhyay, M. (2001). Governance of Indian Education Proposed Reforms. In M. Mukhopadhyay & R. S. Tyagi (Eds.), Governance of School Education in India. NIEPA.

Mukhopadhyay, M. (2012). Leadership for Institutional building in Education (3rd ed.).

Mullick, J., Sharma, U., & Deppeler, J. (2013). School teachers' perception about distributed leadership practices for inclusive education in primary schools in Bangladesh. School Leadership & Management, 33(2), 151-168.

Oduro, G. K. (2004). 'Distributed Leadership in Schools: what English headteachers say about the 'pull' and 'push' factors. British Educational Research Association Annual Conference. Manchester.

Panda, B. K. (2013). Role of School Heads.

Panda, B. K. (n.d.). Heads of Schools, Positions, Powers, Functions ad Recruitment.

Price, H. E. (2015). Principals' social interactions with teachers: How principal-teacher social relations correlate with teachers' perceptions of student engagement. *Journal of Educational Administration*, 53(1), 116–139.

Spillane, J. (2006). Distributed Leadership. San Francisco: Jossey Bass.

Van Maele, D., & Van Houtte, M. (2015). Trust in school: a pathway to inhibit teacher burnout? *Journal of Educational Administration*, 53(1), 93–115.

Whitby, G. (2006). Distributive leadership as an emerging concept, Australian Centre for

Yukl, G. (1999). An evaluation of conceptual weaknesses in transformational and charismatic leadership theories. *The leadership quarterly*, 10(2), 285-305.

Yukl, G. (2006). *Leadership in Organizations* (5th edition). Upper Saddle River, NJ: Pearson prentice hall.

# 17

# Transformative Impact of Classroom Observations on Teacher Development

Mohd Zia Ul Haq Rafaqi

## Introduction

Classroom observations stand as a cornerstone in the realm of teacher development, offering a lens through which educators can reflect on their instructional practices, student engagement, and overall classroom dynamics (O'Leary, 2020). As an integral component of ongoing professional growth, classroom observations contribute significantly to a teacher's commitment to lifelong learning (Strong-Cvetich, 1995). Teacher development is a dynamic process encompassing lifelong learning and continuous improvement (Ingersoll & Strong, 2011). Rooted in adult learning theories (Knowles, Holton, & Swanson, 2015), this process emphasizes the importance of self-directed, reflective practice for educators. Lifelong learning theories posit that teachers should actively engage in ongoing professional development to adapt to evolving educational landscapes (Darling-Hammond, 2017). Moreover, the concept of reflective practice, as articulated by Schön (1983), underscores the significance of educators critically examining and refining their instructional methods. The use of classroom observations as a means of professional development has evolved over time. Historically, observations were often conducted for evaluative purposes, emphasizing compliance rather than fostering growth (Hofer, 2018). However, contemporary perspectives advocate for a shift towards formative observations, emphasizing collaboration and improvement over judgement (Hofer, 2018; Pianta, Hamre, & Allen, 2012). This transformation aligns with the broader paradigm shift in education towards teacher empowerment and continuous improvement. Research consistently suggests that well-designed and supportive classroom observation programs positively impact teacher development (Hattie, 2009). Positive outcomes include enhanced instructional practices, increased teacher self-efficacy, and improved student learning outcomes (Bell, Wilson, Higgins, & McCoach, 2010; Stronge, Richard, & Catano, 2008). Effective feedback during observations plays a critical role in facilitating these improvements (Hattie & Timperley, 2007). Despite the benefits, challenges exist in the implementation of classroom observations. Issues such as observer bias, time constraints, and the potential for observations to be perceived as evaluative rather than formative pose challenges to their effectiveness (Smylie & Denny, 1990). Additionally, the impact of observations may vary based on contextual factors, such as school culture and administrative support (Cruickshank & Haefele, 2001). The study aspires to contribute to the existing body of literature by providing a nuanced understanding of the transformative impact of classroom observations on teacher development. The findings of this study have the potential to inform educational practitioners, administrators, and policymakers about the effectiveness of classroom observations as a tool for teacher development.

## The Study

The primary objectives for the study are as follows:

1. To assess teachers' perceptions of the impact of classroom observations on instructional strategies.
2. To investigate the influence of classroom observations on teachers' classroom management techniques.
3. To explore teachers' perceptions of the impact of classroom observations on student engagement.

### *Methodology*

This study employs a survey-based research design to investigate the impact of classroom observations on teacher development in Kashmir. The survey serves as the primary tool for data collection, allowing for the exploration of teachers' perceptions and experiences related to instructional strategies, classroom management, and student engagement. 299 participants were recruited from diverse schools in the Kashmir region. Inclusion criteria included teachers with a minimum of three years of teaching experience. Stratified random sampling was employed to ensure representation from various geographical areas and school types (urban/rural). Descriptive statistics and inferential statistical methods have been used to identify relationships among variables. Self-structured questionnaire related to instructional strategies, classroom management, and student engagement were framed.

## Analysis and Interpretation

*Objective 1:* To assess teachers' perceptions of the impact of classroom observations on instructional strategies.

Table 1.1 shows mean frequency/quality of observations is 4.25 (on a scale of 1 to 5), indicating a relatively high level. The mean perceived impact on instructional strategies is 4.62, suggesting a positive overall perception.

The intercept (1.20) represents the estimated mean perceived impact when the frequency/quality of observations is zero. The coefficient for the frequency/

**Table 1.1:** Descriptive Statistics for Variables in the Regression Model

| Variable | Mean | Standard Deviation |
|---|---|---|
| Frequency/Quality of Observations | 4.25 | 0.63 |
| Perceived Impact on Instructional Strategies | 4.62 | 0.51 |

quality of observations (0.57) indicates the change in the perceived impact for a one-unit change in the frequency/quality of observations. Both coefficients are statistically significant ($p < 0.001$).

**Table 1.2:** Regression Model Summary Statistics

| *Predictor Variable* | *Coefficient (β)* | *Standard Error* | *t Value* | *p Value* |
|---|---|---|---|---|
| Intercept | 1.20 | 0.35 | 3.43 | < 0.001 |
| Frequency | 0.57 | 0.08 | 7.12 | < 0.001 |

The R-squared value (0.52) suggests that 52% of the variability in perceived impact on instructional strategies can be explained by the frequency/quality of observations. The adjusted R-squared (0.51) adjusts for the number of predictors and is still relatively high. The F test is highly significant F=50.56, indicating that the model is good fit.

**Table 1.3:** Regression Model Summary Statistics

| *Measure* | *Value* |
|---|---|
| R-squared | 0.52 |
| Adjusted R-squared | 0.51 |
| F Value | 50.56 |
| p Value (F Test) | < 0.001 |
| Standard Error of the Model | 0.46 |

The regression analysis demonstrates a significant positive relationship between the frequency/quality of classroom observations and teachers' perceptions of the impact on instructional strategies. The model explains a substantial proportion of the variability in perceived impact, emphasizing the importance of classroom observations in shaping teachers' perceptions of enhanced instructional strategies.

*Objective 2:* To investigate the influence of classroom observations on teachers' classroom management techniques.

**Table 2.1:** Descriptive Statistics for Different Levels of Classroom Observations

| *Observation Level* | *Mean Perception Score* | *Standard Deviation* |
|---|---|---|
| Low | 4.23 | 0.67 |
| Moderate | 4.65 | 0.52 |
| High | 5.12 | 0.45 |

**Table 2.2:** ANOVA Result

| *Source of Variation* | *Sum of Squares (SS)* | *Degrees of Freedom (df)* | *Mean Squares (MS)* | *F Value* | *p Value* |
|---|---|---|---|---|---|
| Between Groups | 215.34 | 2 | 107.67 | 18.72 | $< 0.001$ |
| Within Groups | 352.21 | 297 | 1.19 | | |
| Total | 567.55 | 299 | | | |

The ANOVA test yielded a statistically significant difference in teachers' perceptions of the impact on classroom management techniques across varying levels of classroom observations ($F = (2,297) = 18.72, p < 0.001$).

**Table 2.3:** Post-hoc Tests (Tukey HSD) for Classroom Observation Levels

| *Observation Levels* | *Mean Difference* | *p Value (Adjusted)* |
|---|---|---|
| Low vs. Moderate | -0.42 | 0.087 |
| Low vs. High | -0.89 | $< 0.001$ |
| Moderate vs. High | -0.47 | 0.023 |

Post-hoc tests revealed specific differences between observation levels. Teachers who experienced high levels of classroom observations reported significantly greater perceived impact on classroom management techniques compared to those with low or moderate levels ($p<0.001$).

**Table 2.4:** Effect Size Measure

| *Effect Size Measure* | *Value* |
|---|---|
| Eta-squared | 0.38 |

The effect size measure, Eta-squared ($\eta 2=0.38$), indicates a moderate to large effect. This suggests that 38% of the variability in teachers' perceptions of the impact on classroom management techniques can be attributed to differences in the levels of classroom observations.

The ANOVA results provide robust evidence that the frequency or quality of classroom observations significantly influences teachers' perceptions of the impact on classroom management techniques. Post-hoc tests further specify the nature of these differences, with high levels of observations being particularly impactful. The substantial effect size underscores the practical significance of these findings, emphasizing the importance of considering observation levels in teacher development programs aiming to enhance classroom management techniques.

*Objective 3:* To explore teachers' perceptions of the impact of classroom observations on student engagement.

Table 3.1 mean frequency/quality of observations is 4.31 (on a scale of 1 to 5), indicating a relatively high level. The mean perceived impact on student engagement is 4.55, suggesting a positive overall perception.

**Table 3.1:** Descriptive Statistics for Variables in the Regression Model

| *Variable* | *Mean* | *Standard Deviation* |
|---|---|---|
| Frequency/Quality of Observations | 4.31 | 0.61 |
| Perceived Impact on Student Engagement | 4.55 | 0.48 |

The intercept (1.15) represents the estimated mean perceived impact when the frequency/quality of observations is zero. The coefficient for the frequency/quality of observations (0.42) indicates the change in the perceived impact for a one-unit change in the frequency/quality of observations. Both coefficients are statistically significant ($p < 0.001$).

**Table 3.2:** Regression Model Summary Statistics

| *Predictor Variable* | *Coefficient (β)* | *Standard Error* | *t Value* | *p Value* |
|---|---|---|---|---|
| Intercept | 1.15 | 0.33 | 3.48 | < 0.001 |
| Frequency/Quality of Observations | 0.42 | 0.07 | 6.21 | < 0.001 |

The R-squared value (0.47) suggests that 47% of the variability in perceived impact on student engagement can be explained by the frequency/quality of observations. The adjusted R-squared (0.46) adjusts for the number of predictors and remains relatively high. The F test is highly significant indicating that the model is a good fit. The standard error of the model is 0.50, providing an estimate of the variability of the residuals.

**Table 1.3:** Regression Model Summary Statistics

| *Measure* | *Value* |
|---|---|
| R-squared | 0.47 |
| Adjusted R-squared | 0.46 |
| F Value | 38.68 |
| p Value (F Test) | < 0.001 |
| Standard Error of the Model | 0.50 |

The regression analysis reveals a significant positive relationship between the frequency/quality of classroom observations and teachers' perceptions of the impact on student engagement. The model explains a substantial proportion of the variability in perceived impact, underscoring the importance of classroom observations in shaping teachers' perceptions of improved student engagement. These findings can guide educational practitioners in designing observation programs that specifically target improvements in student engagement for effective professional development.

## Conclusion

This research study delved into the transformative impact of classroom observations on teacher development, focusing on instructional strategies, classroom management, and student engagement. The findings contribute valuable insights to the discourse on effective professional development strategies, shedding light on the nuanced experiences of teachers undergoing classroom observations.

The study's first objective, assessing teachers' perceptions of the impact of classroom observations on instructional strategies, revealed a significant positive relationship. The frequency and quality of observations were strongly correlated with teachers' perceived enhancements in instructional practices. The regression model explained a substantial proportion of the variability in perceived impact, emphasizing the crucial role of classroom observations in shaping teachers' perceptions of improved instructional strategies. Moving to the second objective, investigating the influence of classroom observations on teachers' classroom management techniques, the study employed ANOVA to explore differences across observation levels. The results demonstrated a statistically significant impact, with higher levels of classroom observations associated with greater perceived improvements in classroom management. Post-hoc tests specified these differences, highlighting the effectiveness of high-level observations. The substantial effect size underscored the practical significance of these findings, emphasizing the importance of considering observation levels in teacher development programs. The third objective focused on exploring teachers' perceptions of the impact of classroom observations on student engagement. The results revealed a significant positive relationship, with the frequency and quality of observations correlating strongly with teachers' perceptions of improved student engagement. The regression model explained a substantial proportion of the variability in perceived impact, reinforcing the importance of classroom observations in shaping teachers' views on enhanced student engagement.

In conclusion, this study provides empirical evidence supporting the transformative impact of classroom observations on teacher development. The findings underscore the need for well-designed and supportive observation programs, emphasizing the importance of formative approaches that prioritize collaboration and improvement over judgement. Additionally, the study highlights the role of contextual factors, such as school culture and administrative support, in shaping teachers' perceptions of observation effectiveness.

Educational practitioners, administrators, and policymakers can leverage these insights to design and implement observation programs that cater to the diverse needs of teachers, fostering continuous improvement and contributing to the broader goal of enhancing the quality of education. Ultimately, the study advocates for a holistic understanding of teacher development, considering both the quantitative dimensions of the impact of classroom observations on the professional growth of educators.

## References


Cruickshank, D.R., & Haefele, D. (2001). Good teachers, plural. *Educational leadership, 58*(5), 26-30.

Darling-Hammond, L. (2017). Teacher education around the world: What can we learn from international practice? *European Journal of Teacher Education, 40*(3), 291-309.

Hattie, J. (2009). The black box of tertiary assessment: An impending revolution. *Tertiary assessment & higher education student outcomes: Policy, practice & research, 259*, 275.

Hattie, J., & Timperley, H. (2007). The power of feedback. *Review of Educational Research, 77*(1), 81-112.

Hofer, C.L. (2016). *The impact of classroom observations and collaborative feedback on evaluation of teacher performance, based on the Danielson" Framework for Teaching"*. Wayne State University.

Ingersoll, R.M., & Strong, M. (2011). The impact of induction and mentoring programs for beginning teachers: A critical review of the research. *Review of Educational Research, 81*(2), 201-233.

Knowles, M.S., Holton III, E.F., & Swanson, R.A. (2014). *The adult learner: The definitive classic in adult education and human resource development.* Routledge.

O'Leary, M. (2020). *Classroom observation: A guide to the effective observation of teaching and learning.* Routledge.

Pianta, R.C., Hamre, B.K., & Allen, J.P. (2012). Teacher-student relationships and engagement: Conceptualizing, measuring, and improving the capacity of classroom interactions. In *Handbook of research on student engagement* (pp. 365-386). Boston, MA: Springer US.

Schon, D.A. (1983). *The reflective practicioner: How professionals think in action* (p. 1983). New York: Basic Books.

Smylie, M.A., & Denny, J.W. (1990). Teacher leadership: Tensions and ambiguities in organizational perspective. *Educational Administration Quarterly, 26*(3), 235-259.

Strong-Cvetich, J.R. (1995). *Lifelong teaching: Sustaining and renewing commitment to the classroom* (Doctoral dissertation, The Fielding Institute).

Stronge, J.H., Richard, H.B., & Catano, N. (2008). Qualities of effective teachers. Association for Supervision and Curriculum Development.

# 18

# Continuous Professional Development for Teachers amidst the NEP 2020 Landscape

Amanpreet Kaur

## Introduction

To provide the excellent education to the learners/students is always a first demand at global level and to fulfil this demand, to have the excellent teachers is the prerequisite. Teachers are the backbone of the educational organizations, so to foster the improvements in the teaching; it has become necessary to nurture the teachers through the continuing professional development program. For this worldwide many countries, since long, are organizing the programs, in form of lectures, workshops, seminars and conferences to deliver continuing teacher education to the in-service teacher educators (Louws et al. 2017). Teachers are fulcrums upon which the entire system hangs (Omorghie, 2006); in all education system teachers are at centre point (Misra, 2015). Teachers have direct impact on the classroom activities and learning of students (OECD, 2010). Hammond, 2000 suggested that fully-prepared and well-qualified teachers are needed to successfully implement educational reforms and to accomplish high standards. Till now extensive research has been done globally to determine the success rate of continuing professional development (Guskey, 2009, van Veen et al., 2012, & Darling-Hammond et al., 2017), Nipper et al., 2011 found that teachers' expectations do not match the reality of their experience of CPD. Many researchers have a view point to polish and advance the teacher's competence, the teachers' expectations regarding CPD are necessary to meet with their actual experiences otherwise it will negatively impact it (Kruger et al., 2016, Makopoulou, 2018 & Kennedy, 2016).

The continuing professional development of teachers is always remained at the top priorities while framing the education policies at global level. As many other countries, India also has documented many teachers' learning professional development courses, but these were confined to the in-service education and training (INSET) of teachers which is a restricted vision of continuing professional development program. In previous education policies, continuing professional development of the teachers was seen from the perspective of INSET which focuses to update in-service teachers only through training programs, induction courses, crash courses, faculty development programs (FDP) and workshops.

## Continuing Professional Development (CPD) and its Importance for the Teachers

National Education Policy 2020, asserts to bring the teachers to centre of vital reforms in education system and recognize the prerequisite to refurbish the teachers' respect in the community. The era in which todays' teachers are working is rapidly changing, so it is the pressing situation to expand the key competencies of the education learning that are recommended in sustainable development goals by UNESCO. Today a proficient teacher is not the one who only knows what and how of his content but s/he also is well acquainted with why and when of his practice. Teachers are the imperative part of the teaching-learning process. CPD starts with entry in the teaching profession and goes on all the way through the career as lifelong learning (Panda, 2001). Day, 1999 posited that CPD is a normal regular learning skill with cognizant and deliberate activities which are directly or indirectly beneficial for the education and to its stakeholders. CPD is perceived as continuing training of the teachers; development process after entering the profession which is involves teachers' initiatives and mandatory planned programs by the authorities (Padwad & Dixit, 2013).

## Features of Continuing Professional Development (CPD)

1. It aims to enrich the system of the education by evolving the key competencies, knowledge, and performance of the teachers.
2. It includes both formal and informal experiences of the learning.
3. It may happen anywhere in institution, at home, in virtual mode without any restriction of specific place.
4. Includes both collaborative efforts of individual initiatives and mandatory programs by the institutions.
5. Holistic process including teacher-driven and system-driven instead of INSET-based activities which is single system driven.
6. Teachers are self-driven and responsible for their professional training rather than depending on ready-made courses of same type for all teachers.

Keeping in mind the potential advantages of the CPD, it is imperative to take a look in earlier education policy documents to comprehend how it was observed and formerly endorsed.

## History of Earlier Education Policy Documents

Different policies and educational document made after Independence have focused on the many different professional development programs for teachers at the name of In-service Teacher Education and Training (INSET) activities.

The term CPD is merely used interchangeably for INSET. A summary of earlier document on education policy and recommendations given in it helps to understand this.

**Table 1:** Brief Summary of the Professional Development programs of teachers

| *Serial Number* | *Commission/ Policy/ Scheme* | *Year* | *Advisement on the Professional Development Programs of Teachers* |
|---|---|---|---|
| 1 | Mudaliar Commission (Secondary Education Commission) | 1952-53 | In service education and training started in the teacher training colleges.<br>Established the Extension Services Departments.<br>In-service teacher's training, short term refresher courses and training in specific subjects, workshops and professional conferences organized. |
| 2 | Education Commission (Kothari Committee) | 1964-66 | Established the School Complexes with a Nodal school.<br>At least 2 or 3 months of In-service training during five years.<br>All educational institutions and organizers were required to offer orientation programs like refresher courses, workshops, and seminars for teachers. |
| 3 | Chattopadhyay Commission | 1983-85 | Promoted the consolidation the status of INSET in the country<br>All teachers attend INSET for three weeks in every block once in a time period of five years.<br>Training of teachers considered for the career promotion. |
| 4 | National Policy on Education | 1986-1992 | Established the nodal agency District Institute for Education and Training (DIETs) for providing academic and resource support at the grassroot level for the various programs.<br>600 teachers get training in In-service education for 2 weeks per year.<br>250 College of Education upgraded as College of Teacher Education (CTE) to provide and improve teacher's competency.<br>Strengthening 50 Colleges of Education just as Institutions of Advanced Study in Education (IASE) deemed to be universities.<br>Establishment of Academic Staff Colleges (ASC) in the universities to enable newly appointed lecturers.<br>Establishment of a Statutory body National Council for Teacher Education (NCTE). |

| *Serial Number* | *Commission/ Policy/ Scheme* | *Year* | *Advisement on the Professional Development Programs of Teachers* |
|---|---|---|---|
| 5 | District Primary Education Program (DPEP) | 1995 | Establishment of resource centres at District, Block, and Cluster levels for the elementary/ primary teachers. |
| 6 | National Curriculum Framework (NCF 2005) | 2005 | "In-service education cannot be an event but rather is a process, which includes knowledge development and changes in attitudes, skills, disposition and practice through interactions both in workshop settings and in the school" (NCERT, 2005, p. 112).<br>Suggested to split the fixed number of days in the year of In-service teachers' training to instantaneously apply newly learnt knowledge in their actual teaching practice and pre-service training. |
| 7 | National Curriculum Framework for Teacher Education [NCFTE] (2009) | 2009 | Government of India proposed changes and updates in NCTE for professionalization of teacher education.<br>Vocational education for the teachers.<br>Open and distant learning (ODL) for teachers. |
| 8 | National Education Policy (NEP) | 2020 | Training of teachers under NEP focus on inclusive and equitable education.<br>Recommend the minimum fifty hours training every year for the teachers and h ead teachers driven by their own interest.<br>Offers customized learning paths, expert led training and flexible learning formats for the teachers and blended mode.<br>NISHTHA Online in three versions (1.0, 2.0,3.0) [National Initiative for School Heads' and Teachers' Holistic Advancement].<br>National Professional Standards for Teachers (NPST) is a public statement comprising the guidelines on the phases of the effective and high-quality teaching from trainee to professional lead teacher which also includes performance evaluation, salary, and required skill sets. It aims to equitable access to highest quality education for all.<br>Draft on National Mission for Mentoring (NMM). |

In short, the table reflects on the earlier policy makers have not been emphatic to enact previous documents which can cater the professional development need of the teachers at the different levels. Basically, these policies before NEP 2020 remained stuck to the terminology of in-service education. The education world in other countries has moved from INSET to CPD and from CPD to Continuing Lifelong Professional Learning (CLPL) and earlier Indian education policies and programs still embrace the INSET. In view of above stated education policies, it is imperative to understand how NEP 2020 envisions CPD in contemporary global scenario.

## CPD with Reference to NEP 2020 and Expectations from the Teachers

NEP has recognized the importance CPD for the improvement of the teachers and also accepts the globally used term 'CPD' instead of using timeworn term INSET. It now delves upon to various aspects of CPD to enact it more promisingly. These aspects for teachers are:

1. NEP 2020 proposed different opportunities which cover, "latest pedagogical skills related to literacy and numeracy, formative and adaptive assessment of learning outcomes, experiential learning, arts and sports integrated, storytelling approach etc." (MHRD, 2020, p.22).
2. NEP aims to provide continuous self-improvement chances to the teacher educators to progresses in their profession. These opportunities will be offered to them in blended modes offline as well as online development modules (MHRD, 2020).
3. But NEP 2020 is not clear on whether private school teachers can also take the benefits from it or government school's teachers are only its beneficiary. For the best implementation it should encourage and facilitates the private institutions the same way it provides the benefits to government employees. Policy needs to make more clear guidelines on this for all the teachers serving in private and government sectors.
4. The policy wishes the teachers facilitate active engagement of the students. For this the policy conveys that "Teachers will undergo rigorous training in learner-centric pedagogy and on how to become high-quality online content creators themselves using online teaching platforms and tools" (p. 59).
5. NEP 2020 also emphasizes to utilize the technology and online platforms that help the teachers and suggests "The use of technology platforms such as SWAYAM/DIKSHA for online training of teachers will be encouraged, so that standardized training programs can be administered to large numbers of teachers within a short span of time" (MHRD, 2020, p. 43), also it points up, "A National Mission for Mentoring shall be established, with a large pool of outstanding senior/retired faculty — including those with the ability to teach in Indian languages — who would be willing to provide short and long-term mentoring/professional support to university/college teachers" (MHRD, 2020, p.43).

6. NEP 2020 expects from every teacher, teaching in school or higher educational institutions, must participate in Continuing Professional Development activities. It states "Each teacher will be expected to participate in at least 50 hours of CPD opportunities every year for their own professional development, driven by their own interests" (MHRD, 2020).
7. It also mentions "School Principals and school complex leaders will have similar modular leadership/management workshops and online development opportunities and platforms to continuously improve their own leadership and management skills, and so that they too may share best practices with each other. Such leaders will also be expected to participate in 50 hours or more of CPD modules per year, covering leadership and management, as well as content and pedagogy with a focus on preparing and implementing pedagogical plans based on competency-based education" (MHRD, 2020, p.22).

CPD is important for the improvement of teacher's professional competencies and their voluntary participation in these developmental activities is expected.

## Conclusion

To wrap up the discussion with famous saying which is apt for the teachers is perfectly said by Rabindranath Tagore — A lamp can only lighten another lamp when it continues to burn its own flame." Only a self-committed teacher to lifelong learning is able to comprehend and can gratify to the learning requirements of the learners proficiently. To remain professionally motivated CPD activities are essential to be accepted voluntary as a part of learning with broader view point. Hopefully the vision of CPD suggested in National Education Policy 2020 be implemented and followed up and reviewed from time to time to empower the teaching-learning growth of all stakeholders of the wider learning community and help propel the educational destiny of India towards excellence.

## References

Darling-Hammond, L. (2000). Teacher Quality and Student Achievement. *Education Policy Analysis Archives*, *8*(1), 1. https://doi.org/10.14507/epaa.v8n1.2000

Darling-Hammond, L., Hyler, M., & Gardner, M. (2017). *Effective Teacher Professional Development*. Learning Policy Institute. Retrieved from Learning Policy Institute website: https://learningpolicyinstitute.org/sites/default/files/product-files/Effective_Teacher_Professional_Development_REPORT.pdf

Day, C. (1999). *Developing teachers: the challenges of lifelong learning*. London; Philadelphia, Pa: Falmer Press.

*Guidelines for 50 hours of continuous professional development for teachers, head teachers and teacher educators Based on National Education Policy 2020.* (2022). Retrieved from https://ncert.nic.in/pdf/Guidelines50HoursCpd.pdf

Guskey, T.R. (2009). Closing the knowledge gap on effective professional development. *Educational Horizons*, 87(4), 224-233. (n.d.).

Kennedy, M.M. (2016). How Does Professional Development Improve Teaching? *Review of Educational Research, 86*(4), 945–980. https://doi.org/10.3102/0034654315626800

Kruger, C., Janse van Rensburg, O., & De Witt, M. (2016). Meeting Teacher Expectations in a DL Professional Development Programme — A Case Study for Sustained Applied Competence as Programme Outcome. *The International Review of Research in Open and Distributed Learning, 17*(4). https://doi.org/10.19173/irrodl.v17i4.2458

Louws, M.L., Meirink, J.A., van Veen, K., & van Driel, J.H. (2017). Teachers' self-directed learning and teaching experience: What, how, and why teachers want to learn. *Teaching and Teacher Education, 66*(Teaching and Teacher Education Volume 66, August 2017, Pages 171-183), 171–183. https://doi.org/10.1016/j.tate.2017.04.004

Makopoulou, K. (2017). An investigation into the complex process of facilitating effective professional learning: CPD tutors' practices under the microscope. *Physical Education and Sport Pedagogy, 23*(3), 250–266. https://doi.org/10.1080/17408989.2017.1406463

Misra, P.K. (2015). Teacher education policies, practices, and reform in Scotland: Implications in the Indian context. *Cogent Education, 2*(1). https://doi.org/10.1080/2331186x.2015.1066089

Nipper, K., Ricks, T., Kilpatrick, J., Mayhew, L., Thomas, S., Kwon, N.Y., Hembree, D. (2011). Teacher tensions: expectations in a professional development institute. *Journal of Mathematics Teacher Education, 14*(5), 375–392. https://doi.org/10.1007/s10857-011-9180-1

OECD (2010), PISA 2009 Results: What Makes a School Successful? — Resources, Policies and Practices (Volume IV) http://dx.doi.org/10.1787/9789264091559-en.

Omoreghie, N. (2006). *Inadequacies in teacher education in Nigeria: The way out*. Arts and Education Publications, Benson Idahosa University.

Padwad, A., & Dixit, K.K. (2013). Multiple stakeholders' views of continuing professional development. Continuing professional development: Lessons from India, 11-22.

*Human Rights Education in Indian Schools: Curriculum Development pranati panda.* (n.d.). Retrieved from https://www.hurights.or.jp/archives/pdf/asia-s-ed/v04/11panda.pdf

What Makes Teacher Professional Development Effective? A Literature Review by Klaas van veen, rosanne zwart and Jacobiene Meirink Book Teacher Learning That Matters Edition1st Edition First Published2011 Imprint Routledge Pages19 eBook ISBN9780203805879. (2011). What Makes Teacher Professional Development Effective? A Literature Review. In *Teacher Learning That Matters* (pp. 1–19). New York: Routledge.

Walia, P., & Walia, P. (2022). Continuous Professional Development: A Policy Analysis In Indian Perspective. *Journal of Positive School Psychology, 6*(7), 2624-2633.

*National curriculum framework 2005.* (n.d.). Retrieved from https://ncert.nic.in/pdf/nc-framework/nf2005-english.pdf

Ministry of Human Resource Development. (2020b). *National Education Policy 2020 Ministry of Human Resource Development Government of India.* Retrieved from https://www.education.gov.in/sites/upload_files/mhrd/files/NEP_Final_English_0.pdf

# 19

# Perception of Teacher Educators towards Implementing ITEP

Mohammad Kaif Farooqui
Sajid Jamal

## Introduction

Teacher education now-a-days is considered very important because it enables the prospective teachers to perform on the desired lines in the classroom as well as equip the in-service teachers with necessary skills and competencies. In various parts of the globe the governments have extensive system of training for the pre-service teachers. Our beloved country India has one of the largest education systems of the world and is the most populous country. Needless to say, we should have a robust system of teacher education to cater to the needs of a large number of students in our classroom. Our system of teacher education should ensure the best possible professional preparation of the prospective teachers and should groom them in a way that they can do the needful.

## Historical Background of Teacher Education in India

The history of teacher education in India is as old as the education system itself. In Ancient India, the prospective teachers were trained through the monitorial system, however, the formal teacher training system emerged during the Buddhist period (500 BC to 1200 AD), allowing individuals to become teachers regardless of social level. Teachers were trained to disseminate Buddhist principles and values under the guidance of experienced trainers. They gained knowledge about ethics, behaviour, and Dharma instruction, earning a certificate for teaching fitness. During the medieval period (1200-1700) also we had an organised system of teacher training.

Teachers' training got added importance with the release of Wood's Dispatch in 1854, as it recommended to give allowances to individuals with teaching aptitude and the establishment of training schools in each presidency. In this connection The Indian Education Commission (1882-83) recommended introducing an examination focused on teaching principles and practice and it made completing this examination as necessary for securing a permanent teaching position in any secondary school, regardless of whether it is government-funded or privately supported. The commission also proposed a more concise training programme for recent graduates. Government of India Resolution on Education Policy, 1904 is also considered as a milestone in the field of teacher education in India as it recommended enhancing the teacher training programme and establishing five teacher training colleges in Madras, Kurseong, Allahabad, Lahore, and Jabalpur. It highlights the importance of providing teachers with training in effective teaching methods to improve secondary education. Colleges are anticipated to attract and admit graduates, providing them with the option of either a two-year or one-year program. The training would cover a range of teaching principles and technical skills.

After getting the Independence, the first education commission, which is known as The University Education Commission found that teacher training colleges required a fundamental reorientation and suggested that teacher educators adopt a fresh approach to enhance the quality of training. The commission proposed the integration and mutual support of theory and practice. On the similar lines the Secondary Education Commission (1952–53) recommended to set up teacher training institutions for primary and secondary education, proposing programmes for individuals with school-leaving certificates and graduates. The commission proposed that universities acknowledge and formalize graduate training institutions while a separate board should oversee secondary-grade training institutions. The Kothari Commission (1964-66) highlighted the significance of professional education for teachers in enhancing the quality of the education system and proposed recommendations such as integrating teachers' colleges with universities and schools.

The National Policy on Education in 1986 highlighted the significance of enhancing the quality of teacher education to improve the overall quality of school education. Consequently, specific training schools underwent upgrades to become District Institutes of Education and Training (DIETs). On the other hand, specific training colleges underwent upgrades to become Colleges of Teacher Education (CTEs) and Institutes of Advanced Studies in Education (IASEs). The Yashpal Committee (1993) suggested that the B.Ed. programme should provide specialised secondary, elementary, or nursery education tracks. The program could also be one-year post-graduation or four years after higher secondary education. The program's content should be reorganized to better align with the evolving requirements of school education. It should prioritise the development of self-learning and independent thinking skills among trainees. The National Knowledge Commission (2007) recommended that Teacher Eligibility Tests be conducted at state and centre levels to improve the quality of education. National Curriculum Framework for Teacher Education (2010) emphasized the importance of addressing the demands and expectations placed on teachers in initial and continuing teacher education. It further recommended that The National Council for Teacher Education (NCTE) should take initiatives to improve the quality of teacher education programs, including collaborating with the National Assessment and Accreditation Council (NAAC) to ensure quality assurance and sustenance.

The National Education Policy (NEP) 2020 highlights a revolutionary approach to the education system, emphasizing the crucial role of teacher educators in shaping the future of teaching and learning by prioritizing teacher education and introducing a four-year Integrated Teacher Education Programme (ITEP). These programmes strive to equip prospective teachers with the essential skills and knowledge to facilitate impactful and transformative learning experiences for students. By 2030, the NEP suggests transforming teacher education institutions into multidisciplinary Higher Education Institutions (HEIs) and closing down the substandard standalone teacher education institutions and accrediting all teacher education institutions as multidisciplinary HEIs within the next 3-5 years. It proposes enhancing the education departments in universities to take on a pivotal role in establishing education programmes across all disciplines. The NEP suggests that admission to pre-service training programmes should be based on subject and aptitude tests conducted by the National Testing Agency. This approach aims to maintain consistency and high standards in teacher education. Finally, it suggests creating a nationwide mentoring initiative in which experienced and retired faculty members offer guidance and professional assistance to teachers.

## Integrated Teacher Education Programme (ITEP)

To enhance teacher education in India, the National Council for Teacher Education (NCTE) has implemented the Integrated Teacher Education Programme (ITEP) in 57 Teacher Education Institutions (TEIs) for the upcoming session in 2023-24. This programme, introduced as part of the National Education Policy (NEP) 2020, is a 4-year undergraduate degree that provides options for B.A. B.Ed./ B.Sc. B.Ed. and B.Com. B.Ed. The programme is designed to equip educators with the necessary skills and knowledge to adapt to the new 4-stage school structure (Foundational, Preparatory, Middle, and Secondary). It is currently available in specific Central/State Government Universities/Institutions. ITEP allows students to complete their education in a shorter time frame than the traditional 5-year B.Ed. programme. The programme explores various aspects of education, including innovative teaching techniques, early childhood development, fundamental skills in reading and maths, promoting inclusivity in education, and appreciating Indian cultural values and customs. The said programme aims to improve teacher education significantly, producing teachers equipped with the necessary skills to shape the future of India in the 21st century.

## The Study

***Rationale:*** The successful implementation of Integrated Teacher Education Programme (ITEP) requires dedicated, devoted, and committed teacher educators as they are responsible for preparing and supporting the next generation of teachers, allowing aspiring teachers to choose teaching as a deliberate career path. They are vital in cultivating skilled and compassionate teachers, championing strong teacher education programs, and fostering the ongoing professional growth of in-service teachers. Their impact goes far beyond individual classrooms, as they frequently participate in research, curriculum design, and the creation of educational programmes. Teacher educators are essential in shaping the education system and preparing future educators to meet the diverse needs of students in an ever-changing world. These individuals possess extensive experience and expertise in various education-related fields, including pedagogy, curriculum development, educational psychology, philosophy, and sociology. Their perspectives and opinions regarding ITEP can significantly impact the program's implementation and effectiveness. Through gaining insight into different perspectives, we can pinpoint opportunities for enhancement and provide more effective assistance in implementing the programme. The findings of this study will provide valuable insights for various stakeholders, such as teacher educators, educational institutions, and policymakers.

***Sample*:** The data for the present study was obtained from 100 teacher educators. The participants taught at different central, state, and private universities and teacher training colleges in India. They had sufficient experience in teaching. The researchers created a Google form and sent it to the emails of the respondents. It was ensured to them that this study was only for research purposes and that their identity would be strictly kept confidential. The researchers contacted some teachers personally also to do the needful.

***Research tool*:** The researchers used a self-made questionnaire containing 20 items to collect the data. The respondents were required to answer items 1 to 18 with either "yes" or "no". In contrast, items 19 and 20 are related to the top challenges and solutions respectively in implementing ITEP.

## Results

*Item No. 1 — The Integrated Teacher Education Programme (ITEP) is a good initiative in the field of Teacher Education.*

In response to this item, 92% of respondents said "Yes", whereas 8% of teacher educators responded "No". This means that most teacher educators support ITEP as a good initiative in the field of Teacher Education.

*Item No. 2 — 4-year Integrated B.Ed. Programme is a costly affair in terms of time and money.*

In response to this item, 36% of respondents said "Yes", whereas 64% of teacher educators responded "No". It means a sizeable majority of teacher educators opine that 4-year integrated B.Ed. Programme is costly in terms of time and money.

*Item No. 3 — Implementing ITEP is a challenging task for training colleges in the present condition.*

In response to this item, 83% of respondents said "Yes", whereas 17% of teacher educators responded "No". This means most teacher educators feel ITEP is a very challenging task to implement in training colleges in the present condition.

*Item No. 4 — We have not yet received a clear roadmap for implementing the ITEP.*

In response to this item, 69% of respondents said "Yes", whereas 31% of teacher educators responded "No". This means most of the teacher educators still need to receive a clear roadmap for implementing the ITEP.

*Item No. 5 — There is a need for more infrastructure in training institutions for implementing ITEP.*

In response to this item, 95% of respondents said "Yes", whereas 5% of teacher educators responded "No". It means most of the teacher educators want more infrastructure in training institutions for implementing ITEP.

*Items No. 6 — 125 working days in a semester, as per the NCTE regulations for ITEP, are very difficult to achieve.*

In response to this item the teacher educators were equally divided. 50% of them said "Yes", whereas 50% of them responded "No".

*Item No. 7 — Through ITEP, we can prepare better teachers.*

In response to this item, 88% of respondents said "Yes", whereas 12% of teacher educators responded "No". It means most of the teacher educators feel that through ITEP, we can prepare better teachers.

*Item No. 8 — ITEP gives a chance to those students who want to become a teacher by choice, not by chance.*

In response to this item, 97% of respondents said "Yes", whereas 3% of teacher educators responded "No". It simply implies that most teacher educators feel that ITEP gives a chance to those students who want to become teachers by choice, not by chance.

*Item No. 9 — We can have enough time to guide student-teachers in improving teaching methodology in ITEP.*

In response to this item, 93% of respondents said "Yes", whereas 7% of teacher educators responded "No". It means most teacher educators feel that ITEP will provide enough time to guide student-teachers in improving teaching methodology in ITEP.

*Item No. 10 — ITEP will be as acceptable as other professional courses, such as medicine, engineering, and law.*

In response to this item, 76% of respondents said "Yes", whereas 24% of teacher educators responded "No". It implies that though in minority but a good chunk of teacher educators believes that ITEP will not be as acceptable as other professional courses, such as medicine, engineering, and law.

*Item No. 11 — The 4-year integrated course will make for a more comprehensive integration of subject and pedagogy.*

In response to this item, 95% of respondents said "Yes", whereas 5% of them responded "No". It means majority of the teacher educators feel that 4-year integrated course will make for a more comprehensive integration of subject and pedagogy.

*Item No. 12 — Multi and Interdisciplinary academic environments help student-teachers increase their knowledge in various subjects.*

In response to this item all the respondents went overwhelmingly in favour and they responded "Yes" and no one responded in "No". It simply implies that all teacher educators feel that Multi and Interdisciplinary academic environments help Student-teachers increase their knowledge in various subjects.

*Item No. 13 — Learning content and pedagogical knowledge together will make the student teacher a brighter teaching professional.*

Again, in response to this item all the 100% of respondents said "Yes" and no one responded in "No". It simply implies that all teacher educators feel that learning content and pedagogical knowledge together will make the student teacher a brighter teaching professional.

*Item No. 14 — The physical expansion of training colleges into a 'composite institution' is very challenging.*

Responding to this item, 83% of respondents said "Yes", whereas 17% of teacher educators responded "No". It means all teacher educators feel that the physical expansion of training colleges into a 'composite institution' is very challenging.

*Item No. 15 — Stand-alone training colleges may not exist in the future.*

Responding to this item, 72% of respondents said "Yes", whereas 28% of them responded "No". It means all teacher educators feel that stand-alone training colleges may not exist in the future.

*Item No. 16 — Doing post-graduation in the primary subject will be an issue for ITEP graduates.*

Respondents were divided in response to this item as, 57% of them said "Yes", whereas 43% said "No". It means a plenty of teacher educators have some apprehensions related to the post-graduation in the primary subject for ITEP graduates.

*Item No. 17 — Beginning Teacher Education at the early stage of Higher Education will help to mould fully dedicated professionals in the Teacher Education field.*

Responding to this item, an absolute majority of respondents said "Yes" and a very thin minority said "No". 97% of them said "Yes", whereas 3%

of them responded "No". It means that teacher educators feel that beginning teacher education at the early stage of higher education will help to mould fully dedicated professionals in the teacher education field.

*Item No. 18 — ITEP acts as a filter for creating quality teaching professionals.*

Responding to this item, 90% of respondents said "Yes", whereas 10% of them responded "No". It means that a high majority of teacher educators feel that ITEP acts as a filter for creating quality teaching professionals.

*In response to Item nos. 19 and 20 of the questionnaires, the respondents reported plenty of challenges and solutions for implementing ITEP. For the sake of clarity these are being mentioned in the following table:*

**Table 1:** Challenges and Solutions in implementing ITEP

| | *Challenges in Implementing ITEP* | *Solutions for Implementing ITEP* |
|---|---|---|
| **Infrastructural challenges** | Under this category, the teacher educators mentioned several challenges, such as lack of physical infrastructure, lack of human resources, converting existing institutions into composite ones, and lack of infrastructure for ICT integration in teacher education programs including Internet access during training. | According to them, to overcome the challenge of infrastructure, the government should provide more grants to institutes to meet the infrastructure facility. The government should release a handsome budget to meet out the expenses related to infrastructural development. They also opined that recruitment of required faculty in these institutions should be given the top priority. |
| **Curricular challenges** | Under the curricular challenges category, the teacher educators mentioned: lengthy Syllabus, managing curricular activities timely, designing a cohesive curriculum seamlessly and integrating content from various disciplines, etc. | Giving solution to this challenge they opined that the government should make curriculum available in regional languages. In addition, curriculum development should be prioritized in such a way that a seamless integration of theoretical and practical components may become easy. For this to happen NCERT, NUEPA, and SCERT should collaborate and frame the ITEP curriculum while considering the country's cultural variety, local aspirations, and regional demand, they further suggested to establish a curriculum committee with representatives from each discipline to design a curriculum that aligns with overarching learning goals collaboratively. The regular meetings and feedback sessions should also be conducted to make this integration easy. |

| | | |
|---|---|---|
| **Pedagogical challenges** | Under this category they mentioned lack of professionals in multi and interdisciplinary pedagogy, making a fine balance between concerned subject and Pedagogical Knowledge, credit framework, creating interdisciplinary relationship with other subjects, and lack of subject teachers. | The respondents suggested that interactive and project-based learning experiences should be provided to captivate student interest and they should be provided real-world examples demonstrating the practical application of interdisciplinary knowledge, hence, fostering a sense of relevance and engagement. |
| **Challenges related to attracting quality entrants** | Attracting calibre pupil to ITEP course was found to be one of the most important challenges by the teacher educators. They opined that the dropout rate in ITEP will be higher and students' disinclination towards the teaching profession and attracting good students with teaching aptitude for ITEP are the biggest challenges. They further mentioned that science students will always be more inclined towards their science subject rather and they will pay least attention to teachers training at that moment. | The respondents suggested to implement a proper strategy to reduce the burden on students as the teacher preparation course requires various activities. Teaching should be made as attractive as engineering, medical, and other professions. There should be a guaranteed job after completion of the course and teacher education should be made an optional subject of the civil services exam. Some incentives should also be given during the practice teaching. We should ensure quality at the preparatory level and employ a well-designed and continuous assessment. |
| **Challenges related to the funding** | Under this category the respondents opined that since ITEP will be expensive, hence making more funds available for it will be a big challenge. Further they opined that lack of stakeholder collaboration and resource allocation for ITEP will be other challenges. | The respondents suggested that the government should issue certain guidelines regarding the funds utilisation and the government should provide extra budget for the ITEP program, provide more funds in the education sector, and all the stakeholders should be sensitised about the importance of ITEP. In this connection private entrepreneurs, industrialists and philanthropists should be encouraged to invest in ITEP programme. |
| **Challenges regarding the training of faculty** | The teacher educators opined that there is a lack of experienced faculty, and preparing teachers in regional languages will be a big challenge. Further, continuous professional development of the faculty, lack of collaboration with the faculties of other departments, | There were a variety of suggestions under this category. They suggested that there should be more appointment of subject expert teachers, the teachers who have already been appointed by the government should be provided a bridge course, providing training to the faculty members who will implement |

| | |
|---|---|
| insufficient number of teachers with various specializations, lack of quality teachers in private colleges, teaching practice issues, and a lack of intensive capacity building to align the curriculum with the new policy are some of the other challenges. | ITEP in subject matter expertise and effective pedagogical methods and fostering a culture of interdisciplinary collaboration through workshops, joint projects, and shared resources. For the teachers who possess good academic qualifications, administrators must offer a competitive compensation package and additional benefits such as periodic promotions, salary increases, and support for research initiatives. |
| *Other Challenges and Solutions for Same* | |
| *Other Challenges* | *Other Solutions* |
| The other challenges opined by them were — lack of proper coordination with other academic institutions, unsatisfactory assessment methods, challenges related to standalone institutions, leaving of the students just after completing the graduation, availability of less time for preparation and implementation in the stipulated time 2030, lack of feeder schools, coordination between the Department of Teacher Education and other departments and bringing self-financed institutions to follow the guidelines of ITEP in letter and spirit. | For these challenges the respondents suggested that a strategic plan for faculty recruitment is crucial besides having a well-designed and continuous assessment system to monitor students' progress and providing timely feedback as well as defining subject-wise credit framework. Further, developing assessment rubrics that align with interdisciplinary goals and involve faculty from multiple disciplines in the evaluation process is also very important, implementing diverse assessment methods, including collaborative projects and presentations, to capture the breadth of integrated learning. More focus on practical aspects should be there. They further suggested that the planning at the grass-root level should be done and there should be strict and proper regulations by NCTE. A policy regarding standalone colleges should be made. Institutions should be given more time to adopt ITEP. |

## Conclusion

ITEP is a paradigm shift in teacher education in India. However, there are various apprehensions in the mind of various stakeholders particularly the teacher educators. As they are the main players to implement ITEP, hence their perception regarding it and their opinion about the challenges in implementing it should be given due weightage. The solutions mentioned by them in the present study might be very helpful in successfully implementing ITEP in India.

## References

First Five-year Plan. (1951-56). Planning Commission. Government of India

Kothari Commission Report. (1964-66). Ministry of Human Resource Development. Government of India. New Delhi.

MHRD. (2000). Quality Education in a Global Era: Challenges to Equity and Opportunities for Diversity. Country Paper. Government of India. MHRD. New Delhi.

MHRD. (2004-05). Selected Educational Statistics. MHRD. Government of India, New Delhi.

National Policy on Education. (1986). National Council of Educational Research and Training. Sri Aurobindo Marg. New Delhi.

National Commission on Teachers. (1982-85). Ministry of Human Resource Development. Government of India. New Delhi.

National Curriculum Framework for Elementary and Secondary Education. (1998) National Council of Educational Research and Training. Sri Aurobindo Marg. New Delhi.

National Curriculum Framework for School Education. (2000). National Council of Educational Research and Training. Sri Aurobindo Marg. New Delhi.

National Curriculum Framework for Teacher Education (NCFTE): Towards Preparing Professional and Humane Teacher. (2010). National Council for Teacher Education. New Delhi.

National Curriculum Framework. (2005). National Council of Educational Research and Training. Sri Aurobindo Marg. New Delhi.

National Knowledge Commission Report. (2007). Government of India, New Delhi.

National Policy of Education. (1992). Ministry of Human Resource Development. pp. 43

National Policy on Education. (1986). Ministry of Human Resource Development, Government of India, New Delhi.

NCERT. (1998). Curriculum Framework for Quality Teacher Education. (1998). National Council for Teacher Education. New Delhi.

NCERT. (2000). National Curriculum for School Education. Published at the Publication Department, Secretary, NCERT, New Delhi.

NPE. (1986). Towards an Enlightened and Humane Society: A Review. Government of India. (1990). New Delhi: MHRD.

NEP (2020) (1): Policy document released by Government of India Retrieved from https://www.education.gov.in/sites/upload_files/mhrd/files/NEP_Final_English.pdf on 22 Dec 2023

Report of the Education Commission. (1964-66). Education and National Development. Ministry of Education. GoI. pp. 622.

Report of the Secondary Education Commission. (1952). Ministry of Human Resource Development. GoI. New Delhi.

Report of the University Education Commission — Radhakrishnan. (1948). Ministry of Human Resource Development, Government of India (1948), New Delhi.

Right of Children to Free and Compulsory Education Act. (2009). The Gazette of India, August 27, 2009, New Delhi.

Right to Education Act — 2005. (2009). Ministry of Human Resource Development. New Delhi.

Second Five-year Plan. (1956-61). Planning Commission. Government of India. New Delhi.

Third Five-year Plan. (1961-66). Planning Commission. Government of India.

University Commission. (1892). in Mohanty, J. (2003). Teacher Education New Delhi, Deep and Deep Publications Pvt. Ltd.

Yashpal Committee Report. (1993). Learning Without Burden. MHRD. GoI. pp 26.

# 20

# Teachers Perception on Impact Flipped Teaching on Students Achievements

Ashoshika Bhadoria
Aerum Khan

## Introduction

The teaching-learning process is a two-way process where both teacher and students are involved physically and mentally. An effective teaching-learning process is one where the learners are self-propelled to achieve knowledge and apply it to solve life problems and contribute to society as well. In the 21st century, with the changing landscape, opportunities, and global ecosystem, it is imperative to equip our children with the abilities to think, make correct decisions, take responsibility for their actions, and contribute to the well-being of humanity.

As National Education Policy (NEP) 2020 recommends, "Education thus, must move towards less content, and more towards learning about how to think critically and solve problems, how to be creative and multidisciplinary, and how to innovate, adapt, and absorb new material in novel and changing fields. Pedagogy must evolve to make education more experiential, holistic, integrated, inquiry-driven, discovery-oriented, learner-centred, discussion-based, flexible, and, of course, enjoyable."

To achieve these goals, our country must develop an education system based on equity and gender parity that focuses on the holistic development of its future citizens.

## Teaching Methods

Education is a great leveller and is an important medium for achieving economic and social mobility, inclusion, and equality. The government must ensure timely interventions to create opportunities for all to enter and excel in the educational system irrespective of caste, creed, sex, gender, etc. Keeping this view in mind, the teaching-learning techniques must be designed in such a way that equips the learners with 21st-century skills of critical exploration, collaboration, divergent thinking, decision-making, etc. But the traditional teaching methods fail to meet such requirements and they only prepare students to pass the exam through rote learning. There seems to be no alignment between objectives, activities, and assessments in traditional teaching.

Teaching learning methods can be broadly classified as Traditional and Modern methods based on processes and methods employed in teaching.

## Traditional Teaching Methods

Traditional teaching methods which are also known as conventional teaching methods are still used in schools on a wider scale. In the traditional teaching methods, the classes are teacher-centred and portray the teacher as a sage on stage whose work is to preach and profess. The environment of the traditional class makes students passive listeners rather than allowing them to be active participants.

Traditional teaching methods encourage compliance, and conformity and discourage innovative thoughts and divergent thinking among the students. Rules and regulations are exercised in the classroom in such a way that it keeps students' behaviour in check. Teachers are responsible for imparting knowledge and maintaining the standards of behaviour in the school. Traditional teaching methods emphasized handholding, dictating, constant guiding and even rebuking on mistakes at times. Such guided instructions make students dependent on teachers completely and are a great hindrance to the development of decision-making in students. Student psychology becomes overly dependent on instructions and often leads to underdeveloped thinking processes.

The Education system has been evolving with time. With the advent of science and technology, methods of teaching-learning have gone digital and become more child-focused. In modern teaching methods, teachers teach every student on a different level and adjust their teaching styles to the academic needs of the students. They assume all students are different and apply different educational practices to them individually. Adjusting teaching methods according to student's academic and learning needs leads to differential learning. Unlike old education, progressive teaching methods are based on activity, questioning, explaining, demonstrating, and using collaboration techniques.

## Characteristics of Modern Teaching Methods

1) It is learner-centred
2) Task-based/Activity-based
3) Collaborative
4) Integrative

5) Interdisciplinary
6) Blended that employs both online and offline modes.

One of the very effective teaching-learning methods is Flipped teaching which is also known as Inverted learning. It hinges on the idea that students learn more effectively by using class time for small group activities and individual attention. Teachers then assign students lecture materials and presentations to be viewed at home or outside the classroom day, prioritizing active learning.

According to Kari M. Arfstrom, cofounder of the Flipped Learning Network, flipped learning is all about creating opportunities for active engagement. It is "a pedagogical approach in which direct instruction moves from the group learning space to the individual learning space, and the resulting group space is transformed into a dynamic, interactive learning environment where the educator guides students as they apply concepts and engage creatively in the subject matter."

The flipped learning approach is gaining traction every year. According to a 2014 survey from the Flipped Learning Network, 78 per cent of teachers said they had flipped a lesson, and 96 per cent of those who tried it said they would recommend it to other educators. This indicates that flipped learning inspires teachers to update traditional methods and bring new technology into their classrooms using video, screencasts, and more.

Bergmann and Sams (2012) have described the Flipped Classroom approach in a wider view. According to them, the Flipped Classroom approach is a setting where students take charge of their learning. This increases communication and contact time between students and teachers. The Flipped Classroom approach then gives priority to students where all students are engaged in their learning and the teacher becomes the "guide on the side" and not the "sage on the stage" as described by Baker (2000).

A flipped classroom does not restrict itself to sharing online videos, pictures, lectures, or tutorials rather teacher is also involved in activities both before and after the class. The introduction of the content beforehand with the help of a small lecture or by playing quizzes and games ensures equal participation of teachers and students.

Bergmann and Sams (2012) believe that if an educator implements micro-lecture for his or her class before coming to class, the in-class activities can be varied by guiding students in groups or individually, answering questions, mastering learning, or giving remediation depending on the student's progress in the topic.

The in-class time in a flipped classroom is usually noisy and disorganized as compared to traditional classes. In the Flipped Learning model, there is a switch from a teacher-centred classroom to a student-centred approach where class time is determined for exploring the content of the topic to a greater extent and creating a richer learning environment.

In the Flipped Learning model, Professional Educators are more important than the traditional method of teaching as educators must be skilled and wise enough to convert a lecture-based class into an activity-based class which requires more planning and creativity. In this way, face-to-face sessions between teachers and students can be maximized.

## Essential Components of Flipped Classroom

Moreover, lessons should include four major components to be entitled as the Flipped Classroom (Flipped Learning Network [FLN], 2014). First, educators should restructure the learning environment and time in a flexible way, considering individual and group expectations and needs. Second, instructors need to teach the contents in detail, adopting a learner-centred approach and providing rich learning opportunities and activities reflecting a particular learning culture for specific groups of students. Third, educators should regularly keep track of the difficulty level of the contents and the notes taken by the students as well as their progress, and they also apply active learning strategies that will maximize the conceptual understanding of the students. Finally, the instructor should be a professional educator who continuously monitors students in their learning processes, immediately provides feedback, and assesses students' outputs.

## Research Design

The study involved an investigative descriptive survey design. The survey has been conducted on the sample population comprising teachers at Delhi Government School. The survey involved the distribution of a Questionnaire and collection of responses from the teachers of Morning shift and Evening shifts to study their views on Flipped teaching methods. The design has been intended to collect data simultaneously from all the intended respondents of the study.

*Sample of the proposed study included the following*:

- The Questionnaire was administered to 15 Teachers who taught classes 6-12 in morning and evening shift school. Some of them used blended teaching techniques while others did not.

**Table 1:** Population and Sample of the Study

| *Components* | *Teachers* | *Total* |
|---|---|---|
| Population | 15 | 15* |
| Sample | 15 | 15* |

*Note:* * Indicates that the entire population formed the sample of the study, as the total size of the population itself is small.

1) The items of the questionnaire have been prepared by consulting the literature related to the experiences of faculty/teachers involved in blended mode teaching-learning, examinations, and evaluation at different levels. The draft questionnaire for teachers was prepared keeping in mind that the teacher-respondents comprise both kinds of teachers- those who employed Flipped teaching and others who used both.
2) The questionnaire was administered to teachers before the start of the winter break and their responses were collected when the school reopened after 15 days. This time duration was sufficient for the teachers to register their responses after thoughtful consideration.

## Analysis and Interpretation of data collected

The questionnaire comprising 10 Items was shared with 15 Teachers of Evening and Morning shift teachers who used both Traditional and Blended ways of teaching in their classes to know their opinion about the benefits of Flipped teaching over the traditional methods.

The questionnaire was shared with the teachers in November 2022, and they were given 15-20 days to answer the questions. Since these teacher respondents were from different shifts of the same school, hence the questionnaire was answered and collected within the prescribed time. The items of the questionnaire were discussed in detail with the teacher respondents and their views were collated and interpreted after a detailed analysis.

**Table 2:** Sample Questionnaire

| *Item No* | *Items* | *Alternatives* | *No of teacher-respondents* | *Percentage of respondents* |
|---|---|---|---|---|
| 1. | A) Have you heard about flipped teaching? | A) Yes | 12 | 80% |
| | | B) No | 03 | 20% |
| 2. | Do you ever share any study material with your students before the class/beforehand? | A) Yes | 10 | 86.66% |
| | | B) No | 01 | 6.66% |
| | | C) Sometimes | 04 | 26.66% |
| 3. | Which methods do you employ for the introduction of the chapter? | A) Sharing content online | 05 | 33.33% |
| | | B) Administering small test | 05 | 33.33% |
| | | C) Conduct Discussion to test students' previous knowledge | 03 | 20% |
| | | D) Playing Quiz | 02 | 13.33% |

| | | | | |
|---|---|---|---|---|
| 4. | When do you conduct assessments of students? | A) After the completion of the chapter? | 04 | 26.66% |
| | | B) Both at the beginning and completion of the chapter? | 11 | 73.33% |
| 5. | How is a flipped classroom better than a traditional one? | A) Better preparedness of students | 05 | 41.66% |
| | | B) Saves time and energy | 03 | 20% |
| | | C) Improves oratory skills of students | 01 | 6.66% |
| | | D) All of the above | 06 | 40% |
| 6. | Do you think flipped teaching helps in interdisciplinary study among subjects? | A) Yes | 12 | 80% |
| | | B) No | 03 | 20% |
| 7. | Is flipped teaching a success in traditional classroom setups? | A) Yes | 03 | 20% |
| | | B) Maybe | 05 | 33.33% |
| | | C) No | 07 | 46.66% |
| 8. | Are there any disadvantages of flipped teaching methods? | A) If Yes, then What? | 03 | 20% |
| | | 1) Code1-Requires smart boards | 01 | 6.66% |
| | | 2) Code2-teachers must have technical knowledge | 02 | 13.33% |
| | | B) No, then why? | 12 | 80% |
| | | 1) Code 1-Saves time and energy | 08 | 53.33% |
| | | 2) Code 2-Makes learning fun | 02 | 13.33% |
| | | 3) Code 3-Child-centered | 02 | 13.33% |
| 9. | Will you put extra effort into making online content videos for students? | A) Yes | 12 | 80% |
| | | B) Not sure, sometimes | 03 | 20% |
| 10. | Will you recommend flipped teaching methods to other teachers? | A) Yes | 14 | 93.33% |
| | | B) No | 01 | 6.66% |

## Findings

The findings after analysis of responses (refer Table 2 above) from teachers lead to the following conclusions:

1) The sample population consisted of 15 Regular teachers, PGTs, and TGTs teaching both shifts. Subjects of teachers — Maths, English, Science, Commerce, Political Science respectively.
2) About 12 teacher respondents (80%) have heard about flipped teaching and 03 teachers (20%) said they have not heard about it.
3) About 10 teacher respondents (86.6%) said Yes that they share study material with their students before class, 01 (6.6%) said No while 04 teachers (26.6%) said Sometimes.
4) Out of 15 teachers' respondents, 05 teachers (33.3%) said that they introduce chapters by sharing content online, another 05 teachers (33.3%) said they administer the small test, 03 teachers (20%) said they conduct discussions in class to test previous knowledge of students while 02 teachers (13.3%) said that they play quiz in the class.
5) About 04 teachers (26.6%) said they conduct assessments of students after the completion of the chapter while 11 teachers (73.3%) said they conduct assessments both at the beginning and completion of the chapter.
6) About 05 teachers (41.6%) answered that Flipped teaching is better than traditional as it leads to better preparedness of students, 03 teachers (20%) say it saves time and energy, 01 teacher (6.6%) says that it improves oratory skill of students, 06 teachers (40%) chose the option All of the above.
7) About 12 teachers (80%) say that "Flipped teaching helps in the interdisciplinary study among subjects", 03 teachers (20%) say "No". From teachers' responses, it can be inferred that Flipped teaching helps students understand interrelated concepts among different subjects and establish cause-effect relationships.
8) On the question of assessing the success of Flipped teaching methods in traditional classroom setups, 03 teachers (20%) say "Yes", 05 teachers (33.3%) say "Maybe" while 07 teachers (46.6%) say "No".
9) About 03 teachers (20%) said Yes there are some disadvantages of flipped teaching methods. The reasons are coded based on similarity and patterns.
   Code1 — 01 teacher says it requires smart boards while,
   Code 2 — 02 teachers say it requires technical know-how.
   About 12 teachers say flipped teaching does not have any disadvantages. The reasons are coded based on similarity and patterns.
   a. Code 1 — 08 teachers (53.3%) say it saves time and energy.
   b. Code 2 — 02 (13.3%) teachers say it makes learning fun.
   c. Code 3 — 02 (13.3%) teachers say it is child-centred.

10) The teachers' responses indicate that most of them believe that Flipped teaching methods have no disadvantages.
11) About 12 teachers (80%) say Yes that they will put extra effort into making online content videos for students while 03 teachers (20%) say Not sure, sometimes.
12) About 14 teachers (93.3%) say that they will recommend Flipped teaching methods to other teachers while 01 teacher (6.6%) says No.

## Conclusion

The idea of the study gained ground during the lockdown when the Department of Education directed the teachers to resort to online modes of learning to maintain continuity in teaching-learning processes. The teachers (mostly senior teachers), who lacked the technical know-how to conduct online classes, were provided training on digital tools and techniques to be used in online classes by the Department of Education.

The teacher-student ratio in government schools is far from ideal, therefore, to manage large classes in an effective way many teachers resorted to blended modes of learning and assessment. The alternative ways of teaching-learning saved the time and energy of the educators and helped in achieving learning outcomes with little effort.

Moreover, the assessments of students through Google Forms acted as a quick check on how effectively the students understood the content.

The teachers preferred making personalized videos on difficult topics rather than sharing random YouTube videos to simplify the content for students. Besides, personalized videos were designed to cater to specific difficulties faced by students hence it was preferred over the online videos available online.

The teachers (PGTs and TGTs) of the morning shift taught various subjects and used flipped teaching methods in their classes as it saved both time and energy and developed self-studying habits among the students. Moreover, flipped teaching methods facilitate interdisciplinary studies as they enable exploration, comparison, and analysis of a wide range of data available on various online and offline platforms.

It was observed that the students who were taught using blended modes of learning performed better than those who were taught through the traditional methods as they developed a passion for knowledge exploration through various online modes.

The flipped teaching methods have advantages over the traditional methods of learning and hence most of the teachers agreed to recommend this method in their fraternity.

## References

Baker, W. (2000). The Classroom Flip: Using Web Course Management Tools to Become the Guide by the Side. In 11th International Conference on College Teaching and Learning (pp. 9–17). 2. Bergmann, J., Overmyer, J., & Wilie, B

Bergmann, J., Overmyer, J., & Wilie, B. (2013). The Flipped Class: Myths vs. Reality. Retrieved March 24, 2016, from http://www.thedailyriff.com/articles/theflipped-class-conversation-689.php

Bergmann, J., & Sams, A. (2012). Flip Your Classroom: Reach Every Student in Every Class Every Day. International Society for Technology in Education.

Bergmann, J., & Sams, A. (2014). Flipped Learning. Learning & Leading with Technology, 41(7), 18–23. http://doi.org/10.

Jessica Yarbro, George Mason University Patrick McKnight, Ph.D., George Mason University Katherine McKnight, Ph.D. Pearson's Center for Educator Learning & Effectiveness FLIPPED LEARNING Kari M. Arfstrom, Ph.D. Executive Director, Flipped Learning Network

Bloom B, Englehart MD, Furst EJ, Hill WH, Krathwohl D. The classification of educational goals. In: Taxonomy of Educational Objectives Handbook I: The Cognitive Domain. New York: Longmans, 1956.

Barker, D., Quenners`tedt, M., & Annerstedt, C. (2013). Inter-student interactions and student learning in health and physical education: A post-Vygotskian analysis.

Physical Education and Sport Pedagogy, (ahead-of-Uzunboylu, H., & Karagozlu, D. (2015). Flipped classroom: A review of recent literature. 147

Bergmann, J., & Sams, A. (2012). Before You Flip, Consider This. Phi DelBergmann, J., Overmyer, J., & Wilie, B. (2015). The Flipped Class: Myths vs. Reality - THE DAILY RIFF - Be Smarter.

Butt, A. (2014). Student Views on The Use of A Flipped Classroom Approach: Evidence From Australia. Business Education & Accreditation.

Enfield, J. (2013). Looking at the Impact of the Flipped Classroom Model of Instruction on Undergraduate Multimedia Students at CSUN. Techtrends, 57(6), 14-27.

Hung, H. (2015). Flipping the classroom for English language learners to foster active learning. Computer Assisted Language Learning,

NEP 2020

# 21

# Awareness of TPACK Framework among Pre-service Teachers

Mohd Haroon Salmani
Dori Lal

## Introduction

Teaching is a complex process that includes learning, imparting knowledge, and experience, which is organized within a discipline. A teacher performs teaching purposefully and systematically. A teacher must have competency in teaching. Teachers' role in the 21st century has become wider and more complex in this changing world where knowledge is multifaceted and multidisciplinary (NEP 2020). Firstly, in brief, Mishra (1998) introduced the TPCK by combining content, pedagogy, and technology knowledge. Shulman constructed Pedagogical Content Knowledge (PCK) that includes technological knowledge with content and pedagogical knowledge. Many researchers in the U.S. & Canada have worked on any one of these three domains of the TPACK framework before 2009. Teaching Competency is the set of knowledge and skills. Mishra and Kohler (2006) presented a theoretical framework for comprehending teacher knowledge. The abbreviation for technological pedagogical content knowledge is the TPACK framework. It has three domains: content, pedagogical, and technological knowledge (Thompson & Mishra, 2007-2008). By integrating technology into teaching activities, the TPACK framework integrates instructors' existing knowledge with their pedagogical approaches. It has become imperative for teachers worldwide. It is anticipated that educators will develop into technologically oriented and responsible (Amin, 2016).

In the rapidly evolving era of education, the anticipation of technology plays an important role in efficient instruction and learning. The Technological Pedagogical Content Knowledge (TPACK) framework emerges as a crucial theoretical lens, giving a thorough grasp of the intricate interactions that exist between content, pedagogy, and technological knowledge in educational settings. Pre-service teachers stand at the forefront of this transformative phase, tasked with the responsibility of not only mastering their subject matter but also adeptly incorporating technology into their pedagogical practices.

This study investigates the level of awareness of the TPACK framework among pre-service teachers, recognizing the pivotal role it plays in shaping their preparedness for contemporary education. Mishra and Koehler (2006) introduced TPACK, which indicates the relationship between content, pedagogical, and technical knowledge. It emphasizes the dynamic and integrated nature of these knowledge domains, emphasizing that a sophisticated understanding is necessary for using technology in education.

Determining the degree to which pre-service teachers are prepared to handle the opportunities and problems posed by technology integration in the classroom requires investigating their knowledge of the framework. Advancement of technology changes every aspect of society, educators must be equipped with the knowledge and skills to harness its potential for enhancing student engagement, learning outcomes, and overall educational experiences.

This study aims to shed light on the TPACK framework of pre-service teachers in the current level of awareness. By examining their perceptions, attitudes, and understanding of the TPACK framework, identify potential areas for improvement in teacher education programs, with the ultimate goal of fostering a generation of educators who are well-prepared to meet the demands of 21st-century classrooms.

If any researchers combine these three core aspects of teaching-learning, they found seven domains (Fig. 1) which are as follows:

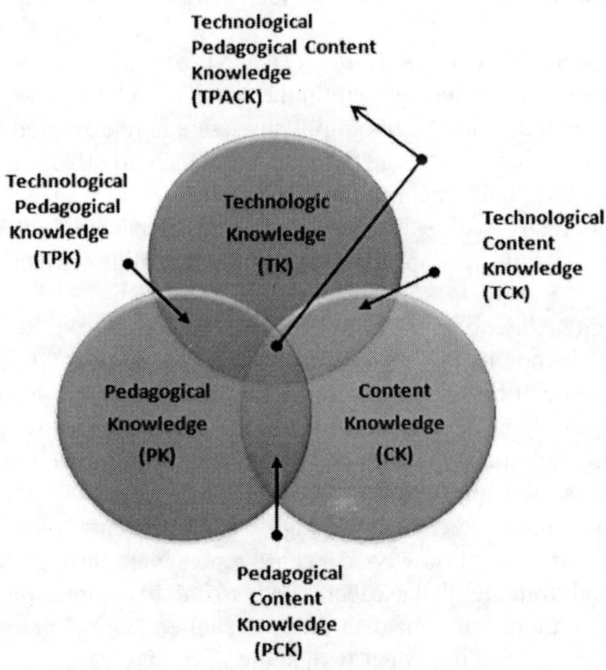


**Figure 1:** TPACK Model

1. *Content Knowledge (CK)*: The knowledge of facts, theories, concepts, ideas, principles, and vocabulary — that educators need to grasp to be productively employed is referred to as content knowledge. Teachers are expected to have a deep understanding of both the curriculum and the subject matter that they teach. Content knowledge refers to the understanding of a specific subject that will be delivered.
2. *Pedagogical Knowledge (PK):* Pedagogical knowledge refers to how to deal with and process content knowledge effectively. Teachers should be professionally competent. Professional competencies include cognitive abilities (professional knowledge, general pedagogical knowledge, content knowledge, pedagogical content knowledge) and affective-motivational characteristics (motivation, self-regulation, professional beliefs about teaching and the subject content) (Blomeke and Delaney, 2012).
3. *Technical Knowledge (TK):* Technological knowledge consists of the knowledge of different technologies, implications in educational settings, proper integration of technology, and various tools and software.
4. *Pedagogical Content Knowledge (PCK):* To assist students in creating helpful cognitive maps, connecting ideas, and clearing up misconceptions, teachers need to be well-versed in the subject matter and able to adapt to changing circumstances to teach all pupils following today's standards. According to Schulman (1986), PCK is based on how teachers relate their pedagogical knowledge to their subject matter and other disciplines in daily life.
5. *Technological Content Knowledge (TCK):* It provides a way how to use the technological knowledge within the specific content. The interface of content knowledge and technology knowledge is represented by TCK. It is a certain type of knowledge that educators have to effectively integrate technology into their teaching practices within specific academic content areas. This also involves knowing how to select and use appropriate technological tools, resources, and strategies that align with their teaching content.
6. *Technological Pedagogical Knowledge (TPK):* The term "technological pedagogical knowledge" describes the understanding of how different technologies can be employed in the classroom and the awareness that doing so may alter the way educators teach. TPK places a strong emphasis on knowing how to use technology to improve learning and instruction.
7. *TPACK:* It is the center point of three core components — technological knowledge, pedagogical knowledge, and content knowledge. An in-depth awareness of how concepts are represented through technology, pedagogical strategies that use technology to impart content constructively, information about what makes concepts challenging or simple to learn, and how technology may deal with some of the issues that students face

are all necessary for effective technology-based education. Additionally, knowledge about students' prior knowledge and epistemological theories is also necessary.

## Reviewed Studies

*Kayathri (2023)* evaluated the awareness about TPACK among prospective teachers. Data were collected from 300 prospective teachers from five colleges in Chennai. A normative research design was selected for this study. Findings revealed that prospective teachers possess a high awareness of TPACK. Based on gender, types of management of institutions, and locality, there were no significant differences found among prospective teachers. TPACK framework is a model that enables teachers to use their knowledge effectively to teach and engage students.

*Thappa & Baliya (2021)* explored the awareness of pre-service teachers between UG and PG from the Jammu division. A descriptive exploratory design has been used. Findings revealed that the least number of students were aware of this framework. The results looked at various proposals and ideas for merging technology and took part in regional and national educator training programs that use interactive pedagogy. The study's conclusions support the current perspective on policy development for teacher education.

*Tyarakanita, A., Kurtianti, E., & Fauziati E. (2020)***,** pre-service teachers are intended to improve the three TPACK domains. The objective of this study is to elucidate the domains included in the lesson design for aspiring teachers. In the TPACK domain, pre-service teachers demonstrated their plan, but still, few were left to cover. According to this study, the pre-service teachers' main source of difficulties was their need for prior teaching experience.

*Schmidt et al. (2009*) "*Technological Pedagogical Content Knowledge (TPACK)*: *The Development and Validation of an Assessment Instrument for Pre-service Teachers*." This research aimed to develop and verify a tool for evaluating the TPACK and related knowledge domains that pre-service teachers self-assess as part of the framework. A pilot study on 124 pre-service teachers was conducted. The findings of this study are the development and validation of an assessment framework to assess pre-service teachers' development is valid and reliable after applying Cronbach's alpha statistics.

*Durdu, L., & Dag, F. (2017)* investigated pre-service teachers' TPACK development and analyzed technology-based instruction and learning. Mathematics courses according to TPACK were designed and implemented. From 71 pre-service teachers data were collected through a parallel mixed method approach. The results showed that the adopted teaching procedures had a good impact on the development of pre-service teachers. Regarding Technology Knowledge, Technological Content Knowledge, Technological Pedagogical Knowledge, and TPACK in general, there were notable changes between the pre and post-course periods. Pre-service teachers ought to take more courses that require them to create computer-based lesson plans and implement those plans in small-group instruction.

*Koehler & Mishra (2009)* presented a TPACK framework for teachers. This paradigm builds on Lee Shulman's idea of pedagogical content knowledge (PCK) by adding technology knowledge. The paper addresses the ineffective structure of instruction. How do educators integrate pedagogical and content expertise with technology literacy? TPACK framework provides a complex intersection among three domains. Theoretically and practically combined, these banks of knowledge create the kinds of adaptable knowledge required to successfully incorporate technology into instruction.

## The Study

### *Significance*

Many factors make a teacher competent but in this era schools, institutions, colleges, and universities are more inclined toward technology that is usable in educational settings. The teaching competency of pre-service teachers is a variable of my research title. Pre-service teachers must be competent in Technology Knowledge, Pedagogical Knowledge, and Content Knowledge.

Examining the pre-service teachers who are familiar with TPACK are better able to recognize areas in which they may require assistance to integrate these components successfully. TPACK knowledge gaps in pre-service teachers could be found and filled using specially created training programs. This study seeks potential gaps in knowledge ensuring that future educators are equipped with the necessary skills for a technology-enhanced learning environment.

### *Objectives*

1. To study the level of awareness of the TPACK framework among B.Ed. pre-service teachers.
2. To study the level of awareness of the TPACK framework among D.El. Ed. pre-service teachers.
3. To analyze the level of awareness of the TPACK framework among pre-service teachers (B.Ed. & D.El.Ed).
4. To study the level of awareness regarding the domains of the TPACK framework among pre-service teachers.
5. To compare the awareness between B.Ed. and D.El.Ed. pre-service teachers of the TPACK framework.

### *Hypothesis*

1. There is no significant difference between B.Ed. and D.El.Ed. pre-service teachers in awareness of the TPACK framework.

### *Methodology*

This research aims to investigate how pre-service teachers use and acquire Technological Pedagogical Content Knowledge in their teaching practices or teacher preparation courses. This study is a Survey Research (Normative Research Design). A random sampling technique was used for this study.

### *Reliability: Cronbach's Alpha*

To determine the reliability of this survey with the Likert Scale, the researcher used Cronbach's alpha tests. It will indicate whether the designed test accurately measures the relevant variables or not. In this survey, the researcher selected 40 items. After calculating through SPSS 20 the reliability is derived .831 which falls within the scope of excellent internal consistency.

Intrinsic Validity coefficient was computed by taking the square root of the reliability coefficient.

**Table 1:** Details of Questionnaire

| *Tool* | *No. of Items* | *Validity* | *Reliability* |
|---|---|---|---|
| Questionnaire | 40 | .91 | .83 |

The test has a face validity. Items of the test were validated by five experts.

### *Population*

The study's participants have been chosen from the Jamia Millia Islamia., who are pursuing their B.Ed. & D.El.Ed. 2nd-year students only. By random sampling, 103 B.Ed. (53 Pre-service Teachers) & D.El.Ed. (50 Pre-service Teachers) 2nd-year students have been randomly selected.

### *Instrumental Design*

This research design is adapted from the study by Schmidt et al. (2009) on the topic of "*Technological Pedagogical Content Knowledge (TPACK): The Development and Validation of an Assessment Instrument for Pre-service Teachers*." After reviewing the literature, the researcher has modified the items. It is being used for the self-assessment of pre-service teachers. The objective of this research is quite clear while constructing items up to what extent pre-service teachers are utilizing all seven aspects of the TPACK framework in educational settings. It would measure the pre-service self-assessment. The researcher has modified the items and added some items keeping in mind the level of advancement of digitalization and pre-service teachers under the supervision of experts. The total items for this study were 40. All the items are based on a five-point Likert Scale: Strongly Disagree, Disagree, Neutral, Agree, Strongly Agree. In 40 items 05 items are negative.

**Table 2:** Number of items in each dimension

| *S. No.* | *Dimensions* | *Number of Items* |
|---|---|---|
| 1 | Technology Knowledge (TK) (1-7) | 7 |
| 2 | Content Knowledge (CK) (8-12) | 5 |
| 3 | Pedagogical Knowledge (PK) (13-18) | 6 |
| 4 | Pedagogical Content Knowledge (PCK) (19-23) | 5 |
| 5 | Technological Content Knowledge (TCK) (24-28) | 5 |
| 6 | Technological Pedagogical Knowledge (TPK) (29-33) | 5 |
| 7 | TPACK (34-40) | 7 |

This questionnaire has seven domains as shown in the above table. This instrumental design is developed for pre-service teachers (B.Ed., D.El.Ed.).

## Discussion

### *Objective 1*

To study the level of awareness of the TPACK framework among B.Ed. pre-service teachers.

**Table 3:** Level of awareness of the TPACK framework among B.Ed. pre-service teachers

| *S. No.* | *Level of Awareness* | *Score Range* | *No. of Pre-service Teachers* | *Percentage* |
|---|---|---|---|---|
| 1. | Low | 40-93 | 0 | 0 |
| 2. | Average | 94-147 | 19 | 35.84 |
| 3. | High | 148-200 | 34 | 64.16 |

19 pre-service teachers were found to have an average level of awareness and 34 were found to have in high level of awareness. There were no B.Ed. pre-service teachers who lie in low awareness.

### *Objective 2*

To study the level of awareness of the TPACK framework among D.El.Ed. pre-service teachers.

**Table 4:** Level of awareness of the TPACK framework among D.El.Ed. pre-service teachers.

| *S. No.* | *Level of Awareness* | *Score Range* | *No. of Pre-service Teachers* | *Percentage* |
|---|---|---|---|---|
| 1. | Low | 40-93 | 0 | 0 |
| 2. | Average | 94-147 | 33 | 66 |
| 3. | High | 148-200 | 17 | 34 |

33 Pre-service teachers were found in the score range of average level of awareness and 17 pre-service teachers were scored in the range of high awareness level. No pre-service teacher was found at a low awareness level.

## Objective 3

To analyze the level of awareness of the TPACK framework among pre-service teachers (B.Ed. & D.El.Ed).

**Table 5:** The level of awareness of the TPACK framework among pre-service teachers (B.Ed. & D.El.Ed)

| *S. No.* | *TPACK Awareness of Ppre-service Teachers* | *Score Range* | *No. of Pre-service Teachers* | *Percentage* |
|---|---|---|---|---|
| 1. | Low | 40-93 | Nil | 0 |
| 2. | Average | 94-147 | 51 | 49.52 |
| 3. | High | 148-200 | 52 | 50.48 |

52 Pre-service teachers were found within the average TPACK awareness category, constituting 49.52%. This indicates that many pre-service teachers have a moderate level of TPACK awareness. Notably, no pre-service teachers are in the low TPACK awareness category (score range 40-93). This might suggest that the education program or training for these teachers has effectively ensured a baseline level of TPACK awareness. Even if there are 52 or 50.48% of pre-service teachers in the high TPACK awareness category, this means that half of them have an effective understanding of how to integrate content, instructional methods, and subject knowledge.

## Objective 4

To study the level of awareness regarding the domains of the TPACK framework among pre-service teachers.

**Table 6:** Level of awareness regarding the domain of the TK among pre-service teachers.

| *1.* | *Level of Awareness* | *B.Ed.* | *D.El.Ed.* |
|---|---|---|---|
| TK | Low (7-21) | 18.86% (18) | 40% (20) |
| | High (22-35) | 81.14% (43) | 60% (30) |

Following data analysis, it was shown that pre-service B.Ed. teachers had a higher awareness of technology knowledge (81.14%) than pre-service D.El. Ed. pre-service teachers (60%). In the low score range, 18.86 and 40 per cent of pre-service teachers fall under low awareness of technological knowledge. A significant difference appears in the B.Ed. and D.El.Ed. pre-service teachers.

**Table 7:** Level of awareness regarding the domain of the CK among pre-service teachers

| *1.* | *Level of Awareness* | *B.Ed.* | *D.El.Ed.* |
|---|---|---|---|
| TK | Low (5-15) | 7.54% (4) | 18% (9) |
| | High (16-25) | 92.45% (49) | 82% (41) |

From the data analysis of the content knowledge domain, low awareness of B.Ed. & D.El.Ed. pre-service teachers are 7.54 and 18 per cent respectively. High awareness of pre-service teachers is 92.45 and 82 per cent respectively. B.Ed. pre-service teachers are more aware of content knowledge than D.El.Ed.

**Table 8:** Level of awareness regarding the domain of the TK among pre-service teachers

| *3.* | *Level of Awareness* | *B.Ed.* | *D.El.Ed.* |
|---|---|---|---|
| PK | Low (6-21) | 19.98% (9) | 30% (15) |
| | High (22-36) | 83.02% (44) | 70% (35) |

Pedagogical Knowledge of B.Ed. & D.El.Ed. pre-service teachers with high and low awareness are 83.02 & 70 and 16.98 & 30 respectively.

**Table 9:** Level of awareness regarding the domain of the PCK among pre-service teachers

| *4.* | *Level of Awareness* | *B.Ed.* | *D.El.Ed.* |
|---|---|---|---|
| PCK | Low (5-15) | 15.09% (8) | 16% (8) |
| | High (16-25) | 84.91% (45) | 84% (42) |

**Table 10:** Level of awareness regarding the domain of the TCK among pre-service teachers

| *5.* | *Level of Awareness* | *B.Ed.* | *D.El.Ed.* |
|---|---|---|---|
| TCK | Low (5-15) | 11.32% (6) | 26% (13) |
| | High (16-25) | 88.68% (47) | 74% (37) |

**Table 11:** Level of awareness regarding the domain of the TPK among pre-service teachers

| *6.* | *Level of Awareness* | *B.Ed.* | *D.El.Ed.* |
|---|---|---|---|
| TPK | Low (5-15) | 13.20% (7) | 32% (16) |
| | High (16-25) | 86.80% (46) | 68% (34) |

Similar results are coming for the domain of PCK, TCK, and TPK per cent of B.Ed. pre-service teachers are higher than D.El.Ed. pre-service teachers. The number of pre-service teachers with low awareness of the domain is greater than B.Ed. pre-service teachers.

**Table 12:** Level of awareness regarding the TPACK among pre-service teachers

| *7.* | *Level of Awareness* | *B.Ed.* | *D.El.Ed.* |
|---|---|---|---|
| TPACK | Low (7-21) | 16.98% (9) | 30% (15) |
| | High (22-35) | 83.02% (44) | 70% (35) |

Finally, the intersection of each domain is presented by the TPACK framework. In this domain B.Ed. pre-service teachers' awareness is very high as compared to D.El.Ed. pre-service teachers these are 83.02 and 70 per cent. In low awareness of the framework, they are 16.98 and 30 per cent this implies that D.El.Ed. pre-service teachers are less aware of the framework.

### *Objective 5*

To compare the awareness between B.Ed. and D.El.Ed. pre-service teachers of the TPACK framework.

Hypothesis: There is no significant difference between B.Ed. and D.El.Ed. pre-service teachers of the TPACK framework.

**Table 13:** Numerical analysis of Data

| *Major* | *N* | *Mean* | *SD* | *df* | *t-value* | *F* | *Sig.* | *Remarks* |
|---|---|---|---|---|---|---|---|---|
| B.Ed. | 53 | 149.26 | 18.90 | 101 | 2.53 | 1.143 | .288 | Significant |
| D.El.Ed. | 50 | 140.72 | 15.02 | | | | | |

The calculated value is 2.53, it does not equal or exceed the t critical value necessary for rejection of the null hypothesis at the .01 level for 101 degrees of freedom; the hypothesis is not rejected (accepted), and the conclusion is that there is no significant difference.

Had the .05 level of significance for 101 degrees of freedom been used, the t critical value necessary for rejection would be 1.98, and the null hypothesis could have been rejected, for the calculated t critical ratio of 2.63 exceeds the 1.98 t-table value. There is a significant difference between B.Ed. and D.El.Ed.

## Findings

1. The data suggests that 50% of pre-service teachers have an average and 50% have a high level of TPACK awareness. This could be an opportunity for targeted interventions or further professional development to enhance the TPACK skills, particularly for those in an average category who may benefit from additional support.
2. The absence of pre-service teachers in the low TPACK awareness category may indicate the success of the current educational program in imparting a basic level of TPACK awareness. Ongoing assessment and adjustments to the program can ensure that the quality of TPACK awareness is maintained or improved.
3. At each domain of the TPACK framework B.Ed. pre-service teachers percentage or the number of pre-service teachers are more aware than D.El.Ed. pre-service teachers. It may be due to the advancement of the curriculum as compared to D.El.Ed. and it is compulsory for B.Ed.

pre-service teachers to attend a workshop based on the understanding of the TPACK: a framework for the usage of technologies or the eligibilities differences.

4. The researcher has categorized the B.Ed. and D.El.Ed. pre-service teachers and applied t-tests, a significant difference was found between them at 0.05 level.
5. Separately observing the data of B.Ed. and D.El.Ed. pre-service teachers, the percentage of high awareness in B.Ed. is greater but the percentage of low awareness is greater in D.El.Ed.

## Conclusion

Through a thorough investigation, this research provides insights that can inform curriculum development, instructional practices, and professional development initiatives to enhance pre-service teachers' awareness and proficiency in applying the TPACK framework. The findings of this study may serve as a valuable resource for educators, teacher education institutions, and policymakers committed to ensuring that the upcoming generation of teachers is adequately equipped for the transformative power of technology in education. It permits curriculum and training method modifications to prepare upcoming teachers better to use technology in the classroom. Teachers who are proficient in TPACK are more likely to design stimulating and productive learning environments. It will contribute to the larger scholarly discussion on pedagogy a educational technology. It can provide factual information and new perspectives for more in-depth academic research in the area.

## Reference

Amin, N., & Dr. Kumar J. (2016) Redefining the role of Teachers in the Digital Era. *International Journal of Indian Psychology*. 3.10.25215/0303.101.

Ayegi D.D. & Vooget J.M. (2011) Pre-service Mathematics Teachers' Learning and Teaching of Activity-Based Lessons Supported with Spreadsheets

Blömeke, S. & Delaney, S. (2012). Assessment of teacher knowledge across countries: A review of the state of research. ZDM Mathematics Education, 44, 223-247

Durdu, L., & Dag, F. (2017). Pre-Service Teachers' TPACK Development and Conceptions through a TPACK-Based Course. *Australian Journal of Teacher Education*, 42(11). Retrieved from http://ro.ecu.edu.au/ajte/vol42/iss11/10

Kayathari K., & Ansari N.K. (2023) Awareness about TPACK among prospective teachers *International Journal of creative research thoughts (IJCRT)* ISSN: 2320-2882

Koehler, M. & Mishra, P. (2009). What is Technological Pedagogical Content Knowledge (TPACK)? Contemporary Issues in Technology and Teacher Education, 9(1), 60–70.

Koehler, M.J., & Mishra, P. (2009). What is technological pedagogical content knowledge? *Contemporary Issues in Technology and Teacher Education*, *9*(1).https://citejournal.org/volume-9/issue-1-09/general/what-is-technological-pedagogicalcontent-knowledge

Koehler, M.J., Mishra, P., & Cain, W. (2013). What is technological pedagogical content knowledge (TPACK)? Journal of Education, 193(3), 13–19. https://doi.org/10.1177/00220 57413 19300 303.

Mishra, P. (1998). Flexible learning in the periodic system with multiple representations: The design of a hypertext for learning complex concepts in chemistry. (Doctoral dissertation, University of Illinois at Urbana — Champaign). Dissertation Abstracts International, 59(11), 4057. (AAT 9912322).

Mishra, P., & Koehler, M.J. (2006). Technological pedagogical content knowledge: A framework for integrating technology in teachers' knowledge. Teachers College Record, 108(6), 1017–1054.

Murtafiah, W. & Lukitasari, M. (2016). Developing pedagogical content knowledge of mathematics pre-service teachers through microteaching lesson study. *Jurnal Pendidikan Matematika*, 13 (2), 201-218.

NEP (2020), National Policy on Education, MHRD, GOI.

OECD. (2005). Teachers Matter: Attracting, Developing, and Retaining Effective Teachers. Paris: OECD Publishing

OECD. (NA). Teachers' Pedagogical Knowledge and the Teaching Profession

Schmit D.A., Baran E., Thompson A.D., Mishra P., Koehler M.J., and Shin T.S. (2009), "*Technological Pedagogical Content Knowledge (TPACK): The Development and Validation of an Assessment Instrument for Preservice Teachers*." JRTE, 42(2), 123-149, International Society for Technology in Education

Thappa, S. R. ., & Baliya, J. N. (2021). Exploring Awareness for Technological Pedagogical and Content Knowledge (TPAC) in Pre-Service Teacher Education Programme. *MIER Journal of Educational Studies Trends and Practices*, *11*(1), 1–14. https://doi.org/10.52634/mier/2021/v11/i1/1765

Thompson, A., & Mishra, P. (2007–2008). Breaking news: TPCK becomes TPACK! *Journal of Computing in Teacher Education*, 24(2), 38–64.

Tyarakanita, A., Kurtianti, E., & Fauziati E., (2020), A case study of pre-service teachers' enabling TPACK knowledge: lesson design projects, *ELS Journal on Interdisciplinary studies in Humanities*, 3(2), 158-169, DOI: 10.34050/els-jish.v3i2.10006

Waynesville, NC USA: Society for Information Technology and Teacher Education. Retrieved November 7, 2020, from https://www.learn techl ib.org/prima ry/p/29544 /. 409 1 3 J. Comput. Educ. (2021) 8(3):395–410

Yang X. &, Kaise G. (2022) The impact of mathematics teachers' professional competence on instructional quality and students' mathematics learning outcomes. *Elsevier* https://doi.org/10.1016/j.cobeha.2022.101225

https://policytoolbox.iiep.unesco.org/glossary/content-knowledge/#:~:text=Content%20knowledge%20refers%20to%20the,curriculum%20(subject%20content%20knowledge).

https://intime.uni.edu/teachers-depth-content-knowledge

# 22

# Blended Approaches in Teachers' Continuing Professional Development

Kiran Joshi

## Introduction

The field of education is undergoing a profound transformation, driven by technological advancements, shifting student dynamics, and an expanding knowledge landscape. In this era of constant evolution, the professional development of teachers is a fundamental pillar, ensuring educators stay proficient in employing cutting-edge pedagogical practices. Recognizing the necessity for educators to adapt to the multifaceted demands of contemporary education, the integration of blended approaches in teachers' continuing professional development (CPD) has emerged as a progressive and transformative strategy.

Blended learning, marked by the seamless fusion of traditional face-to-face instruction with online and technology-mediated components, exemplifies the dynamism required by the educational landscape. As a response to the diverse learning needs of both educators and students, blended approaches not only bridge the gap between traditional and digital methodologies but also provide a flexible and personalized avenue for sustained professional growth.

## Concept of Blending Learning

Blended learning in teacher education is an instructional approach that combines traditional face-to-face teaching methods with online activities. A directive from the UGC suggests that 40% of any higher education course should be delivered online, while the NEP-2020 emphasizes the importance of recognizing both digital and in-person learning in teacher training.

The concept of blended learning in teacher education involves crafting a pedagogical framework that integrates face-to-face instruction with technology-supported teaching. This approach encompasses diverse methods such as direct and indirect instruction, collaborative teaching, and individualized computer-assisted learning tailored to the needs of future educators.

Blended learning in teacher education empowers aspiring teachers to embrace technology, utilizing tools like interactive presentations, virtual classrooms, and video lectures to enhance their teaching skills. This approach contributes to improving the overall quality of teacher education, ensuring effective assimilation of instructional content, and making the training process more efficient and productive.

The benefits of teacher professional development in a blended learning context include the development of advanced teaching skills, increased access to relevant information, increased satisfaction with the learning experience, and opportunities for both collaborative learning and preparation to teach others.

The blended face-to-face class model, adapted for teacher education, is grounded in the physical classroom. While a significant portion of classroom time is replaced by online activities, the importance of in-person interactions remains. This model optimizes class time for engaging in higher-order learning activities, fostering discussions, and facilitating collaborative projects among future educators.

## Concept of Continuous Professional Development

Continuous professional development (CPD) in the context of teacher education refers to the ongoing learning initiatives and activities undertaken by educators to enhance their knowledge, skills, competence, and expertise. It serves as a documentation of the discoveries, experiences, and applications in the field of education. Teachers engaging in continuous professional development become proactive in integrating newly acquired skills and information, contributing to more effective and dynamic teaching practices rather than adopting a reactive and passive approach. To advance their careers, educators actively participate in conferences, workshops, online training sessions, and e-learning courses tailored to the field of teacher education.

CPD ensures that educators possess the necessary information and abilities to perform their teaching responsibilities effectively within a specific educational setting. This form of training is designed to achieve three primary objectives:

1. Elevate existing teaching skills to a new level.
2. Reinforce and sharpen current teaching skills.
3. Acquire new teaching skills and knowledge.

Commonly, CPD activities for teachers are offered by various entities, including specialists in the field, commercial training providers, independent coaches, and educational institutions. Teacher education programs, universities, colleges, and schools often play a pivotal role in providing CPD opportunities internally.

Mandated by educational institutions, CPD training is crucial for teachers in schools and colleges. These institutions actively encourage and support their teaching staff in continuous professional development, recognizing it as a fundamental element in ensuring effective teaching performance and fostering a culture of lifelong learning in the field of teacher education.

## NEP 2020 and Teachers' Professional Development

The National Professional Standards for Teachers (NPST) play a crucial role in shaping the teaching career and fostering professionalism. It is instrumental in defining aspects related to teacher career management, professional development, salary advancements, performance appraisals, teaching audit reports, and more.

The responsibility for implementing the teacher training program under the National Education Policy (NEP) is entrusted to the National Council of Educational Research and Training (NCERT). Functioning as a catalyst, NCERT actively contributes to the ongoing expansion and enhancement of professional development within the teaching profession. NEP 2020 incorporates dedicated sections focusing on annual Continuous Professional Development (CPD), emphasizing the importance of continuous learning and growth in the teaching field.

According to the Justice J.S. Verma Commission (2012), over 10,000 stand-alone Teacher Education Institutions (TEIs) are primarily selling degrees without a serious commitment to teacher education. Regulatory efforts have failed to curb malpractices, and instead, hindered excellence and innovation. Urgent revitalization is needed to raise standards, restore integrity, and ensure high-quality teacher education.

1. Teacher education programs, requiring diverse inputs, must be conducted in composite multidisciplinary institutions. All multidisciplinary universities and colleges are mandated to establish education departments collaborating with various disciplines for cutting-edge research and offering B.Ed. programs. Stand-alone Teacher Education Institutions (TEIs) are required to transition to multidisciplinary institutions by 2030 to provide the mandated 4-year integrated teacher preparation program.
2. In-service professional development for college and university teachers will be enhanced and expanded through existing institutional arrangements. Technology platforms like SWAYAM/DIKSHA will be encouraged for online teacher training to efficiently deliver standardized programs to a large number of educators in a short timeframe, ensuring quality education.
3. As a professional development requirement, both heads and teachers are expected to undergo a minimum of 50 hours of Continuous Professional Development (CPD) annually. This commitment is integral to their

lifelong learning journey throughout their teaching careers, serving not only institutional goals but also aligning with their individual self-interests.

4. Teachers should receive capable mentor support to enhance and align their skills with the academic environment in which they play a pivotal role. The involvement of experienced experts with a diverse skill set is crucial in adding value to teacher training programs.
5. The National Initiative for School Heads' and Teachers' Holistic Advancement (NISHTHA) is an initiative led by NCERT aimed at capacity building for teachers and school principals. The program spans elementary to secondary levels, starting at the elementary stage to enhance school education quality and curriculum development.
6. Numerous tutorial training programs, research activities, and reporting initiatives exist in teacher training. These modules can be fully implemented or tailored to specific skills, contributing to candidates' personal and professional development.

### *Government Programmes Promoting Continuous Growth in Teachers' Professional Development*

The Pandit Madan Mohan Malaviya National Mission on Teachers and Teaching (PMMMNMTT) focuses on enhancing higher education teaching quality through professional development and innovation. The National Initiative for School Heads' and Teachers' Holistic Advancement (NISHTHA) trains 42 lakh teachers to improve skills and adopt innovative teaching methods. The Integrated Scheme on School Education (ISSE) emphasizes in-service teacher training at the elementary and secondary levels. The National Programme for the Education of Girls at Elementary Level (NPEGEL) addresses girls' educational needs through teacher support. Rashtriya Madhyamik Shiksha Abhiyan (RMSA) enhances secondary education quality with financial assistance. Various National Council of Educational Research and Training (NCERT) initiatives provide resources and training for teachers, while the Online Teacher Professional Development (OTPDI) platform offers digital resources. The Scheme for Providing Quality Education in Madrasas (SPQEM) improves Madrasa education quality through teacher training and infrastructure support. National Council for Teacher Education (NCTE) conducts programs and initiatives, setting standards for teacher training and recognizing institutions.

## Models of Blended Learning

1. *Flipped Model:*
    - Inverts traditional classroom instruction.
    - Pre-learning outside class; in-class focuses on activities.
    - Promotes personalized, interactive learning.

2. *Face-to-Face Driver Model:*
    - Resembles traditional classroom training.
    - Classroom-based with instructor guidance.
    - Provides individualized support.
3. *Rotational Model:*
    - Learners rotate through various modalities.
    - Flexibility in scheduling based on progress.
    - Accommodates diverse learning styles.
4. *Flex Model:*
    - Offers learner autonomy and control.
    - Combines online learning with in-person support.
    - Adaptive platform for self-paced learning.
5. *Enriched Virtual Model:*
    - Predominantly online with periodic face-to-face sessions.
    - Balances virtual and in-person engagement.
    - Provides individualized instruction and group opportunities.

## The effectiveness of Blended approaches in teachers' Continuing Professional Sevelopment (CPD)

1. *Flexibility and Accessibility*: Blended learning provides teachers with flexible access to learning materials, allowing them to engage with professional development activities at their own pace and convenience.
2. *Increased Interaction*: Blended learning environments create opportunities for heightened interaction among teaches. This interactive platform enhances the overall learning experience.
3. *Personalization of Learning*: The adaptive nature of blended learning accommodates diverse learning styles and preferences, enabling teachers to tailor their CPD experiences to meet individual needs.
4. *Collaborative Opportunities:* Online components of blended learning foster collaboration among educators, creating communities of practice where teachers can share insights, resources, and experiences, thereby enriching their professional development.
5. *Immediate Application of Knowledge:* Teachers can apply newly acquired knowledge and skills directly to their classrooms, translating theory into practice immediately, which enhances the relevance and impact of CPD.
6. *Cost-Effectiveness:* Blended learning can offer cost-effective alternatives to traditional CPD models, reducing expenses related to travel, venue, and materials.
7. *Mastering Digital Learning Skills:* Blended learning play a pivotal role in equipping teachers with the proficiency to use a variety of technologies. As digital learning skills become imperative for lifelong learning, blended learning acts as a catalyst for mastering these essential skills.

## Barriers to implementation of Blended approaches in Teachers Continuous Professional Development

The implementation of Blended Learning in Continuous Professional Development (CPD) for teachers faces specific barriers that are crucial to acknowledge and address. These obstacles can impact the effectiveness of CPD initiatives. Here are some key barriers:

1. *Inadequate Training for Educators:* Teachers participating in CPD programs may lack the necessary training to navigate and leverage technology effectively. Insufficient preparation can lead to discomfort with online tools and hinder the seamless integration of blended learning.
2. *Resistance to Technology Adoption:* Teachers may resist incorporating technology into their professional development, especially if they are accustomed to traditional, face-to-face methods. Overcoming this resistance requires addressing concerns and showcasing the benefits of blended learning.
3. *Limited Time for CPD:* Teachers often face time constraints due to their demanding schedules. Finding time for CPD, including both face-to-face and online components, can be challenging, affecting the depth and breadth of professional development.
4. *Lack of Customization and Personalization*: CPD programs may not cater to the diverse needs and preferences of individual educators. The one-size-fits-all approach may not effectively address the unique learning styles and professional goals of each teacher.
5. *Insufficient Resources for Blended Learning*: Inadequate funding and resources may hinder the development and implementation of blended learning initiatives in CPD. This includes funding for technology tools, training programs, and ongoing support.
6. *Evaluation and Assessment Challenges:* Determining the effectiveness of blended learning in CPD can be challenging. Developing appropriate evaluation metrics and assessing the impact of online and face-to-face components on teacher development may require careful consideration.
7. *Organizational Culture and Leadership:* The culture within educational institutions and the leadership's attitude toward technology and innovation can influence the success of blended learning. A supportive organizational culture is essential for overcoming resistance and fostering a positive learning environment.
8. *Data Security and Privacy Concerns:* Teachers may express concerns about the security and privacy of their personal and professional data when engaging in online CPD. Ensuring robust data security measures is crucial for building trust.

## Technology in supporting teachers' Continuous Professional Development

Blended learning in continuous professional development for teachers involves integrating traditional face-to-face instruction with online or digital learning experiences. Various emerging technologies contribute to the effectiveness of this approach. Some notable examples include:

1. *Learning Management Systems (LMS):* Platforms like Google Classroom, Moodle, Canvas, and Blackboard help organize and deliver course content. They serve as centralized hubs for resources, assignments, assessments, and communication, streamlining and enhancing the learning experience.
2. *Mobile Learning Apps:* Mobile apps offer flexibility and accessibility, allowing educators to access materials, participate in discussions, and complete assignments on-the-go. This promotes continuous and convenient learning, aligning with the demands of a teacher's professional schedule.
3. *Social Media Integration:* Utilizing platforms like Twitter, Facebook, or specialized educational networks enables teachers to connect, share resources, and engage in professional discussions. Social media complements formal learning experiences and contributes to a broader, more collaborative professional community.
4. *Video Conferencing and Webinars:* Platforms such as Zoom, Microsoft Teams, or Google Meet facilitate synchronous online interactions. This is particularly valuable for remote or distance learning components, enabling educators to engage in live discussions, virtual meetings, and collaborative activities.
5. *Gamification:* Incorporating gamification elements into professional development courses, such as badges, points, and leaderboards, enhances engagement and motivation. This fosters a positive and competitive atmosphere, making the learning experience interactive and enjoyable.
6. *Interactive Whiteboards and Smart Technologies:* Tools like interactive whiteboards, tablets, and smart devices support dynamic presentations and interactive activities. Educators can create engaging multimedia content, and participants can actively engage in discussions and collaborative projects, even in an online setting.
7. *Virtual and Augmented Reality (VR/AR):* VR and AR technologies offer immersive experiences for teacher training. VR simulations allow educators to practice classroom management and engage in realistic teaching scenarios in a controlled environment. AR applications provide additional context or interactive elements in real-world environments.

8. *Artificial Intelligence (AI) for Personalized Learning:* AI tools analyze individual learning styles, providing personalized feedback and recommendations. Adaptive learning platforms use AI algorithms to tailor content to the needs of each educator, allowing them to progress at their own pace.

Blended learning, enriched with these emerging technologies, creates a dynamic and engaging environment for continuous professional development, equipping educators with the skills and knowledge needed for the evolving demands of modern classrooms.

## Conclusion

The educational landscape is experiencing a profound transformation, necessitating a corresponding evolution in the professional development of teachers. The adoption of blended learning, seamlessly integrating traditional face-to-face teaching with online and technology-mediated components, emerges as a forward-thinking strategy aligned with the dynamic demands of modern education. The endorsement of blended learning by the New Education Policy 2020 and the University Grants Commission highlights its significance, prompting a reassessment of teachers' continuous professional development (CPD) to align with this visionary policy. In this context, prioritizing the CPD of teachers becomes crucial, ensuring they acquire advanced skills, access relevant information, and meet the heightened expectations of contemporary learners. Models of blended learning offer flexibility, accessibility, and personalized learning opportunities for educators. The effectiveness of blended approaches in CPD is demonstrated through increased interaction, collaborative opportunities, and the immediate application of acquired knowledge. Despite these benefits, addressing barriers to implementation, such as limited technology integration and time constraints, is essential to unlock the full potential of blended learning. Enriched by technology, blended learning emerges as a dynamic force propelling teachers toward continuous improvement and lifelong learning in the ever-evolving field of education.

## References

Bowman, J.D. (2017). Facilitating a class Twitter chat. Edutopia. Retrieved from https://www.edutopia.org/article/facilitating-class-twitter-chat

D Janse van Rensburg, E., & Oguttu, J.W. (2022). Blended teaching and learning: exploring the concept, barriers to implementation and designing of learning resources. *South African Journal of Higher Education,* 36(6), 285-298.

Deivam, M., & Devaki, N. (2015). Effectiveness of blended learning approach in teaching of educational psychology among b. ed trainees'. Int. J. Dev. Res, 5(09), 5558-5561.

Nachimuthu, K. (2020). Effectiveness of Blended Learning For Degree Students. *Journal Of Critical Reviews*, 7(15), 1440-1444.

Namyssova, G., Tussupbekova, G., Helmer, J., Malone, K., Mir, A., & Jonbekova, D. (2019). Challenges and benefits of blended learning in higher education.

NEP(20202) Final English document available at: https://www.education.gov.in/sites/upload_files/mhrd/files/NEP_Final_English_0.pdf

Saber, H., Manaf, R.A., Basman, A. T., Sanip, S., Yein, L.P., Kamalludeen, R., ... & Amin-Nordin, S. (2022). Challenges and Barriers of Blended Learning Among Asian Health Sciences Students: A Pilot Study. *Education in Medicine Journal*.

Sayed, M., & Baker, F. (2014). Blended learning barriers: An investigation, exposition and solutions. *Journal of Education and Practice*, 5(6), 81-85.

Seema & Vasantha, (2018). Effectiveness of Blended Learning in Higher Education, *Jour of Adv Research in Dynamical & Control Systems*, Vol. 10, 07-Special Issue, https://www.researchgate.net/publication/341992585_Effectiveness_of_Blended_Learning_in_Higher_Education

Wolpert-Gawron, H. (2017). Extending classroom management online. Edutopia. Retrieved from https://www.edutopia.org/article/extending-classroom-management-online

Yilmaz, Y., Durak, H.I., & Yildirim, S. (2022). Enablers and Barriers of Blended Learning in Faculty Development. Cureus, 14(3).

# 23

# Concerns regarding Teacher Education in Indian Discourse from B.Ed. to ITEP

Masooda Haseeb

## Introduction

The approach to reforming teacher education (TE) employed in India's National Education Policy (NEP) 2020 is subject to analysis by numerous researchers aiming to delve deeper into the matter and facilitate the implementation of the policy recommendations in the field. It is of utmost importance to prioritize the role of educators in fundamental educational reforms. Innovations in teacher education extend beyond mere adaptation to policy changes; they encompass the provision of educationalists with the necessary devices, wisdom, and conviction to influence the direction of Indian education growing ahead. The objectives of this approach are to comprehensively enhance the Indian teacher education system and cultivate dedicated professionals in the field. An educational institution that is duly recognized and offers courses in various subject areas, or integrates and incorporates multiple disciplines, is referred to as a "multidisciplinary institution." In order to acknowledge the Integrated Teacher Education Program, multidisciplinary universities and colleges shall collaborate to establish education departments that not only conduct cutting-edge research in various educational fields, but also administer the program. These departments shall work in conjunction with other departments or fields in the liberal arts, humanities, social sciences, commerce, or mathematics, as relevant. Teacher education plays a critical part in the transformation of students and the national school system, as teachers constitute the most pivotal element in any educational program. The National Curriculum Framework 2005 underscores the necessity for both initial and continuing teacher education to address the demands and expectations placed upon teachers. Teacher education programs have various modalities in India, the current issue is the four-year integrated teacher education program from current two-year B.Ed. program which already faces various challenges and have concerns with regards to the high pace changing skill market.

## Studies Highlighting Reforms in Teacher Education

The investigation by G. Sharma, R. Mittal (2023) explored the underlying knowledge traditions and global education policy (GEP) discourses that inform the anticipated modifications. Furthermore, it evaluated how the core reform concepts are translated into the national regulatory framework for effective enactment. In the initial part of the study, the findings reveal the knowledge traditions and influences of GEP that are inherent in the policy. The argument suggests that NEP's reform approach is a combination of fundamentally contradictory discourses. In the subsequent part, the study scrutinizes the governing rules and paradigms of the NEP-recommended TE program in order to identify its distinctive features in comparison to ongoing programs. The analysis concludes that the proposed program is essentially an altered version of India's conventional TE approaches. Additionally, the article unveils the impact of global education policy (GEP) on India's NEP 2020, which strengthens the proposed reforms in teacher education (TE).

The developing topography in the area of teacher training and development encounters the pressing need for pioneering tactics and methodologies preparing the craft in future educators so as to be well-equipped to meet unprecedent trials of the 21st century. And hence globally as well India attempts to refurbish their education system and specifically the teacher education system through edifying investigation for meeting the high bars lifted to aim.

## NEP 2020 Appeal to Multidisciplinary Approach

The new education policy 2020 envisions to the existing TEIs conducting teacher training programmes to function as multidisciplinary institutions by 2030. This approach shall enable the future teachers under training to receive access to rich resources, pedagogy as complete package in content/knowledge/technology/skills TPACK training along with experience in formulating inquiries. The NEP 2020 proposes dual-major degree programme in education which demands heedful contemplation in the field of teacher education (TE) along with training, education to be imparted in TEIs.

Maseeh M. in the year 2023 extensively explored the dynamic progression of teacher training and advancement, shedding light on the urgent need for pioneering approaches in equipping educators to tackle the distinctive challenges of the 21st century. Overall, the article highlighted the potential for modifications, innovations, and novel reforms in the field of teacher education in the near future, in accordance with the national education policy of 2020.

## Teacher Education and Areas of Concerns

### *Teacher Education and ICT/ Post Pandemic*

The utilization of information and communication technologies (ICTs) employed to facilitate student-cantered constructivist learning has recommendations by many educators. Post pandemic increase in the use of ICT in education has been with minimal changes in the instructional methods used. The focus on conveying information through traditional teaching approaches are still prevalent, albeit with the inclusion of ICT. To tackle this matter, schools have endeavoured to integrate ICT into teacher education programs that emphasize constructivist practices. (Murthy, Iyer, Warriem, 2015)

It is a significant challenge moving towards the "new normal" in the educational system, especially following the outbreak of COVID-19. It is an arduous undertaking that our contemporary societies have encountered and will persistently confront in the time to come. The various aspects of the post-COVID experience in academia, effective collaboration with the educational system, and the involvement of partakers have a key role to play for academic excellence and sustenance. Customarily non-formal education has been a means to be utilized in supporting and including individuals less privileged for being unable to attend formal education; or may have attended but still require the practical accessibility that non-formal education offers, providing them with a "second chance at education." (Egbosiuba, 2023)

### *Teacher Education and Vocational Education*

During and after India's independence, a number of education commissions recommended changes to the country's general and vocational education systems. Wood's Despatch was the first to note the necessity of instituting vocational education at the secondary school level in pre-independent India (1854). Following this, the Sargent Report (1944), the Sapru Enquiry Committee (1934), the Hunter Commission (1882), the Hartog Review Committee (1929), and the Wood-Abbot Advisory Committee (1936) all stressed the critical role that vocational education played in the nation's economic development (Dey & Srivastava, 2022).

The foundations of RPL (Recognition of Prior Learning) are equity and inclusion adopted by GoI's (Government of India) Ministry of Skill Development and Entrepreneurship (MSDE), enabling individuals without formal education to obtain a formal qualification. Nevertheless, a paucity of studies exists that would examine how different forms of informal education shape the interplay between an individual and society (Egbosiuba, 2023). This research through participatory observation with an NGO in Spain conducted by Egbosiuba contributes to the existing body of literature by investigating the nexus between identity, inclusivity, and non-formal education. It highlights the sociology of education in tandem with efficient engagement of educational system and participants for ensuring academic-based sustainability along with well-being in crisis and unprecedented times.

The Pandit Sunderlal Sharma Central Institute of Vocational Education (PSSCIVE) has formulated the curriculum for vocational education courses. As of the academic year 2019/20, these courses are being offered in 10,158 schools throughout various Indian states. The Vocational Education First State of the Education Report for India 2020, reports a significant impact of the initiative touching lives of 1,201,896 students by means of explicit emphasis on Technical and Vocational Education and Training (TVET). On the contrary, null enrolments have also been reported in certain secondary schools with approved vocational education in states such as Bihar, Uttar Pradesh, Uttarakhand, and Union Territory like Lakshadweep. This is a matter of great concern as it deprives learners in these states of the ongoing educational opportunities. In secondary schools, the failure to effectively implement vocational education, even after its approval, can lead to increased dropout rates and disinterested students in the classroom (Dey & Srivastava, 2022).

### *Teacher Education and Inclusivity*

The investigation into how variables such as attitudes and efficacy of educators' impact or correlate with real teaching practices in inclusive classrooms is limited; although substantial body of research has examined these variables of educators. In one of the scarce observational studies that establishes a link between attitudes, efficacy, and actual teaching practice, Sharma and Sokal (2016) discovered that both perceived efficacy for inclusion and positive attitudes toward inclusion exhibited a correlation with inclusive classroom practices.

The extent to which a learner with diverse abilities, e.g. disability, is genuinely included in regular classrooms is contingent upon factors encompassing the ability of school educators to fulfil the educational and social needs of all students, their willingness to include learners with diverse abilities, and the availability of the necessary support systems to facilitate the education of all students together (Sharma, 2018). School management too presumes a crucial part in the establishment of a supportive inclusive environment (Billingsley & Banks, 2019; Author, 2020). The gap lies in determination of the extent to which a learner is truly included as per recent research conducted by DeVries, Voss, and Gebhardt (2018).

### *Teacher Education and Pedagogy for Interdisciplinary Approach*

Approaches to equip students with the skills to succeed in the 21st century is another concern in TE. Home Science based curriculum in Finland Japan and Sweden through STEM/ STEAM activity integrate Science, Technology,

Engineering/English, Art, and Mathematics linking it to day-to-day activities. Some curriculums have restrained STEAM to robotics. STEAM activities conducted in groups involve use of critical thinking, problem solving, reasoning, empathy, collaboration, analysis, integrity, global citizenship, and various terms come under the umbrella of 21st century skills. This brings the student on stage (SOS) giving learner the opportunity to learn real life situation in a real-life setting.

Herro & Quigley (2017) study was to compare the attitudes and behaviours of teachers before and after a professional development session where the political, social, economic, environmental, and historical context of a nearby river was used to examine STEAM integration. Digital media was utilised by participants for data collection and analysis, project creation and sharing, peer and mentor collaboration, and communication. The findings indicate that instructors gained a better grasp of STEAM to teach material and thought the STEAM professional development was a good starting point for changing practices. They also mentioned the significance of technology that is directly incorporated into the learning process and collaboration. The study's implications provide other teacher educators with important ideas for creating effective STEAM professional development, which will impact effective STEAM instruction.

### *School/Stakeholders/Community Coherence with Teacher Education*

The methods used by study programme leaders (SPLs) in TE to attain coherence have not been extensively studied. A study used an ethnographic method to investigate how SPLs in two particular TE institutions in Norway view coherence and what approaches they employ to develop programmes that are cohesive. Short-term observations made over the course of a single school year provided support for it. The analysis identified six techniques that SPLs employ to manage ongoing obstacles within a varied and independent faculty in their ongoing efforts to promote coherence in TE programmes, adding to the sparse but emerging literature on how SPLs conceptualise coherence.

Aalde, O., & Staal Jenset, I. (2023) suggested six primary strategies for enhancing coherence in teacher education programs. Employing steering documents as a means to establish a unified vision between policy makers and ground workers. Utilizing interdisciplinary themes and developing integrated courses to foster collaboration among faculty members was suggested. Employing instructional models to exemplify coherence and establish a shared vision was a strategy recommended. Utilizing organizational structures and meetings to cultivate a collective understanding among stakeholders and teacher educators was seen essential for coherence in TE. Cultivating interpersonal relationships amongst key personnels such as subject coordinators, TE enthusiasts, faculty, partnership with school and teachers under training. Employing evaluations and assessments to monitor candidates' perceptions of coherence through their self-evaluation on preparedness from university coursework before entering school. Which may also answer the preparation of candidates in heading to be learning facilitators rather than knowledge disseminators.

## International Research-based Overview on Professional Functioning of Teacher Educators

A recurring global problem faced by teacher education (TE) is its disintegration and detachment from school practice (Hammerness et al., 2020, 2023).

The opportunities that need to be made available to candidates /student-teachers for linking their practice to national curriculum, examining their students' learning, availing opportunities to rehearse their teaching, revisiting their recordings or transcripts of class talk to exercise from experiencing their teacher educators modelling best practices. Analysing artifacts and resources from real classroom and teaching recordings or transcripts of classroom talk etc. to extend learning opportunities through discussion and replication in practice.

The Pedagogical behaviour of teacher educator to be adapted to adult learning as they train prospective teachers and not the students in school. It has not been easy to put in practice for the teacher educators to promote active, self-directed, and meaningful learning in student teachers. Explicit display of exemplary behaviour of good practices by teacher educator to support affective development and strike right balance in complex situations bridging the reality, theory, and practice for student teachers.

## Concerns regarding Shift to ITEP

As there is a pressing need to upskill, reskill teachers through in-service and pre-service pursuits to suit the dynamics of 21st Century; which the TEI's alone adhering to policies will not make the expected vast difference. The concerns left unaddressed for all these years shall snowball and add to the shift in restructuring the two-year B.Ed. program to function along multidisciplinary universities and colleges. This would not only lead to shutting down of many TEI's but also create a chaos by increase in unemployment rate (Mohtany, 2022). As majority teacher educators do not hone multidisciplinary skills themselves due to the educational set up, they first would require a faculty development crash course to deliver in the astronomical anticipated mode. As Hammerness et al. (2020, 2023) have vividly stated a global problem with teacher education (TE) is its disintegration and detachment from school practice. Inclusive education in India is still a dream, vocational education is under discussion by systematic efforts of governmental bodies; National Skill Development Corporation (NSDC), Sector Skill Council (SSCs), and the Ministry of Education (MoE) for integrating vocational education across schools in the states of India. Both the NHEQF (National Higher Education Qualification Framework) and NCFSE (National Curriculum Framework for School Education) together with the National Skills Qualification Framework (NSQF) are in capacity to impart the horizontal and vertical mobility of students in a better order. The shortcomings in the way TVET (Technical and Vocational Education and Training) provisions are being implemented are also addressed by NEP.

A structured approach in measuring the areas of concern is demanded and a problem-solving agency to help catalyse sustaining the pace of the ever-changing economy, skillset requirement in the work market, addressing needs of the learners along with coherence of stakeholders and policy makers.

## Conclusion

The method employed in India's National Education Policy (NEP) 2020 for reforming teacher education (TE) is a subject that numerous individuals aim to analyse in order to delve deeper into the matter and facilitate the implementation of the policy recommendations in the field. It is of utmost importance to prioritize the role of educators in fundamental educational reforms. Innovations in teacher education extend beyond mere adaptation to policy changes; they involve equipping educators with the necessary tools, knowledge, and mindset to shape the future of education in India. The objectives of this approach are to comprehensively enhance the Indian teacher education system and cultivate dedicated professionals in the field. An educational institution that is duly recognized and offers courses in various subject areas, or integrates and incorporates multiple disciplines, is referred to as a "multidisciplinary institution". To acknowledge the Integrated Teacher Education Program, multidisciplinary universities and colleges shall collaborate to establish education departments that not only conduct cutting-edge research in various educational fields but also administer the program. These departments shall work in conjunction with other departments or fields in the liberal arts, humanities, social sciences, commerce, or mathematics, as relevant. Teacher education has a significant impact on the transformation of students and the national school system, as teachers are the most pivotal element in any educational program. The National Curriculum Framework 2005 emphasized the need for both initial and continuing teacher education to address the demands and expectations placed upon teachers. This would also help in upskilling and reskilling teacher's in-service and pre-service professional development to adapt to the changing needs of the learners through inclusivity, ICT enabling, vocationalization, coherence with community, stakeholders etc. There is dearth of research in measuring teaching practices in various areas due to absence of valid instruments.

## References

Aalde, O., & Jenset, I.S. (2023). Study Program Leaders' Perceptions of Coherence and Strategies for Creating Coherent Teacher Education Programs. *Journal of Teacher Education.* https://doi.org/10.1177/00224871231208683

Billingsley, B., & Banks, A. (2018). Leadership for inclusive schools 1995–2015. In *Handbook of leadership and administration for special education* (pp. 196-220). Routledge

Dey, S., & Srivastava, A. (2022). Reimagining Technical and Vocational Education and Training in India: Prospects and Challenges. *University News*, *60*(20), 3-8 Egbosiuba, C. A. (2023). Sociology of Education: Wellbeing And Resilience in the Times of Crisis. In *Shaping self-society nexus through non-formal education. Participatory observation with Ecocompartimos NGO in Spain.*

Floden, R.E., Carter Andrews, D.J., Jones, N.D., Marciano, J., & Richmond, G. (2021). Toward new visions of teacher education: Addressing the challenges of program coherence. *Journal of Teacher Education*, *72*(1), 7-10.

Govinda, R. (2020). NEP 2020: A Critical Examination. *Social Change*, *50*(4), 603–607. https://doi.org/10.1177/0049085720958804

Hammerness, K. (2013). Examining features of teacher education in Norway. *Scandinavian Journal of Educational Research*, *57*(4), 400–419. https://doi.org/10.1080/00313831.2012.656285

Hammerness, K., Klette, K., Jenset, I. S., & Canrinus, E. T. (2020). Opportunities to study, practice, and rehearse teaching in teacher preparation: An international perspective. *Teachers College Record*, *122*(11), 1-46.

Herro, D., & Quigley, C. (2017). Exploring teachers' perceptions of STEAM teaching through professional development: implications for teacher educators. *Professional Development in Education*, *43*(3), 416-438.

Lüke, T., & Grosche, M. (2018). What do I think about inclusive education? It depends on who is asking. Experimental evidence for a social desirability bias in attitudes towards inclusion. *International Journal of Inclusive Education*, *22*(1), 38-53.

Maseeh, M. (2023). Innovations and New Reforms In Teacher Education: Adapting To Vision of National Education Policy (NEP) 2020. Vidya — *A Journal of Gujarat University*, 2(2), 262– 266. https://doi.org/10.47413/vidya.v2i2.269

Mohanty, S.B. (2022). Should the Nation Go Ahead with Introduction of 4 Year Integrated Teacher Education Programme (ITEP) In a Multidisciplinary Environment? *University News*, *60*(09), 28.

Rakshit S., & Mete J. (2022, July 30). Effects' of National Education Policy 2020 on Future of Teacher Education of India. *International Journal of Recent Research in Social Sciences and Humanities* (IJRRSS, Vol. 9, (3), 80–85. https://doi.org/10.5281/zenodo.6943845

Sahana Murthy, Sridhar Iyer, & Jayakrishnan Warriem. (2015). ET4ET: A Large-Scale Faculty Professional Development Program on Effective Integration of Educational Technology. *Journal of Educational Technology & Society*, 18(3), 16–28.

Sharma, G., Mittal, R., & Zayan. (2023). Teacher Education in India's National Education Policy 2020: Knowledge Traditions, Global Discourses and National Regulations. *Contemporary Education Dialogue*, *20*(2), 256-282.

Sharma, U., & Sokal, L. (2016). Can Teachers' Self-Reported Efficacy, Concerns, and Attitudes Toward Inclusion Scores Predict Their Actual Inclusive Classroom Practices? *Australasian Journal of Special Education*, 40(1), 21–38. doi:10.1017/jse.2015.14

Shirley, L.M., & Kohler, J. (2012). Clothing and Textiles: Reinforcing STEM Education through Family and Consumer Sciences Curriculum. *Journal of Family & Consumer Sciences Education*, 30(2).

UNESCO, D. (2021). Preliminary report on the first draft of the recommendation on the ethics of artificial intelligence. *https://unesdoc.unesco.org/ark:/48223/pf0000374266.*

Verma, S., & Mitima Sachdeva, D.A.B. (2023). Exploring The Level of Awareness for Integrated Teacher Education Programme in Young Pupil Teachers. *Journal of Pharmaceutical Negative Results*, 130-134.

# 24

# Science Educators' Perspectives and Practices on Integrating Art into Science Teaching

Shaista Tanveer

## Introduction

In the pursuit of sustainable economic growth amidst pressing global challenges such as unemployment and public debt, nations have increasingly turned to innovation as a catalyst for change. This tactic is in absolute accord with the fundamental principles of the National Education Policy 2020 (NEP 2020), which promotes a comprehensive and interdisciplinary educational framework. NEP 2020's progressive initiatives include the integration of arts into science education, referred to as STEAM (Science, Technology, Engineering, Arts, and Mathematics). By incorporating artistic creativity into the study of science, STEAM education not only fosters a deeper understanding of scientific concepts but also cultivates the very spirit of innovation that nations seek. This unprecedented educational technique stimulates scholars to think imaginatively, solve intricate puzzles, and investigate uncharted territories where science and art blend. By fostering such interdisciplinary skills from an early age, NEP 2020's STEAM education aligns seamlessly with the overarching goal of equipping the workforce with the innovative mindset required to address economic challenges, drive sustainable growth, and propel nations towards a more prosperous and resilient future.

John Dewey, however, took it a step further by contending that science, in and of itself, constituted a type of art. In his work Experience and Nature (1929), he posited that the evolution of the arts could be traced through the annals of human experience. Dewey regarded the conscious pursuit of fine art as exceptionally valuable due to the fact that the genesis of the artistic process could be attributed to the spontaneous reactions of individuals to situations that did not necessarily involve art. From this vantage point, art represents a form of experimentation that facilitates the emergence of novel modes of perception, thereby expanding and enhancing human vision. (Graham, 2016). In the publication entitled "Research and Resources in Arts Education", Soren discovered a research study which reported that 90% of parents indicated that their children were more motivated to learn when art was incorporated into their academic curriculum (p. 141) (Stough, 2018).

Teachers who are contemplating incorporating the arts into their STEM education programs may experience apprehension and discomfort owing to their lack of knowledge or experience with the arts (Chandler, 2018). When considering the integration of arts into STEM education programs, educators often experience uncertainty and unease. This apprehension is frequently rooted in their limited familiarity or experience with artistic disciplines. STEM teachers typically possess expertise in Science, Technology, Engineering, and Mathematics, where artistic elements may be perceived as unfamiliar territory. The seamless blending of creative and technical subjects can appear daunting, as it challenges their comfort zone and necessitates a departure from their accustomed teaching methods. The potential lack of confidence in their understanding of artistic concepts may lead to a fear of inadequacy in conveying accurate information to students. Additionally, the practical aspects of orchestrating art-infused activities within an already demanding curriculum can amplify concerns.

The effective incorporation of the arts by educators leads to a noticeable enhancement of students' cognitive abilities, class participation, and attendance, as evidenced by various studies (Cattrell, 1998; Horowitz, 2005; Rooney, 2004; Stevenson & Deasy, 2005). By integrating the arts into the learning and teaching process, a stimulating and enriched environment is created where instructors can serve as facilitators of purposeful and captivating activities and lessons that promote academic success among students. (Williams, Attitudinal Factors of Teachers regarding Arts Integration, 2013). The integration of the arts within the educational process fosters a dynamic and enriched academic environment. This methodology enables educators to act as proficient facilitators, guiding pupils through exercises that seamlessly merge creativity and scholarship. By incorporating artistic elements into various subjects, instructors encourage intellectual curiosity and active engagement. Through visual arts, performance, and creative assignments, students grasp complex concepts from diverse perspectives, promoting analytical thinking and problem-solving. The classroom becomes an interactive forum that inspires pupils to explore, question, and express their thoughts, thereby improving comprehension. This comprehensive approach nurtures emotional intelligence, cultural appreciation, and effective communication skills. As students engage profoundly and meaningfully, academic achievement is no longer limited to rote memorization but instead emerges as a natural consequence of an immersive, captivating, and interconnected learning experience, consolidating the interdependent relationship between the arts and scholastic success.

## NEP 2020 and Art Integrated Science Education

The NEP 2020 presents an innovative outlook on education that places a priority on vital skills such as critical thinking, problem-solving, creativity, interdisciplinary studies, innovation, adaptability, and the absorption of new information in emerging fields (ibid., p.3), rather than just emphasizing content. As per the stated statement, the NEP 2020 has a vision that a change in teaching methods is crucial to enable a more hands-on, all-encompassing, interwoven, inquiry-based, discovery-focused, student-centred, discussion-oriented, adaptable, and pleasurable learning experience. Moreover, it is necessary that the academic program consists of not just science and mathematics but also fundamental arts, crafts, humanities, games, sports and physical fitness, languages, literature, culture, and values to encourage the growth of all aspects and abilities of pupils. This shall facilitate education to become more comprehensive, valuable, and satisfying for the student (ibid., p.3). To fully comprehend the potential of science instruction integrated with art, as envisioned by NEP 2020, it is crucial to examine the perceptions and experiences of educators regarding the amalgamation of art into science education. This strategy is noteworthy for its support of art-infused education, an atypical pedagogical approach that combines artistic and academic disciplines to encourage analytical thinking, innovation, and hands-on learning. In the context of science education, this entails incorporating artistic elements into scientific concepts, which fosters a better understanding and engagement among students. Investigating how teachers view the integration of art into science instruction, the difficulties they confront, and the methods they employ may offer valuable insights into effective implementation. By understanding teachers' perspectives, we can identify supportive measures, tailor professional development, and facilitate a smoother integration process. The investigation of instructors' perspectives and experiences towards the incorporation of art into science instruction is indispensable to fully realizing the potential of art-integrated science teaching, as envisioned by NEP 2020.

The draft NEP of 2019 has incorporated Art-Integrated Learning as a significant pedagogical initiative in response to the insights and considerations presented. This step was formalized through Circular No. Acad-12/2019, which was issued on March 8, 2019. The CBSE subsequently provided further support and guidance to its affiliated schools by issuing comprehensive Guidelines on Art-integrated Learning through Circular No. Acad-22/2019 on April 18, 2019. These directions were created to provide educators and school administrators with a structure for effectively executing Art-integrated Learning as a powerful instructional tool, with the main goal of promoting experiential and pleasurable learning experiences in the classroom environment and, as a result, cultivating an overall atmosphere of delightful learning within the entire school. Moreover, recognizing the importance of a comprehensive approach, the CBSE published a manual titled "Art Integration — Towards Experiential Learning" in 2019. This manual serves as a practical resource, aiding educators in the seamless incorporation of art across different subjects and grade levels, thereby facilitating the implementation of Art-integrated Learning in a coherent and effective manner.

## The Study

### Research Questions

1. What perception do the sample science teachers have about art integration in science teaching?
2. What kind of experiences have the sample science teachers had with their efforts at integrating art in science teaching?

### Objectives

1. To study the Perception of sample science teachers about the idea of art-integrated science teaching.
2. To study the ways in which the sample science teachers have attempted to integrate art in their science teaching.

### Methodology

The present study is descriptive and quantitative in nature. The population of the study will comprise In-service Teachers of schools of Aligarh, Prayag Raj, New Delhi. For this standardized tool, Likert type Five scales is used developed by the researcher itself to measure perception and experiences of science teachers. The tool was validated by the experts and the reliability was done by Cronbach's Alpha of social networking usage which was approximately (=0.789).

**Table 1:** Perception of Science Teachers

| *S. No.* | *Item* | *SDA* | *DA* | *N* | *A* | *SA* |
|---|---|---|---|---|---|---|
| 1 | Art integration enhances students' understanding of scientific concepts | 0<br>0 | 2<br>3.3 | 16<br>26.7 | 15<br>25.0 | 27<br>45.0 |
| 2 | Art integration improves students' critical thinking skills in science. | 0<br>0 | 7<br>11.7 | 11<br>18.3 | 21<br>35.0 | 21<br>35.0 |
| 3 | Art-integrated science teaching improves students' critical thinking skills. | 2<br>3.3 | 8<br>13.3 | 1<br>1.7 | 19<br>31.7 | 30<br>50.0 |
| 4 | Art integration allows for interdisciplinary connections between science and other subjects. | 4<br>6.7 | 9<br>15 | 11<br>18.3 | 15<br>25 | 21<br>35 |
| 5 | Art integration facilitates students' ability to communicate scientific ideas effectively. | 3<br>5.0 | 8<br>13.3 | 17<br>28.3 | 11<br>18.3 | 21<br>35.0 |
| 6 | Art-integrated science teaching promotes students' appreciation for aesthetics and artistic expression. | 7<br>11.7 | 3<br>5 | 8<br>13.3 | 12<br>20 | 30<br>50 |

| *S. No.* | *Item* | *SDA* | *DA* | *N* | *A* | *SA* |
|---|---|---|---|---|---|---|
| 7 | Art integration does not foster students' curiosity and inquiry in science. | 20<br>33.3 | 14<br>23.3 | 14<br>23.3 | 7<br>11.7 | 5<br>8.3 |
| 8 | Art-integrated science teaching encourages students to think outside the box. | 5<br>8.3 | 4<br>6.7 | 15<br>25 | 14<br>23.3 | 22<br>36.7 |
| 9 | Art integration promotes inclusivity but does not cater to diverse learning styles in science education. | 25<br>41.7 | 11<br>18.3 | 9<br>15.0 | 14<br>23.3 | 1<br>1.7 |
| 10 | Using art integration, the solar system can be taught by memorizing the names of planets in order. | 5<br>8.3 | 6<br>10.0 | 15<br>25.0 | 13<br>21.7 | 21<br>35.0 |

The examiner performed a comprehensive investigation to examine the viewpoints of science educators on the incorporation of art into science instruction. This analysis consisted of 10 items that encompassed both positive and negative aspects. It is worth noting that a significant portion of respondents, namely 45%, strongly agreed that the inclusion of art improves students' comprehension of scientific concepts, with an additional 25% in agreement. With regards to critical thinking skills, 35% agreed and an equal percentage of 35% strongly agreed that the integration of art has a positive impact. A majority of 50% strongly agreed that teaching science with art improves students' critical thinking abilities, a sentiment supported by 31.7% in agreement. While 35% strongly agreed that art integration fosters connections between different disciplines, opinions on the benefits and challenges varied across subsequent items, providing a nuanced comprehension of teachers' perspectives. For instance, 50% strongly agreed that art integration fosters students' appreciation for aesthetics, whereas 33.3% strongly disagreed that it fails to cultivate curiosity and inquiry in the field of science. In terms of inclusivity, 41.7% strongly disagreed that art integration caters to diverse learning styles, and 35% strongly agreed that the solar system can be taught through memorization by incorporating art. These findings collectively offer valuable glimpses into the attitudes of educators, showcasing both support and skepticism towards the integration of art in science education.

**Table 2:** Ways of Integrating Art in Science Teaching

| *S.No.* | *Item* | *SDA* | *DA* | *N* | *A* | *SA* |
|---|---|---|---|---|---|---|
| 11 | I frequently integrate art into my science lessons. | 4<br>6.7 | 5<br>8.3 | 16<br>26.7 | 16<br>26.7 | 19<br>31.7 |
| 12 | I have incorporated visual arts (e.g., drawings, paintings) in my science lessons. | 1<br>1.7 | 2<br>3.3 | 9<br>15.0 | 21<br>35.0 | 27<br>45.0 |
| 13 | I have not used sculptures or three-dimensional art forms to explore scientific concepts. | 22<br>36.7 | 12<br>20.0 | 6<br>10.0 | 13<br>21.7 | 7<br>11.7 |

| S.No. | Item | SDA | DA | N | A | SA |
|---|---|---|---|---|---|---|
| 14 | I have integrated digital media to enhance science instruction. | 8<br>13.3 | 13<br>21.7 | 6<br>10.0 | 12<br>20.0 | 21<br>35.0 |
| 15 | I have not incorporated music or sound as a means to teach science concepts. | 24<br>40.0 | 15<br>25.0 | 9<br>15.0 | 6<br>10.0 | 6<br>10.0 |
| 16 | I have used dance or movement to reinforce scientific principles. | 6<br>10.0 | 11<br>18.3 | 5<br>8.3 | 12<br>20.0 | 26<br>43.3 |
| 17 | I have encouraged students to create science related poetry or creative writing pieces. | 2<br>3.3 | 7<br>11.7 | 5<br>8.3 | 18<br>30 | 28<br>46.7 |
| 18 | I have not used drama or role-play to explore scientific scenarios. | 20<br>33.3 | 12<br>20.0 | 16<br>26.7 | 9<br>15.0 | 3<br>5.0 |
| 19 | I have not collaborated with art teachers to create interdisciplinary projects combining science and art | 29<br>48.3 | 16<br>26.7 | 6<br>10 | 8<br>13.3 | 1<br>1.7 |
| 20 | Art integration promote a holistic and well-rounded approach to science education. | 2<br>3.3 | 2<br>3.3 | 9<br>15 | 13<br>21.7 | 34<br>56.7 |

The investigation examined the practices of science teachers in incorporating art into their lessons, revealing a wide range of involvement with different forms of art. It is worth noting that 31.7% of participants strongly agreed that they frequently include art in their science lessons, and an additional 26.7% agreed. A significant majority (45%) strongly agreed that they have integrated visual arts, such as drawings and paintings, into their science instruction, while 35% agreed. In relation to three-dimensional art forms, 36.7% strongly disagreed that they have not utilized sculptures, with varying responses in smaller proportions. Positive feedback was received for the integration of digital media, with 35% strongly agreeing and 20% agreeing. However, when it comes to incorporating music or sound, a majority (40%) strongly disagreed. Dance or movement received support, with 43.3% strongly agreeing. The encouragement of science-related poetry or creative writing was affirmed by 46.7%, while 33.3% strongly disagreed about the use of drama or role-play. Collaboration with art teachers for interdisciplinary projects was reportedly low, with 48.3% strongly disagreeing. Nonetheless, a substantial majority (56.7%) strongly agreed that the integration of art promotes a holistic and well-rounded approach to science education, supported by 21.7% in agreement. These percentages provide a comprehensive perspective on the diverse levels of involvement and attitudes among science educators in incorporating various forms of art into their instructional practices.

**Table 3:** Overall Perception Towards Art Integrated Science Teaching

| | *Dimension Wise Description of Perception* | | | | |
|---|---|---|---|---|---|
| | *Statistic* | *Statistic* | *Tool* | *Statistic* | *Statistic* |
| Perception | 35 | 15-50 | 10-50 | 38.30 | 9.883 |
| Ways | 33 | 17-50 | 10-50 | 38.12 | 9.499 |

### *Perceptions of sample science teachers about the idea of art-integrated science teaching*

In the perception dimension, a range of values from 15 to 50 is observed, with a recorded minimum and maximum of 15 and 50, respectively. The tool used reports values ranging from 10 to 50 in this dimension. The average value in the perception dimension is calculated to be 38.30. The data exhibits a standard deviation of 9.883, highlighting a notable dispersion of values around the mean, indicating variability in perceptions. Overall, the perception dimension reflects a diverse range of values, with the recorded statistics providing insights into the distribution and central tendency of the observed data.

### *Ways in which the sample science teachers have attempted to integrate art in their science teaching Ways Dimension*

In the analyzed dimension, a range of values spanning 33 is observed, with recorded minimum and maximum values of 17 and 50, respectively. The tool reports values ranging from 10 to 50 in this dimension, and the calculated average is 38.12, with a standard deviation of 9.499 indicating dispersion around the mean. Shifting focus to the integration of art in science lessons, the data suggests a substantial number of respondents have embraced various forms of art, such as visual arts, digital media, dance/movement, creative writing, and interdisciplinary collaborations. This integration reflects a holistic and well-rounded approach to science education, fostering a multidimensional understanding of the subject while nurturing creativity and interdisciplinary connections among educators.

### *Effects of Art Integration in Science Education*

The data strongly suggests that integrating art into science education holds several positive effects on students' comprehension of scientific concepts. Notably, this integration is linked to the enhancement of critical thinking skills, fostering interdisciplinary connections between art and science, facilitating effective communication of ideas, nurturing an appreciation for aesthetics, and encouraging students to think creatively beyond conventional boundaries. In summary, the findings highlight the multifaceted advantages of incorporating art into science education, providing a comprehensive approach that goes beyond traditional methods and promotes a holistic development of students' cognitive and creative abilities.

## Conclusion

In conclusion, the study delves into the perceptions and practices of science teachers regarding the integration of art into science education. The findings reveal a dynamic landscape where a significant number of teachers express positive attitudes and engage in diverse forms of art integration in their science lessons. Notably, the majority of respondents acknowledge the benefits of art integration, including enhanced understanding of scientific concepts, improved critical thinking skills, and the promotion of interdisciplinary connections between science and art. The data also highlights areas where art integration has been less common, such as using sculptures, music, drama, and collaborative projects with art teachers. The study underscores the alignment of art-integrated science teaching with contemporary educational policies, such as the National Education Policy 2020 (NEP 2020), which emphasizes the importance of multidisciplinary education and the integration of arts into STEM education. The NEP 2020's vision of cultivating well-rounded individuals capable of navigating a rapidly changing world resonates with the positive perceptions of teachers towards art integration as a method of inquiry. Despite the overall positive attitudes, the study also reveals challenges and areas where teachers may feel less confident or encounter difficulties in incorporating art into science education. These challenges include the infrequent use of certain art forms, potential discomfort, or apprehension among teachers with limited artistic experience, and concerns about the practical aspects of integrating art within a demanding curriculum. In essence, the findings suggest that art integration has the potential to create a dynamic and inclusive learning environment that fosters creativity, critical thinking, and a profound appreciation for science. To further support and enhance art-integrated science teaching, targeted professional development, collaborative efforts, and ongoing support mechanisms may be beneficial. Overall, the study contributes valuable insights into the complex interplay between art and science education, providing a foundation for future research and initiatives in this evolving educational landscape.

## References

Alberts, R. (2010). Discovering science through art-based activities. *Learning Disabilities: A Multidisciplinary Journal, 16*(2), 79-80.

Ambrož, M., Pernaa, J., Haatainen, O., & Aksela, M. (2023). Promoting STEM Education of Future Chemistry Teachers with an Engineering Approach Involving Single-Board Computers. *Applied Sciences, 13(5), 3278.*

Busch, K.C., Kudumu, M., & Park, S. (2023). Pedagogical content knowledge for informal science educators: Development of the ISE-PCK framework. *Research in Science Education, 53(2), 253-274.*

Crawford, L. (2004). *Lively learning: using the arts to teach the K-8 curriculum.* Greenfield,

Dhanapal, S., Kanapathy, R., & Mastan, J. (2014, December). A study to understand the role of visual arts in the teaching and learning of science. In *Asia-Pacific Forum on Science Learning and Teaching*, *15*(2), 1-25). The Education University of Hong Kong, Department of Science and Environmental Studies

Dickinson, D. (2002). Learning through the arts. *New Horizons for Learning*, *3*(3), 1-14.

Downloaded from: http://www.edweek.org/tm/articles/2014/11/18/ctq-jolly-stem-vssteam.

Edwards, L.C. (2010). *The creative arts: a process approach for teachers and children.* Boston:

Flores, M. (2005). The alchemy of art. *The Science Teacher*, *72*(1), 48.

Gadsden, V. (2008). The arts and education: Knowledge generation, pedagogy, and the

Graham, N.J., & Brouillette, L. (2016). Using arts integration to make science learning memorable in the upper elementary grades: A quasi-experimental study. *Journal for Learning through the Arts*, *12*(1).

Graham, N.J., & Brouillette, L. (2016). Using Arts Integration to Make Science Learning Memorable in the Upper Elementary Grades: A Quasi-Experimental Study. *Journal for Learning through the Arts, 12(1), n1.*

Green, K., Trundle, K.C., & Shaheen, M. (2018). Integrating the arts into science teaching and learning: A literature review. *Journal for Learning through the Arts*, *14(1).*

Green, K., Trundle, K.C., & Shaheen, M. (2018). Integrating the arts into science teaching and learning: A literature review. *Journal for Learning through the Arts*, *14(1).*

Haatainen, O., Turkka, J., & Aksela, M. (2021). Science teachers' perceptions and self-efficacy beliefs related to integrated science education. *Education Sciences, 11(6), 272*

http://www.huffingtonpost.com/vidcode/the-importance-of-steam-l_b_9488898.html

http://www.p21.org/news-events/p21blog/1900-why-steam-is-great-policy-for-the-future-of-education-

https://cbseacademic.nic.in/web_material/Circulars/2019/art_integration.pdf

Hunkins, M.M. (2019). The art of science; an exploration of art integration in a science classroom. *Middle Grades Review, 5(2), 6.*

Jolly, A. (2014, November 18). STEM vs. STEAM: Do the arts belong? *Education Week.*

Klopp, T, Rule, A., Schneider, J. & Boody, R. (2014). Computer technology integrated

Li, Y.; Wang, K.; Xiao, Y.; Froyd, J.E. Research and trends in STEM education: A systematic review of journal publications. Int. J.

Lovejoy, V., Prain, V., Musk, C., Poljak, L., Roberts, D., & Stewart, I. (2021). What teachers learn from science and arts integration in a design-based learning framework: An Australian study. *Issues in Educational Research, 31*(1), 149-165.

Margot, K.C.; Kettler, T. Teachers' perception of STEM integration and education: A systematic literature review. Int. J. Stem Educ.

Mathematics, Sciences, and Technology. Can. J. Sci. Math. Technol. Educ. **2014**, 14, 346–358.

Moghal, S., Asma, S., & Usman, Z. (2020). Transforming the teaching of early years Science and Mathematics through the integration of STEAM education: What in-service teachers think?. *International Journal of Elementary Education, 19(3), 2336-2344.*

National Science Teachers Association — NSTA. (2004, October). NSTA Position Statement.

Pool, J., Dittrich, C., & Pool, K. (2011). Arts Integration in Teacher Preparation: Teaching the Teachers. *Journal for Learning through the Arts, 7(1), n1.*

Samson, G. From Writing to Doing: The Challenges of Implementing Integration (and Interdisciplinarity) in the Teaching of school. *Interchange, 46*(4), 323-343.

Soule, H. (2016, March 31). Why STEAM is Great Policy for the Future of Education. Retrieved

Stem Educ. 2020, 7, 11.

Stephens, P., & Walkup, N. (2000). *Bridging the curriculum through art: interdisciplinary*

Stough, A. (2018). Art in the science classroom: art integration.

Suganda, E., Latifah, S., Sari, P.M., Rahmayanti, H., Ichsan, I.Z., & Rahman, M.M. (2021, February). STEAM and Environment on students' creative-thinking skills: A meta-analysis study. In *Journal of Physics: Conference Series* (Vol. 1796, No. 1, p. 012101). IOP Publishing.

Turkka, J., Haatainen, O., & Aksela, M. (2017). Integrating art into science education: a survey of science teachers' practices. *International Journal of Science Education, 39(10), 1403-1419.*

V. (2016, March 17). The Importance of STEAM Learning. Retrieved March 30, 2017, from

Williams, S. E. (2013). *Attitudinal factors of teachers regarding arts integration.* The University of Southern Mississippi.

# 25

# Elevating Teachers' Creative Problem Solving Skills

## *Capacity-Building Strategies*

Priyanka Singh

### Introduction

*"The destiny of India is now being shaped in her classrooms."*

— *Kothari Commission (1964-1966)*

*Do the teachers possess the abilities and capacities to meet the demands of the learners?* The teacher is the agent who can bring the changes in the system through education. All domains of learning can be developed through the education system. If one wants to turn educational policies and reforms into realities, capacity building of the teachers becomes imperative. Teachers are the pillars of the education system. Systematic reforms and policies require that teachers and students must change their ways (Ibara, n.d.-a). Teachers must adapt according to the new demands of the education system. Before the COVID-19 pandemic education society was unaware of the online education system, but the necessity of learning created a way through it and education became accessible. Teachers were trained in the use of technology (Duraku & Hoxha, n.d.).

Capacity is the ability to understand or do something; the building is an increase in the amount of something over time. Our teachers must be trained to keep pace with the changes in educational needs. Capacity building is a lifelong process, not a once-in-a-lifetime one (Bhowmik & Bhattacharya, n.d.). The *NEP 2020* aims to make "India a global Knowledge Superpower". The policy also aims to ensure that all students at all levels of school education are taught by passionate, motivated highly qualified, professionally trained, and well-equipped teachers (*National Education Policy 2020 Ministry of Human Resource Development Government of India*, n.d.).

*SDG 17.16* specifically calls for strengthening the global partnership for sustainable development, complemented by multi-stakeholder partnerships that mobilize and share knowledge, expertise, technology, and financial resources. SDG 17, "Partnerships for the Goals," envisions collaborative efforts to achieve sustainable development (Rica et al., n.d.). Developing teachers' capacity is essential to achieving this goal. Building teachers' ability to incorporate creative teaching strategies, sustainability principles, and critical problem-solving abilities into their lessons is crucial because they are the ones forming the future of education. Equipping teachers with the requisite abilities produces a new generation of socially and ecologically conscious citizens and empowers them to serve as change agents in their local communities (Moneva et al., 2020).

Teacher education is divided into two phases: (a) In-service teacher Education, and (b) Pre-service teacher education. These two are the important phases of making a teacher a professional teacher. Teachers selected for positions in schools go through a rigorous pre-service teacher training program designed by teaching colleges and universities. Pre-service training does not, however, constitute the ultimate level of teacher preparation. This first training imparts the fundamental knowledge and abilities required for a teaching vocation, acting as an early stage of self-preparation. Qualified teachers need to translate and actualize theories, knowledge, and abilities into useful instructional applications. Teachers are faced with this challenge: if post-teacher training self-development and learning processes halt, they may get stuck and become ineffective and inefficient.

Jacques Delors, a French economist, and politician submitted a report to UNESCO considering the four main pillars of education. Delors in his report entitled *Learning: The Treasure Within* to UNESCO reviews the four main pillars of education: (a) learning to Know, (b) Learning to Do, (c) Learning to live Together, (d) learning to Be. These four pillars consider the growth of education, Lifelong learning, and cultivation of key competencies. The Report supports the idea that teacher education is a continuous process of capacity building rather than a static process limited to initial training. To effectively navigate the intricacies of contemporary education and promote the holistic development of their students, teachers — who are lifelong learners — need ongoing support and opportunities for professional development (Delors, 2013).

Creative Problem Solving (CPS) is a tested and proven method that supports and helps generate novel and unique ideas. Irrespective of the problem or challenge to solve CPS can be applied to any field domain or practice whether it be health, engineering, design, Technology, Education, etc. CPS is the widely known process for formulating new and interesting ideas for solving a problem. Running a problem through this process ensures creativity and a concrete and applicable plan of action that is ready to implement to get one step ahead of solving the challenge.

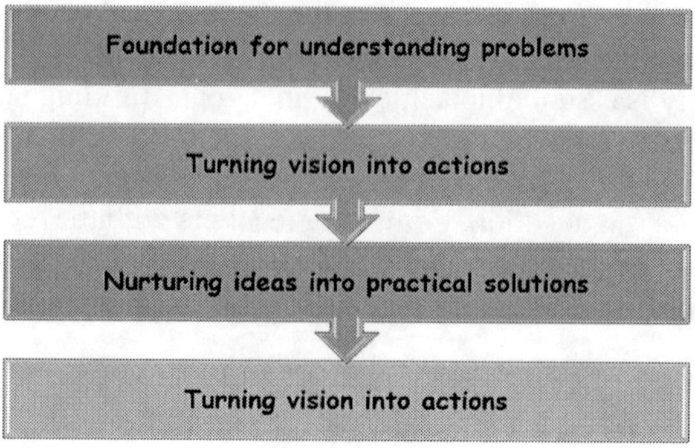


**Figure 1:** Steps for Creative Problem-solving

A key component of creative thinking abilities is the ability to learn from a variety of sources, and this has significant implications for teacher capacity for creative problem-solving. In education, creative thinking is the complex process of applying different cognitive processes to address problems, items, settings, or behaviours in new ways. Creative problem-solving abilities go beyond conventional academic knowledge for teachers (Davarpanah, 2020; Ho et al., 2023). Developing thoughtful and creative ideas is necessary to overcome challenges and efficiently solve issues. Using creative thinking to modify their teaching strategies in response to changing difficulties, the specific requirements of each student, and the learning environment, successful teachers navigate the full range of cognitive processes. Teachers with creative problem-solving abilities can investigate novel ideas and solutions, going beyond traditional methods and creating a dynamic and captivating learning environment (Veysel, 2015). In the end, using creative problem-solving techniques improves teachers' efficacy by enabling them to handle the intricacies of education with resourcefulness and flexibility. In his 1926 book *The Art of Thought*, social psychologist Graham Wallas put out one of the first formal models of the creative process (Wallas, n.d.). Four essential phases make up Wallas' model, which throws light on how people go about the process of coming up with original ideas:

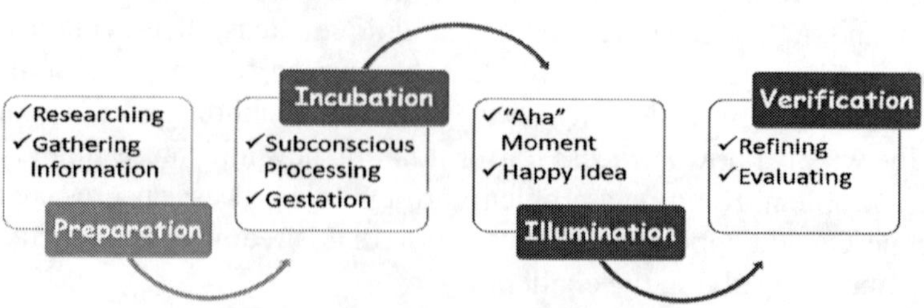


**Figure 2:** Graham Wallas's Model of Creative Process

To equip teachers with the skills to face the constantly changing demands of the classroom, it is essential to combine innovative problem-solving techniques with capacity building. Within the larger context of capacity building, creative problem-solving acts as a dynamic catalyst, providing instructors with the tools they need to manage difficulties efficiently (Burns & Gottschalk, 2020). In addition to gaining necessary information and abilities, teachers who participate in capacity-building programs develop a mindset that views creative problem-solving as the cornerstone of their pedagogical approach (Hajiyakhchali, 2013).

Teachers who have undergone capacity building are better able to manage their classrooms, master their subjects, and integrate technology. Incorporating creative problem-solving into capacity-building initiatives simultaneously motivates teachers to investigate cutting-edge pedagogies, adjust to a range of learning preferences, and design customized responses to new problems (Eragamreddy, n.d.). The combination of these methods guarantees that teachers not only have the required knowledge and abilities but also the attitude to use them in innovative ways. This integration fosters a culture of continual development and flexibility in the ever-changing educational landscape by creating a transformative educational environment where teachers are not only well-prepared but also agile and imaginative.

## Literature Review

The study conducted by Eze & Nwagu, 2021; Orgovanyi-Gajdos concludes that Teachers demonstrate a strong potential for innovation, a learner-centred approach, and educational resources. No matter their gender, location, degree, or length of teaching experience, teachers of all subjects have a high need for capacity-building regarding learner-centred practices and instructional materials.

Related to the subject Erdem, n.d. — a concluded the view held by English teachers employed in public schools — that solving creative problems advances their professional development. This research suggests that innovative approaches to problem-solving by teachers of English may pave the way for new opportunities in their career growth. English teachers in public schools believe they solve problems efficiently through creative problem-solving when they come across them in the course of their work. This data suggests that English teachers are capable of applying creative problem-solving to address their work-related issues. Researchers concluded that Enhancing student's problem-solving abilities is one of the main objectives of mathematics education. The work of Eragamreddy, n.d.; Erdem, n.d.-b; Kareem et al., 2011 states that the research has led to the requirement that we provide training in mathematics education for aspiring maths teachers and CPS scenarios. The program met its objectives and helped aspiring maths teachers gain the pedagogical subject understanding needed to help students improve their CPS skills. They highlighted the significant effects of the creative program on behaviour, attitude, and performance as well as on divergent thinking and problem-solving.

Few researchers related to the educational requirements of 21st century learners conclude that it is important to foster creativity and invention in 21st century learners to adequately equip them for the future. North, n.d.; Steiner & Belski, 2011 conclude that Promoting innovation and creativity in learners requires problem-solving abilities. Various methods, including project-based learning, experiential learning, cross-disciplinary cooperation, and technology integration, can be employed by teachers to foster problem-solving abilities. Teachers are considered to be a powerful support for learners. Amran et al., 2019; Md, 2019; Moneva et al., 2020 results focussed that when encouraging innovation and creativity in learners, teachers must also take into account other elements like motivation, curiosity, and enthusiasm. Prioritizing problem-solving abilities allows teachers to assist students in acquiring the competencies required to thrive in the twenty-first century. Teachers are considered as the powerful support for the learners.

The analysis of the data gathered by Nehal & Khan, 2014 in Aligarh District of secondary school English teachers showcased the areas in which teachers demand training on capacity building: (a) Adapting materials for instruction, (b) Enhancing communication within the classroom, (c) exploring innovative language teaching approaches, (d) delivering content effectively through structured lesson plans, (e) creating engaging and accessible teaching materials, (f) fostering enthusiasm for reading and writing amongst students, (g) facilitating proficiency in speaking, reading, writing and comprehension of English texts, (h) boosting students motivation to engage with texts, (i) incorporating technology and multimedia to enhance the effectiveness of texts, (j) developing skills in team building and networking.

Research conducted by Hamza & Griffith, 2006; J. Pentang et al., 2022; J.T. Pentang & Bautista, n.d. have indicated that the focus on improving teachers' capacities comes as a critical strategy for closing the gap inside the educational system and trying to accomplish learning goals. This strategy includes setting standards for professional development to improve teacher abilities. Dewan, n.d.; Ibara, n.d.-b; Osuji, 2014 analysed that Keeping up with international standards for sustainable education involves governing and facilitating access to professional development, providing modern curriculum and instructional materials, encouraging outside partnerships for technical and scientific support, and making sure that schools have 21st century infrastructure. It also involves allocating resources within the educational sector in an effective and organized manner.

## The Study

### *Need and Importance*

Though many studies have reflected that capacity building, creativity, problem-solving strategies, creative problem-solving skills, etc. are beneficial for students, studies related to teacher educators that focussed on the above-mentioned skills are still negligible. Many types of research talked about the capacity building of students according to 21st century skills, but teacher educators are not talked about enough. *How one can make the students ready for 21st century global learning without the teacher being the consumer of it?* It is equally important for teachers to enhance their teaching skills by the need of the present dynamic educational system. Different studies that focussed on teaching creative thinking skills to students (Eragamreddy, 2013), The benefit of fact-finding and problem-solving skills among students (hooijidonk, 2020), views of teachers related to critical problem-solving scenarios (Kanedmir, 2009), 21st century problem skills amongst students (Rahman, 2020), capacity building of teachers helps urban children (Kyalo, 2019). Various studies show that students should be prepared for the 21st century, but they cannot without the help of teachers and their professional growth. So, the need to experiment with the teachers and educators related to their capacity building and its influence on creative problem skills was preferred by the researcher.

The key component of every educational reform is the teacher, who plays a pivotal role in the learning process. Hence, many initiatives have been taken by the government to work on the teacher's training and capabilities in the form of different workshops, Faculty Development Programs, MOUs, Seminars, Conferences, etc. Many initiatives were launched by governing bodies like NCERT, NIEPA, SCERT, NCTE, CIET, etc. Different BRCs and CRCs acted as the additional layers for the professional development of teachers. Recently, considering the vision of NEP 2020 dynamic integration between the Human Resource Development Centres (HRDC), under the University Grants Commission (UGC), and the Pandit Madan Mohan Malviya Mission (PMMMM) was done. This integration envisioned the capacity-building programs for the Educators of higher education. 111 Malviya Mission Centres were initiated for this program. Various themes were identified under this mission: (a) Indian Knowledge System (IKS), (b) Research and Development, (c) Student Diversity and Inclusive Education, (d) Information and Communication Technology, etc. The study is highly relevant and significant in the context of education. This study focuses on the critical role that teachers' capacity-building techniques play in addressing the urgent need for ongoing improvement in the education sector. By concentrating on improving teachers' creative problem-solving abilities, the study recognizes that teachers have a crucial influence on how students learn. This research is significant because it has the potential to equip teachers with the skills and knowledge needed to successfully negotiate the challenges of contemporary learning environments.

### *Sample*

Twenty teacher educators from Amity University, Noida were considered as the sample for the study. The experiment was conducted in the confronted situation in one section only. The sampling strategy employed was purposive. The targets were student teachers who were getting ready for their internships in different schools. Data was gathered via the distribution of questionnaires both offline and online. Questionnaires were sent out based on participant availability.

### *Method and Procedure*

Before this experiment, at first, the test was conducted to analyse the level of creative problem-solving skills of teacher educators. Results of the conducted test indicated that the creative problem-solving skills among teacher educators were not sufficient to handle the impromptu problems in the classrooms. For this research, one group pre-test and post-test design was chosen as the method. This method includes one group shot study wherein a selected group was given intervention. The data was collected in two phases — one before the intervention and one after the intervention from the same group. Researchers have used different capacity-building strategies to check the effect it has on the creative problem-solving skills of teacher educators. A 12 day (2 Periods each day) was selected as the intervention period. To study the effect, a self-made questionnaire was applied to the teacher educators as a post and pre-test. Likert scale was formed consisting of 28 items. The researchers have prepared the experiment by analysing the need for an hour for the teacher educators about the NEP 2020.

### *Variables*

1. *Independent Variable*

As the effect of different capacity-building strategies was to be studied, capacity-building strategies were used as an independent variable.

2. *Dependent Variable*

Creative problem-solving skills were analysed and evaluated. The effect of different strategies was calculated on creative problem-solving skills. Hence, creative problem-solving skills are the dependent variable.

3. *Intervening Variable*

Certain variables which may affect the experiment are considered as 'intervening variables'. They are controlled during the experiment.

1. Gender: The sample chosen was restricted to female teacher educators.
2. Department: The samples selected were from the one department of Amity University, Noida.
3. Year: The year level was kept constant by selecting B. Ed. students (5th Semester) for the experiment.
4. Teacher: Due to the limited days of the experiment, sessions were taken by both researchers. A total of two periods were organized for a day. Daily one period was taken by each researcher.
5. Intelligence level: Samples were chosen according to the result of 02 years (04 semesters) of the B.Ed. course. The pool of the average students was selected out of which 20 teacher educators were randomly selected.
6. Duration of Intervention: Teacher educators went through an intervention phase for 12 days. No one was absent during the experiment phase.

### *Tools Used*

An achievement test was implemented by the researchers to gather data and assess the treatment's efficacy on the research samples. The researchers created a non-standardized tool under the guidance of the research supervisor since there was no readily available standardized tool that could be used for the study. The researchers constructed the Likert scale related to the creative problem-solving skills of teacher educators.

## Analysis

1. *Need of the experiment:* Before the experiment, an analysis was done by the researcher to study the need for an experiment. The capacity building of teacher educators has been studied based on creative problem-solving skills. Different dimensions were studied under it. The major outcomes indicated that 54.02% of teacher educators were aware of continuing professional development, 56.06% of teacher educators were aware of research and evidence-based practices, 59.83% of teacher educators were aware of leadership development, 63.04% of teacher educators were competent enough to use technology integration in the classroom, etc. the results showed that teacher educators were not fully aware of the strategies to be used in the classroom. Hence, these results indicated that these teacher educators should be trained enough for classroom teaching so that they can become competent enough to deal with different problems in classroom settings.
2. *Context Analysis:* Through the test, the researchers have identified that the teacher educators are not competent enough to solve the problems in the classroom very effectively and creatively. So, an experiment was

planned to see the effect of different capacity-building strategies on the creative problem-solving skills of teachers.

3. *Learner Characteristics:* There was little demographic information gathered by the researchers before the experiment. Their age lies between 20-25 years approximately. They all were voluntarily interested in taking part in the intervention process. It was identified that the teacher suggested experimenting before their internship. So, that they can use the learned strategies during the internship in classroom learning. Almost all the teacher educators were comfortable with the medium used and time selected for the intervention process.
4. *Analysis of the Content Ddelivered:* The researcher identified the different strategies that focussed on the creative problem-solving skills of teacher educators (Okute, n.d.; Van Hentenryck & Coffrin, 2014). The different outlined strategies were discussed with the experts. With the help of the gathered opinions, a few were shortlisted for the experiment to be done. The selected strategies are as follows: (a) Assessment and evaluation, (b) Classroom management, (c) Continuing professional development, (d) peer review and collaboration, (e) leadership development, and (f) Research-based practices.
5. *Design of Experiment:* The experiment was conducted based on the results gathered. A 12-day intervention was given to the teacher educators that was based on the training of their creative problem-solving skills. The researchers have the following objectives in mind during the intervention process:
    1. To identify the specific areas where teacher educators may face challenges in applying creative problem-solving skills.
    2. To evaluate the alignment between the different capacity-building strategies and the creative problem-solving skills.
    3. To identify the different catalyst factors that improve creative problem-solving skills.
    4. To explore teacher educators' experiences during and after participating in capacity-building interventions.
6. *Instructional Strategies:*
    1. The discussion method was used by the researchers for the content delivery.
    2. Various multimedia tools were also used wherever needed by the researchers.
    3. Exchange of ideas amongst the teacher educators and researchers before and after each intervention period was done.
    4. A cooperative and unified learning environment was created through Google Docs and forms for writing their opinions.

5. Activities were assigned to teacher educators after each session, to check the effectiveness of it.

7. *Assessment Strategies:* Assessment was done after the session through activities and discussion. The researchers assessed the activities done by the teacher educators and the problems were exchanged in the classroom amongst the teacher educators and they were later solved in the next session along with the brainstorming techniques.
8. *Experimentation:* The experiment was conducted as per the scheduled sessions. During the experimental phase, the researchers delivered the content according to the prepared plans and suggested instructional methods.
9. *Evaluation:* As the researcher used a one-shot pre-post-test strategy evaluation was done in two phases to compare the before and after effects of the intervention. For evaluation, the self-made Likert scale was used. Before the experiment, the pre-test was done and after the experiment, the post-test was done.
10. *Statistical Analysis:* The data obtained from the conducted test was analyzed with the help of a "t-test" to test the significant difference between the mean score of the test of teacher educators before and after experimentation.

### Result Analysis

**Table 1:** Summary of t-test Difference among the Pre and Post-test Scores

| *Intervention* | *N* | *Mean* | *SD* | *Df* | *"t" Value* | *Significance* |
|---|---|---|---|---|---|---|
| Pre-test | 20 | 20.72 | 7.1 | 38 | 8.8 | Significant* |
| Post-test | 20 | 38.32 | 5.4 | | | |

*Significant at both levels (0.05 &0.01)

The computed value of "t" is 8.8, and the computed critical value of "t" with 38 degrees of freedom at both levels (0.05 and 0.01) is significant. The critical values are 2.02 (0.05) and 2.71 (0.01) with 38 degrees of freedom. The high computed value shows that the difference between the means is significant at both levels. Hence, the researchers failed to accept the null hypothesis at both levels so it can be stated that there is a significant difference between the means. This shows that the intervention given to teacher educators has proven that improvement has been given to them. This concluded that the exposure of teacher educators to creative problem-solving skills has improved due to the given intervention. Therefore, it confirmed that capacity-building strategies have a positive and increasing effect on the creative problem-solving skills of teacher educators.

## Discussion

In the given intervention, the findings have indicated the proportional relationship between the capacity-building strategies and creative problem-solving skills of teacher educators. This result complements the earlier globally conducted experiments on the teacher educators related to their professional development. (*Capacity Building in the Sciences: Imperatives for Teacher Education in Nigeria*, n.d.; Murray & Vanassche, 2019; Warner, n.d.) also concluded that professional development opportunities for teacher educators foster collaboration, capacity building, and self-reflection. Capacity-building strategies have a seamless connection between effective teaching and learning.

(Egbo, 2011; Klentschy, 2005) reached similar conclusions that teacher professional development programs must focus on improvement in the practitioner knowledge and their collaborative approach. The focus should be on capacity building which allows the profession to improve the teaching-learning process.

## Educational Implications

1. Schools and Educational institutions can design and implement targeted professional development programs.
2. The curriculum for teacher preparation can be modified to better meet the needs of the educational environment by emphasizing innovative problem-solving techniques.
3. Strategies for enhancing capacity foster high-quality instruction in the classroom. The research can help curriculum designers about the importance of incorporating activities and content that promote creative problem-solving skills.
4. Educational institutions can reconsider their assessment strategies to ensure that they adequately measure and encourage creative problem-solving skills.
5. Research can encourage teachers to adopt diverse teaching methods that foster creativity and problem-solving skills.
6. This research stresses the need for continuous professional growth of teachers by participating in development programs.

## Recommendations

Capacity building for teachers is the new trend. After the NEP 2020, a lot more focus is given to the professional development of teachers. There is a great need to conduct further research on the concept to understand it in a better way and with different perspectives. The present study has the delimitation related to creative problem-solving skills only. It can further be studied with the creativity of teachers, technology integration, pedagogical knowledge, subject expert guidance, content knowledge, etc. Therefore, the present study opens new windows for conducting further research. Based on the present research, researchers recommend that similar studies be conducted in different departments/institutions, districts, and states of India. This study was delimited to the particular institution. Studies can be conducted to find the effect of capacity-building strategies on different dimensions. Other studies may differ in the selection of the intelligence level of the teacher educators, gender, and study year of the teacher educators. Moreover, this experiment was conducted on the pupil teachers, further, the experiment can be conducted on the in-service teachers in the form of workshops and seminars. Above mentioned suggestions provide an idea to fellow researchers that more studies should be conducted on teachers so that more work can be done on their professional development. The input given to the teachers will resemble the output received from the students.

## Conclusion

Teacher educators who were given intervention have marked the change in their problem-solving skills. These capacity-building strategies concluded to be a productive way of enhancing the professional development of teacher educators. It is evident that investing in strategies that enhance teachers' abilities to solve problems creatively is critical as we traverse the ever-evolving world of education. The implications of these findings reach beyond the confines of individual classrooms, necessitating a more comprehensive commitment to incorporate them into curriculum creation, educational policies, and continuous teacher training. This research highlights educators' critical role in developing the next generation of creative thinkers and problem solvers, acting as a catalyst for good change. Though many teacher education institutions lack many factors of professional development, we should encourage teacher educators to continuously work on themselves be it content or pedagogy as they are the torchbearers of the next generation. They should be accepting of the dynamic approach to learning and the needs of 21st century learners. They should update themselves with the new approach of teaching and learning and institutions, governments and various other stakeholders should accompany them. They should inculcate a positive attitude towards the change.

## References

Amran, M.S., Kutty, F.M., & Surat, S. (2019). Creative Problem-Solving (CPS) Skills among University Students. *Creative Education, 10*(12), 3049–3058. https://doi.org/10.4236/ce.2019.1012229

Bhowmik, S., & Bhattacharya, D. (n.d.). *Implementation of NEP 2020 and Capacity Building of Teachers at Foundation Stage: An Analysis with Empirical Evidence*. https://www.researchgate.net/publication/359878728

Burns, T., & Gottschalk, F. (Eds.). (2020). *Education in the Digital Age*. OECD. https://doi.org/10.1787/1209166a-en

*Capacity Building In The Sciences: Imperatives For Teacher Education In Nigeria*. (n.d.).

Davarpanah, S.H. (2020). *The Role of Teacher Leadership in Improving Students' Problem-Solving Skills by Considering the Mediating Role of Creative Thinking*. https://doi.org/10.22108/nea.2020.110155.1208

Delors, J. (2013). The treasure within Learning to know, learning to do, learning to live together, and learning to be. What is the value of that treasure 15 years after its publication? *International Review of Education, 59*(3), 319–330. https://doi.org/10.1007/s11159-013-9350-8

Dewan, H.K. (n.d.). *In-Service Capacity Building of Teachers*. https://www.researchgate.net/publication/328389922

Duraku, Z.H., & Hoxha, L. (n.d.). *Chapter 1 The impact of COVID-19 on Education and the well-being of teachers, parents, and students: Challenges related to remote (online) learning and opportunities for advancing the quality of education*. https://orcid.org/0000-0002-8268-3962

Egbo, B. (2011). Teacher Capacity Building and Effective Teaching and Learning: A Seamless Connection. In *Mediterranean Journal of Social Sciences* (Vol. 2, Issue 5).

Eragamreddy, N. (n.d.). Teaching Creative Thinking Skills IJ-ELTS: International Journal of English Language & Translation Studies Vol: 1, Issue: 2 Teaching Creative Thinking Skills Eragamreddy, Nagamurali. *International Journal of English Language & Translation Studies, 1*(2). www.eltsjournal.orgwww.eltsjournal.org

Erdem, A.R. (n.d.-a). *The views of English teachers on creative problem solving and its influence*. https://www.researchgate.net/publication/357434435

Eze, E., & Nwagu, E.K.N. (2021). Dimensions of Teachers' Expressed Capacity Building Needs on Climate Change Education Strategies. *Interdisciplinary Journal of Environmental and Science Education, 17*(4), e2251. https://doi.org/10.21601/ijese/10982

Hajiyakhchali, A. (2013). The Effects of Creative Problem-solving Process Training on Academic Well-being of Shahid Chamran University Students. *Procedia - Social and Behavioural Sciences, 84*, 549–552. https://doi.org/10.1016/j.sbspro.2013.06.602

Hamza, M.K., & Griffith, K.G. (2006). Fostering Problem Solving & Creative Thinking in the Classroom: Cultivating a Creative Mind! In *National Forum Of Applied Educational Research Journal-Electronic* (Vol. 19).

Ho, V. T., Tran, V. D., Nguyen, V. De, Phan, T. N., & Cao, T. H. (2023). The process of developing professional capacity for teachers. *Journal of Education and E-Learning Research, 10*(3), 489–501. https://doi.org/10.20448/jeelr.v10i3.4892

Ibara, E. (n.d.-a). *Teachers' capacity building skills and learning outcome*. https://www.researchgate.net/publication/357596207

Kareem, O.A., Bing, K.W., Jusoff, K., Awang, M., & Yunus, J.N. (2011). Teacher capacity building in teaching and learning: The changing role of school leadership. *Academic Leadership, 9*(1). https://doi.org/10.58809/bkay8655

Klentschy, M.P. (2005). *Designing Professional Development Opportunities for Teachers that Foster Collaboration, Capacity Building, and Reflective Practice* (Vol. 14, Issue 1).

Md, M.R. (2019). 21st Century Skill "Problem Solving": Defining the Concept. *Asian Journal of Interdisciplinary Research*, 64–74. https://doi.org/10.34256/ajir1917

Moneva, J.C., Miralles, R.G., & Rosell, J.Z. (2020). Problem-Solving Attitude and Critical Thinking Ability Of Students. *International Journal of Research —Granthaalayah*, *8*(1), 138–149. https://doi.org/10.29121/granthaalayah.v8.i1.2020.261

Murray, J., & Vanassche, E. (2019). Research capacity building in and on teacher education: developing practice and learning. *Nordisk Tidsskrift for Utdanning Og Praksis*, *13*(2), 114–129. https://doi.org/10.23865/up.v13.1975

*National Education Policy 2020 Ministry of Human Resource Development Government of India*. (n.d.).

Nehal, R., & Khan, I. (2014). *Assessing Training Needs and Capacity Building of Secondary School English Teachers at Aligarh*. https://www.researchgate.net/publication/343862079

North, D. (n.d.). Building Capacity For Developing Statistical Literacy In A Developing Country: Lessons Learned From An Intervention *4*. http://iase-web.org/Publications.php?p=SERJ

Okute, A.L. (n.d.). *Capacity building needs of vocational education teachers for qualitative teaching and development of attitude in technical colleges in Nigeria*. https://www.researchgate.net/publication/333419394

Orgovanyi-Gajdos, J. (n.d.-a). *Teachers' professional development on problem-solving: theory and practice for teachers and teacher educators*.

Osuji, C.U. (2014). Capacity Building of Teachers as a Strategy in Bridging the Gap in The Nigerian Educational System. In *African Education Indices* (Vol. 7, Issue 1).

Pentang, J., Bacangallo, L., Buella, R., Rentasan, K., & Bautista, R. (2022). Creative Thinking And Problem-Solving: Can Preservice Teachers Think Creatively and Solve Statistics Problems? *Studies In Technology and Education*, *1*(1), 13–27. https://doi.org/10.55687/ste.v1i1.23

Pentang, J.T., & Bautista, R. (n.d.). *Creative Thinking and Problem-Solving: Can Preservice Teachers Think Creatively and Solve Statistics Problems?* https://www.azalpub.com/index.php/ste

Rica, C., Vincent, S., & Grenadines, the. (n.d.). *4 7*.

Steiner, T., & Belski, I. (2011). *Do We Succeed in Developing Problem-solving Skills — The Engineering Students' Perspective*. https://www.researchgate.net/publication/224060659

Van Hentenryck, P., & Coffrin, C. (2014). Teaching creative problem-solving in a MOOC. *SIGCSE 2014 — Proceedings of the 45th ACM Technical Symposium on Computer Science Education*, 677–682. https://doi.org/10.1145/2538862.2538913

Veysel, T. (2015). The problem-solving skills of the teachers in various branches. *Educational Research and Reviews*, *10*(5), 641–647. https://doi.org/10.5897/err2014.2059

Wallas, G. (n.d.). *Celebrating Giants and Trailblazers in Creativity Research and related Fields Graham Wallas: A Giant Standing On Giants Fredricka Reisman*.

Warner, R. (n.d.). *Education Policy Reform in the UAE: Building Teacher Capacity*. http://mbrsg.ae/home/publications.aspx

# 26

# Reflections on Alternate Education in Contemporary Context

## *A Study of Digantar Institute, Jaipur*

Shama Norien Major
Ayushi Sinha
Anwesha Rai

### Introduction

Education aims at producing engaged, productive, and contributing citizens for building an equitable, inclusive, and plural society as envisaged by our Constitution (NEP 2020, p. 5). Education should focus more on learning how to solve problems by thinking critically than just on its content. Quality education must be provided to all children, irrespective of their place of residence, as envisaged by NEP 2020, with specific reference to historically disadvantaged, marginalised, and underrepresented groups. The Sustainable Development Goals of 2015 also seek to "ensure inclusive and equitable quality education and promote lifelong learning opportunities for all" by 2030 (NEP 2020, p. 3). Since education acts as a vehicle for achieving both social and economic mobility and inclusion in society, therefore, initiatives must be taken to ensure that all the children from such groups are provided opportunities to not only enter but excel in the education system. (NEP 2020, p. 4). One of these initiatives, which NEP 2020 emphasises, is to place various centres in cooperation with civil society to promote alternative education to ensure that children of marginalised groups will get education (NEP 2020, p. 27).

During the late colonial period, the concept of alternative education emerged. There were many zealous nationalists who promoted the revival of local languages, literature, and culture (Vittachi, S., & Raghavan, N., 2007, p. 25). Alternative education provides children with opportunities to explore their paths of interest, which are suitable according to the children's pace and context. It extensively helps children learn through innovative approaches and methods. This paper explores the innovative features of the alternative school situated in Digantar, Jaipur, in light of the National Education Policy 2020.

## The Study

### *Context of the study*

This is a case study on Digantar, an institute that provides alternate education in Jaipur, Rajasthan. The field visit is part of the 3rd year practicum: Classroom management and material development of the Bachelors of Elementary Education, a four-year teacher education programme at Delhi University.

### *Philosophical and Historical Context of Digantar*

It began in 1978, and registered in 1989. A family in Jaipur started it all by looking for a school that provided an ideal education, which brought them to David Horsburgh in Neel Bagh. Digantar was founded with the intention of offering "ideal education" for people. Digantar strives for autonomy based on reason, democracy, egalitarianism, the development of children's skills and the dignity of work, nurture self-motivated and independent learners, who are sensitive and sensible human beings (https://www.digantar.org/).

Current Digantar Secretary Rohit Dhankar and Director Reena Das Roy were trained as teachers by David Horsburgh before opening an experimental school in Jaipur. Even though there are now quite a few government and private schools in the area, Digantar has continued to deliver high-quality education to children who come to the Vidyalaya from adjacent villages and hamlets over the years thanks to their unique practices. Digantar's organisational philosophies include: putting educational theories and notions to practical test; creating instructional strategies and materials that are in line with these strategies; supporting educational research; offering educational support to individuals and institutions engaged in the field of education; and working to advance culture (https://www.digantar.org/).

The vision of Digantar is to help individuals create a society that is pluralistic and democratic at its core, which safeguards the rights of every individual and provides them with justice, equity, autonomy, and the basic dignity that every being deserves (https://www.digantar.org/).

The institution believes they are not teaching children but providing them with independence of mind. As they follow a process-centric approach, they prepare the child for rational thinking in daily life, using learned ideas in practical situations, and developing a sense of sensitivity towards every other existing being.

### *Objectives of the study*

1. To study the need and process of emergence for an alternative school, Digantar in Jaipur, Rajasthan.
2. To study the innovative practices and educational processes of alternate education at Digantar in light of the New Education Policy 2020.

### Research questions

1. Why is there a need to have an alternate school in the context of Digantar, Jaipur, Rajasthan?
2. How does Digantar resonate with the National Education Policy 2020 in terms of its alternate educational processes?

### Method

An exploratory qualitative study was conducted using a case study method.

### Data Collection

Data was collected through observations taken during the field visit, using participatory and non-participatory methods of observation. The data was taken in the form of written field notes. Interviews were conducted with the key people working in the institution and people in the community.

### Innovative Practices of the Institution

*Infrastructure of the school*: The main campus of the school is situated in Todi Ramjanipura. Other than the main school, two Vidyalayas and Shalas are situated in Bandhyali and Kho Dhani. The Bandhyali Vidyalay consists of more than ten non-homogeneous classrooms, a library, a carpentry room, a space for creating the best out of waste, a room for teacher's meetings, and another for maintaining mathematics resources.

*Classroom:* Each classroom had a unique name that the children mutually decided on, like 'Badal', 'Titli', and 'Roshni'. The idea behind naming each classroom was that every student has a name; therefore, their space must also have a name that they associate with.

*Carpentry Room:* This room provided a space for children to unleash their creativity through carpentry. It contained tools required for wood carpentry. The wood was obtained from a particular tree available in the neighbourhood when it dried. Children from the age of seven learned this art, which happened once a week. According to the facilitator, carpentry develops patience, creativity, and a sense of aesthetics in children.

*Mathematics Resource Room:* The resource room contained diverse teaching and learning material in the form of board games, puzzles, charts with labelled diagrams, and blocks to introduce pre-number concepts and place value systems.

*Classroom Structure:* It was found in the observations that there were no chairs or benches in the class, as it helps to dilute the hierarchy in class and also gives learners the liberty to sit wherever they want. This also creates scope for teachers' mobility. The teacher, who facilitates the classroom, also sits with the children in a circle. The bags, water bottles, lunch boxes, and stationery of children are kept in racks in the classroom itself. Each class lasts for 40 minutes, followed by a 10-minute break. The class begins with sabha, where children discuss their previous day experiences, followed by a small meditation practice, which is also one of the practices of the happiness curriculum and resonates with the guidelines of the National Curriculum Framework for Foundational Stage (NCF-FS 2022), children danced and sang folk songs and poems while the facilitator played tabla. children marked their own attendance, and for children who were absent, the facilitator shared the reasons for their absence with others who were present. The children took the lead in organising their teaching and learning material, like workbooks, and making sure their class was tidy and lively. With this, children developed a sense of autonomy, responsibility, and a sense of belonging. The policy document of NEP 2020 also states that a good education institution is one in which every student feels welcomed and cared for, where a safe and stimulating learning environment exists, where a wide range of learning experiences are offered, and where good physical infrastructure and appropriate resources conducive to learning are available to all children (NEP 2020, p. 5).

Curriculum, syllabus, textbooks, teaching materials, and pedagogical approaches: Digantar follows a process-centric curriculum that is uniquely designed to address individual needs, provide autonomy to the teacher to assess pupils, and help them become better. The content and pedagogy are not something coming from an outer body; the institution's curriculum is born out of the child's social context. The curriculum of Digantar is exerted through textbooks, classroom practices, and every act performed by the child on the school premises.

1. There is no concept of "uniformity" in the premise, but there are a bunch of individuals within homogeneous settings.
2. There is no specific level of learning; every individual is assessed and facilitated according to their own understanding.
3. Learning does not take place only in the process of teacher-student interaction; it also promotes self-learning, peer learning, and cooperative learning. Children set their own classroom rules.

*Pedagogical Approaches:* Constructive learning, discovery learning, and inquiry-based learning are used and promoted in Digantar as recommended in NEP 2020. The pedagogy followed in Digantar encouraged sensory, motor, and physical activities. It also gave scope for exploring the child's immediate environment and manipulating it to learn actively and creatively. Teachers play a very important role in using these pedagogical approaches in the classroom. For example, in one of the classes, children were learning about objects that sink and float. The facilitator asked children to bring material from their immediate environment and observe, which objects can float and sink in the water.

*Multi-level Teaching:* Individualised lesson plans based on the curriculum that cater to the specific needs of children were developed. Therefore, in the classroom, level-wise teaching and learning take place. For example, during one of the observations in mathematics classes, children were divided into three groups based on their existing knowledge. One group consisted of children who were to learn the pre-number concept. These children were doing concrete activities with stones. The second group consisted of children who were learning the sequence of numbers. These children were doing pictorial activities. The last group consisted of children who were doing mathematical operations like addition and subtraction. These children were working on the workbooks given to them. Thus, the facilitator was able to cater to the needs of children at different levels.

*Syllabus and Textbooks:* Digantar has developed its own set of textbooks that have a unique outlook towards learning and assessment.

1. *Language: The institution has developed the language curriculum based on the whole language ap*proach, where children are made aware of the language present around them and use it effectively. Although the syllabus is designed with a mixed approach of 'Emergent Literacy' and 'Reading Readiness' perspectives, it promotes the use of colloquial language. Comprehension is taught through various methods, like picture reading, guided writing, and reading comprehension. Digantar works towards providing wider exposure to children's literature other than textbooks, which is one of the effective ways for language development (Sinha, 2012, p. 23). The textbook is designed to familiarize children with words, practice handwriting, and answer on the basis of their understanding. Language learning is promoted in class through a print-rich environment in the classroom and practising poems, discussions, and story-telling (NCF-FS 2022, p. 150). During the sabha (morning assembly) children sing and recite the literature from their own context, it also brings in hidden stereotypes based on gender, appearance, etc. in the classroom. There's no textbook for English. English is the second language for almost all the learners. Hence, to facilitate second language learning, the facilitator draws the curriculum from the first language/mother tongue of the learner. Talk is used as a resource in the language classroom at Digantar.
2. *Environmental Studies:* EVS classes and textbooks are all about making children aware of their surroundings through experiential learning. The objective of EVS classes is to help the learner acquire communication skills, observation skills, the ability to question and reason, and experimentation. The textbooks were designed to invite experiences from children's contexts into classroom contexts and further derive concepts

from them. Teaching materials are used from the learner's immediate surroundings.

3. *Mathematics:* Mathematics teaching has always been a challenge as it requires an understanding of abstract concepts. Young children acquire the ability to think abstractly when they're able to internalise their manipulations of the concept with some concrete experience. Children's needs are identified, and then they are assisted to learn mathematical concepts easily by engaging them in 'learn by doing'. Children are given manipulative concrete objects from their immediate surroundings, like pebbles and wooden sticks, and they're taught the concepts of seriation and classification. They spend a good time learning the "pre-number concepts" so that this can facilitate their understanding of numbers, as the concept of numbers is the key to further mathematical concepts. The textbook uses colloquial language, and the questions are designed to practice the activities learned in the classroom. The learners use manipulatives while solving the textbook questions. The facilitator frequently changes the manipulatives, as young children may associate symbols with concepts, so to break that association and facilitate abstraction, children need to have exposure to different kinds of manipulatives.
4. *Play, Songs, and Poems:* Due importance is also given to play, poems, and songs, and they are an integral part of classroom practices. There are specially curated books for guided play. Play facilitates the spirit of teamwork, engagement, and concentration with the task at hand. The lessons in play textbooks revolve around the values of leadership, democracy, and many more existing social institutions. Children's play provides the facilitator with an insight into the children's world and context.

### Extra co-curricular activities

1. Carpentry: Children over seven years old are taught to make wooden, handcrafted materials. Children's work in the form of artefacts, and their equipment is kept in the carpentry room.
2. Pottery/Clay: Learners are also taught to create handcrafted clay material by applying pressure and grasping these skills.

*Teaching learning material:* TLMs were created by children based on what they are studying. TLMs keep changing. Some of the TLMs that are referred to throughout the year were created by the teacher. The whole class was decorated with children's work.

*Assessment:* Assessment is one of the important elements in the teaching and learning process, as it helps the teacher understand children' learning pace and habits and work on her pedagogy accordingly, moulding it for the children' needs. Problems arise when the very same assessment is used to label children and push them out of the education system. Digantar therefore follows formative assessment that takes place throughout the learning process in the form of observations, discussions, pictorial representation, and communication. The facilitator observes them regularly, making a report of each child's progress without grading them. The children are never ranked or awarded in class based on their academic performance. Children are provided with valuable feedback, which helps both the teacher and children work together towards a common goal. NEP 2020 also emphasises that teachers and schools should build a regular, formative, adaptive, and competency-based assessment that promotes conceptual understanding rather than rote learning and learning-for-exams (NEP 2020, p. 5).

*Classroom management and discipline*: The institution provides the learners with a space where discipline can be directed by the children themselves. Digantar promotes a person-centred classroom where children practice self-discipline and shared leadership. Children resolve their conflicts and differences through dialogues and discussions in the self-created "Bal Panchayat". The process of setting rules and taking charge of their own behaviour was enabled through the panchayat. Even if a rule is broken, there is no punishment given in the class, but the individual shares with the class the reason why such a situation arose. Being an active participant in the process prepares learners to develop the critical awareness required for self-discipline. No rewards are given to any of them, as it is believed that motivation should be intrinsic. Also, in such a setup, all the children have the opportunity to become an integral part of the classroom management process. Children had the liberty to use the resources in the classroom according to their convenience. They were also responsible for the material being used by them. This was an example where providing autonomy to children in a person-centred classroom promoted self-discipline as Carl roger has also mentioned in his book freedom to learn.

*Teacher-student Relationship*: The teacher welcomes the experiences of children in class, engages in a dialogue, and then directs the conversation towards learning using examples from their context. Children respond in class without hesitation, interact freely with the facilitator, respect each other, and are confident about their interactions. Some unique practices followed in Digantar were: children called their teachers by their names affixed with a Hindi word 'Ji', which is used as an expression of respect. The teachers inform children about the reason for the absence of their fellow classmates. Children marked their own attendance. The teachers and children also collaborated on school cleaning duties.

Apart from the school environment, teacher-student relationships were also witnessed in the community environment. As the teachers frequently visited their children' homes and communicated with the family, they also attended community functions like marriages and religious rituals.

*Relationship between the community and the school:* Digantar works on building connections with the local community. The institution's efforts and society's trust and support lead them to share a mutual relationship with each other. The constant interaction between the children's local context and their educational space also benefits their learning.

Digantar believes these community interactions help them understand the child's context and perspective. This interaction process also helps parents know their children's progress and their well-being. Children shared that they love going to this school. They do share about their school experiences with their family members even after returning from there. There is no fear for children related to school. Children use the questioning, reasoning, and other cognitive skills that they have acquired in their daily lives. Children's and their parents' enthusiasm was very evident from their responses during their interactions with the researchers.

Digantar as well as the community have both evolved over the years. There is a gradual increase in the literacy rate of girls, for which various schemes were started by the institution, which led to a change in the communities' mindset. They believed that their girls were safe in Digantar, and education was their right too. Girls are also allowed to work and pursue higher studies. The entire scenario has changed, even in households where people do not discriminate between their children and provide equal opportunities to both genders. The practice of child marriages drastically declined as a result of Digantar's intervention. Digantar's non-participation in any such illegal and unhealthy practice made the community rethink its norms. Digantar is a family for the local community.

## Implications of the Study

Digantar can be projected as a model for providing alternative education that strives to promote and achieve the ideas of equality and sustainability in and for the marginalised and underprivileged sections of society. It also highlights community participation and close collaboration between the school and the community in providing an enriching learning environment. This study also emphasises the importance of educational field trips, which provide opportunities for teachers, educators, and prospective teachers to develop an understanding of the role of the socio-cultural milieu of children in their development and learning. Although National Education Policy 2020 promotes the idea of providing alternative education, it does not specify the processes to overcome the hurdles faced by such institutions.

## Conclusion

On the basis of our on-field observations at Digantar in Jaipur and our understanding of the National Education Policy 2020, it can be concluded that the vision, philosophy, curriculum, and educational processes in Digantar are all based on democratic constitutional values, which makes it a microcosm of the world beyond school and textbooks as the institution prepares children for the outer world on the values of equity, autonomy, justice, and self-governance as suggested by NEP 2020.

## References

Vittachi, S. & Raghavan, N. (2007). *Alternative Schooling in India.* Sage Publication India

Sinha, S. (2012). Reading without meaning: The Dilemma of Indian classrooms

Roger, Carl R. & Freiberg, J.H. (1994). *Freedom* to *learn.* Retrieved from https://archive.org/details/freedomtolearn0000roge

National Education Policy 2020. Retrieved from https://www.education.gov.in/sites/upload_files/mhrd/files/NEP_Final_English_0.pdf

National Curriculum Framework for School Education 2023 — NCERT. Retrieved from https://ncert.nic.in/pdf/NCFSE-2023-August_2023.pdf

National Curriculum Framework for Foundational Stage 2022 — NCERT. Retrieved from https://ncert.nic.in/pdf/NCF_for_Foundational_Stage_20_October_2022.pdf

# 27

# NCERT's Instructional Material
## *Role in School and Teacher Education*

Pooja Jain
Meera

### Introduction

National Council of Educational Research and Training (NCERT) is playing a pioneering role for school and teacher education from the last six decades and striving hard on continuous basis to achieve fourth objective of sustainable development goal of quality education specifically in context of school education. Since its inception, NCERT not only confined to preparation and publication of textbooks but also involved in the development of teacher appropriate material such as teachers' manuals, guide books, source books, reference works, supplementary reading material for students. Broadly, NCERT carried out its programs/proposals in the following four categories to achieve its supreme objective of providing quality education to all children throughout the country:

1. Research
2. Development
3. Training
4. Extension.

NCERT is the national apex autonomous organization under the MoE (Ministry of Education) with an objective to promote research in all branches of school education and its peripheral areas. Simultaneously and equally, NCERT equally involves in the process of development of instructional/educational materials such as textbooks, workbooks, supplementary readers, teacher guide, lab manuals, source books, journals, guidelines, framework, syllabi, courses along with course material, learning outcome, roadmap, activities, kits, supplementary material, reading material, bridge course, exemplar, handbook for teachers, curriculum, question bank, other resource material etc. and in the ICT environment — educational media programs (audio, audio-video, collection of images, interactives, e-content, infographics) online courses, webinar and live session on particular theme and class wise and chapter wise video programs for Classes I to XII and other types of instructional material to improve educational techniques and practices in schools for all level of school education that can be used by for pre service and in-service training of teachers, teacher educators, librarians and other stakeholders of education. NCERT is in continuous process of renewal, evaluation and updating of curriculum and educational materials for all levels of school education and teacher education and making them relevant as per the changing needs of children under the category of development programs. This material is also known as instructional material developed and coordinated in association with eminent experts and professionals in different fields of content and pedagogy.

## Educational/Instructional Material

Educational/ Instructional Material means the learning resources that are developed by the experts of the particular field in print/non-print format to be used by the target group to support and contribute in the teaching-learning process. It covers all curriculum, print and electronic textbooks, supplementary instructional material, training guides/manuals, tools/techniques to enhance understanding the subjects, workbooks. The dissemination of these kinds of educational material to the public from authentic source/organization is also very significant. NCERT is involved in the development of various types of educational material based on the curriculum for students as well as for training of teachers.

## Types of Material Developed by NCERT

There are wide variety of curricula and instructional print and non-print material developed by NCERT as per the various kinds of users' and specific needs in the area of pre-school education, primary education, vocationalist of education, teacher education, inclusive education, science education, language education etc. Following are the types of educational instructional material developed by NCERT during the period of five years under study:

1. Academic Calendar
2. Activity material/Activity Book
3. Audio-video Material
4. Bridge course/ Bridge material
5. Courses (Certificate/Diploma — Online/Physical/Blended mode)
6. Course material
7. Curriculum
8. Compendium
9. Dictionary/Glossary
10. Electronic content

11. Exemplar
12. Guidelines
13. Handbooks
14. Kits
15. Labs
16. Learning outcome
17. Manuals (Lab manual, Practical manual, Kit manual)
18. Other kinds of material (Annual report, Brochure, Bulletin, Compendium, FAQs, Journal, Magazine, Newsletter, Policy, Posters, Question Bank, Roadmap etc.)
19. Resource Material
20. Theme Park
21. Sourcebook
22. Supplementary Material/ Supplementary reading material
23. Tactile book/Kit
24. Teaching-learning material
25. Textbooks
26. Training manual/module/package
27. Video film/guide/programs
28. Webinar
29. Website development
30. Workbook etc.

## The Study

### *Objectives*

The objectives of this study are as follows:

1. To study year wise growth of development projects coordinated by NCERT
2. To study institution-wise contribution towards developmental projects
3. To study type-wise distribution of educational/instructional material developed by NCERT
4. To identify the number of development projects for different stages of school education and teacher education
5. To rank the subjects of education and identify top 10 subjects on which the development projects coordinated by NCERT.

### *Scope and Methodology*

This paper covers the study of 490 development projects coordinated by NCERT faculty members altogether to prepare the various kinds of instructional material (print/non-print format) for the period of five financial years i.e. 2017-2022 (As reflected in the annual report of NCERT prepared on the basis of financial year). The annual reports available on NCERT website has been downloaded in full text form. The link is https://ncert.nic.in/annual-report.php in full-text form. The excel sheets were prepared such as: Title of the Project, Year, Department, Stages of school education and subjects for the projects available under development heading. MS Excel software has been used for further analysis purposes.

## Data Analysis and Interpretation

### 1. *Year-wise distribution of development projects*

**Table 1:** Year wise distribution of development projects conducted by NCERT

| *S. No.* | *Year (Financial Year)* | *No. of Development projects* | *% of Total* | *Cumulative Growth* | *Cumulative %* |
|---|---|---|---|---|---|
| 1. | 2017-18 | 85 | 17.35 | - | |
| 2. | 2018-19 | 92 | 18.77 | 177 | 36.12 |
| 3. | 2019-20 | 94 | 19.18 | 271 | 55.30 |
| 4. | 2020-21 | 105 | 21.43 | 376 | 76.73 |
| 5. | 2021-22 | 114 | 23.27 | 490 | 100 |
| | Total | 490 | 100 | | |

Above chart showed that there is continuous growth from one year to another year from 17.35 % to 23.27% in development projects. However, one important finding is that during pandemic time, school education became the biggest challenge that led NCERT prepared national online programs and live telecast/online session (more than 15,000 programs) through Swayam Prabha for students and training of teachers on different concepts/subjects. These online programs were disseminated by through different platforms (TV channels, you tube, mobile applications etc.) to reach to the remote areas of huge population.

### 2. *Institution-wise contribution of development projects*

There is total eight units under the umbrella of NCERT and Institution-wise contribution in Development Projects is mentioned in the table below:

**Table 2:** Institution-wise Contribution

| *S. No.* | *Name of Institute* | *No. of Projects* | *%* |
|---|---|---|---|
| 1. | National Institute of Education (NIE), Delhi | 292 | 59.59 |
| 2. | Regional Institute of Education (RIE), Ajmer | 22 | 4.49 |
| 3. | Regional Institute of Education (RIE), Bhopal | 23 | 4.69 |
| 4. | Regional Institute of Education (RIE), Bhubaneswar | 17 | 3.47 |

| S. No. | Name of Institute | No. of Projects | % |
|---|---|---|---|
| 5. | Regional Institute of Education (RIE), Mysuru | 12 | 2.45 |
| 6. | North East Regional Institute of Education (NERIE), Meghalaya | 23 | 4.69 |
| 7. | Central Institute of Educational Technology (CIET), Delhi | 59 | 12.04 |
| 8. | Pandit Sunderlal Sharma Central Institute of Vocational Education (PSSCIVE), Bhopal | 42 | 8.58 |
| | Total | 490 | 100 |

Table 2 and Chart 2 reflected that National Institute of Education (NIE), Delhi developed the highest number of materials with 292 development projects i.e. 60% of the total projects and followed by CIET, Delhi and PSSCIVE, Bhopal with 59 and 42 projects. However, other five regional institutes faculty members are having full-time teaching courses and one of the reasons for a smaller number of developmental activities as 97 projects at regional level altogether.

### *3. **Type-wise Distribution of Educational/Instructional Material Developed by NCERT***

**Table 3:** Type-wise distribution of educational/instructional material

| S. No. | Type of Material developed | No. of Projects |
|---|---|---|
| 1. | Activity Book/work book | 11 |
| 2. | Academic Calendar | 09 |
| 3. | Bridge course/ Bridge material | 06 |
| 4. | Courses (Certificate/Diploma) | 24 |
| 5. | Course material/content | 04 |
| 6. | Curriculum development | 15 |
| 7. | Dictionary/Glossary | 04 |
| 8. | E-content (Audio, Audio-Video programmes, Multimedia, E-resources, Infographics, PM e-vidya, Video guide. Webinar, Live sessions, SAHYOG, Webinar series etc.) | 145 |
| 9. | Exemplar | 07 |
| 10. | Framework/Guidelines | 22 |
| 11. | Handbooks | 18 |
| 12. | Kits | 06 |
| 13. | Labs/Resource Centre | 09 |
| 14. | Material developed based on learning outcome | 16 |
| 15. | Manuals (Lab manual, Practical manual, Kit manual) | 08 |
| 16. | Module | 14 |
| 17. | Resource Material | 16 |

| *S. No.* | *Type of Material developed* | *No. of Projects* |
|---|---|---|
| 18. | Theme Park | 06 |
| 19. | Supplementary Material | 23 |
| 20. | Tactile book/Kit | 09 |
| 21. | Teaching-learning material/Teacher Resource Material | 14 |
| 22. | Textbooks | 36 |
| 23. | Training manual/module/package | 14 |
| 24. | Website development | 04 |
| 25. | Miscellaneous (Annual report, Brochure, Bulletin, Compendium, FAQs, Journal, Magazine, Newsletter, Policy, Posters, Question Bank, Roadmap, working paper and not covered in above mentioned category etc.) | 50 |
| Total | | 490 |

Table 3 and above Chart 3 showed that the highest type of material developed is e-content with 145 projects under which thousands of video programs were prepared and disseminated for school education and teacher education. Total 36 new textbooks developed of different subjects and 24 Courses have been run by NCERT during the 5-year period of study.

*4.* ***Distribution of Development Projects among four stages of School Education and Teacher Education***

NCERT main target group is the school education and teacher education. Next table will depict the number of development projects associated with four stages of school education and teacher education. As per NCF 2005 and as per the All-India School Education survey there are following four stages of school education:

1. *Primary stage (Class I to V) (also includes Early childhood care and education).*
2. *Upper Primary stage (Class VI to VIII)*
3. *Secondary stage (Class IX & X)*
4. *Higher Secondary Schools (XI & XII)*

Besides above mentioned four specified stages of school education, the following categories are created to specify the development projects:

1. *All stages of education (Primary and Upper Primary, Secondary and Higher Secondary altogether)*
2. *Combination of two or more of any of the stages (Primary and Upper Primary, Secondary and Higher Secondary, Upper Primary and Secondary, Primary to Secondary)*
3. *Teacher education.*

**Table 4:** Distribution of Development Projects among four stages of School Education and Teacher Education

| *S. No* | *Stages of Education* | *No. of Projects* | *Percentage* |
|---|---|---|---|
| 1. | Primary Stage | 79 | 16.12 |
| 2. | Upper Primary Stage | 34 | 6.94 |
| 3. | Secondary Stage | 58 | 11.84 |
| 4. | Higher Secondary Stage | 83 | 16.94 |
| 5. | Others (Combination of any of the above four stage) | 55 | 11.22 |
| 6. | All stages of Education (Primary, Upper Primary, Secondary and Senior Secondary) | 155 | 31.63 |
| 7. | Teacher Education | 26 | 5.31 |
| Total | | 490 | 100 |

Above table 4 and chart 4 depicts that the highest projects have been done for all stages of education. with 155 projects. 83 projects for Higher secondary stage and followed by 79 projects/material has been developed exclusively for primary education and 58 for secondary stage. The least development work was done in exclusively for Upper Primary stage with 34 projects. Another important observation is 26 instructional material is prepared specifically related for teacher education.

*5. Subject-wise distribution of Development Projects*

**Table 5:** Subject-wise distribution in Development Projects

| *S. No.* | *Subject* | *Total* | *Percentage* | *Rank* |
|---|---|---|---|---|
| 1. | Educational Technology /Application of ICT in Education | 70 | 14.29 | 1 |
| 2. | Teacher Education | 63 | 12.86 | 2 |
| 3. | Science Education | 62 | 12.65 | 3 |
| 4. | Language Education | 50 | 10.20 | 4 |
| 5. | Vocational Education | 38 | 07.76 | 5 |
| 6. | Social Science Education | 27 | 05.51 | 6 |
| 7. | Inclusive Education | 25 | 05.10 | 7 |
| 8. | School Education/Education | 23 | 04.69 | 8 |
| 9. | Mathematics Education | 21 | 04.29 | 9 |
| 10. | Habitat & Learning (Environmental Education) | 20 | 04.08 | 10 |
| 11. | Arts in Education | 19 | 03.88 | 11 |
| 12. | Elementary Education (Early Childhood Care and Education/Pre-school education/Primary Education) | 18 | 03.67 | 12 |
| 13. | Assessment and Evaluation | 13 | 02.65 | 13 |
| 14. | Curriculum Studies | 09 | 01.84 | 14 |
| 15. | Foundational Literacy and Numeracy | 09 | 01.84 | 15 |

| S. No. | Subject | Total | Percentage | Rank |
|---|---|---|---|---|
| 16. | Educational Psychology | 07 | 01.43 | 16 |
| 17. | Gender Studies | 06 | 01.22 | 17 |
| 18. | Health and Physical Education | 05 | 01.02 | 18 |
| 19. | Textbook Analysis | 05 | 01.02 | 19 |
| 20. | Intervention in Education and Evaluation | - | 0 | 20 |
| | Total | 490 | 100 | |

After analysing the content of the development projects, above are the 20 broad subject headings have been identified to study this objective. Total 490 projects have been analysed with type of material and subject analysis revealed that in last five years Educational Technology/ICT in education took first place with 70 (14.29%) projects and followed by Teacher education (12.86%) and Science education (12.65%) with 63 and 62 projects respectively. Above analysis showed that application of ICT in education is visible in Indian education system at the national level.

## Findings and Suggestions

1. Total 490 development projects are completed during the period of five financial years (Financial Year) 2017-2022 as reflected in the annual report published by NCERT. The most productive year is identified is 2021-22 with 114 projects and followed by year 2020-21 with 105. However, continuous growth pattern can be seen from 2017 to 2022 i.e. 17.35% to 23.27%.
2. Total 292 development projects have been taken by National Institute of Education (NIE), Delhi and followed by CIET, Delhi and PSSCIVE, Bhopal with 59 and 42 projects respectively. However, other five regional institutes faculty members are having full-time teaching courses which could be the reason for a smaller number of developmental activities with 97 projects at regional level altogether.
3. The highest type of development material is e-content with 145 projects under which thousands of video programmes were prepared and disseminated for school education and teacher education. Total 36 textbooks have been developed on different subjects and 24 courses have been run by NCERT during the five-year period of study.
4. Total 155 developmental projects are done for all the four stages of school education together which is highest among all stages. 83 projects for Higher secondary stage and followed by 79 projects/material has been developed exclusively for primary education and 58 for secondary stage. The least development work was done in exclusively for Upper Primary

stage with 34 projects. Another important observation is 26 instructional/training material is prepared specifically related for teacher education.

5. Educational Technology/ICT in education received the maximum attention with 70 projects and followed by Teacher education and Science education.

After analysing all the developmental projects for five years, it can be said that NCERT plays a pivotal role at the national level for school and teacher education. It is promoting the development and accessibility of all kinds all kinds of material from text, audio, video, electronic, online, and live session on all areas of school and teacher education. This five year study also includes the pandemic period in which NCERT did exemplary work that includes development of Alternative academic calendar, PRAGYATA guidelines on digital education, NISHTA-National initiatives for school heads and teachers for their holistic advancement (online) for teacher training at mass level, Review of syllabi (course curtailed), Development of online education national level programmes for school education and teacher education, PM eVidya channels (For classes I to XII for each Subjects), Orientation programmes on educational technology through webinar series for teachers and other stakeholders of education, production and dissemination of e-contents for children with special needs, Development of the guidelines/booklet for cyber safety and cyber bullying for students, parents and teachers, MANODARPAN cell created to provide psychosocial support for mental health and well-being of students during the COVID-19 outbreak and beyond, Counselling Services for Schoolchildren, Live interactive sessions called 'SAHYOG', Guidance for Mental Well-being of Children, Online Quizzes for Students and Teachers, Continuous Professional Development (CPD) Courses on DIKSHA, Created a SSP mobile app (Android) for delivery of e-contents, Community radio in remote areas where no online education access is available.

## Conclusion

NCERT is playing the most pioneering role in the Indian education system. It is serving as the apex body and critical knowledge resource for various stakeholders operating in the education system continuously evolving and contributing immensely to address new emerging issues in the present scenario and supporting and building a robust and resilient education system in India. At present, NCERT is focussed towards addressing the mental health of children, promote inclusive education, develop gender neutral syllabus (transgender concerns) and building and learning e-learning methodologies and tools for wider outreach and contribute effectively to NEP 2020. NCERT is concentrating its efforts in publishing latest education material and make it accessible through NCERT website and various new age digital tools for wider dissemination.

## References


Anderson, J. and Lightfoot, A. (2019). *School education system in India.* Delhi, British Council. pp.18-42.

National Council of Educational Research and Training. (2018). *Annual Report of NCERT 1962 63.*pp-1-40

National Council of Educational Research and Training. (2001). *In pursuit of equity and excellence NCERT 1986-2000.* Delhi, NCERT.pp-1-50

National Council of Educational Research and Training. (2005). *National Curriculum Framework.* Delhi, NCERT. pp.12-126.

National Council of Educational Research and Training. (2018). *NCERT Annual Report 2017-18.*https://ncert.nic.in/pdf/annualreport/Annual_report_17_18.pdf

National Council of Educational Research and Training. (2020). *NCERT Annual Report 2018-19.* https://ncert.nic.in/pdf/annualreport/Annual_Report_18_19.pdf

National Council of Educational Research and Training. (2021). *NCERT Annual Report 2019-20.* https://ncert.nic.in/pdf/annualreport/Annual-Report-2019-20.pdf

National Council of Educational Research and Training. (2022). *NCERT Annual Report 2020-21.* https://ncert.nic.in/pdf/annualreport/AnnualReport2020-21.pdf

National Council of Educational Research and Training (2022). *NCERT Annual Report 2021 22.* https://ncert.nic.in/pdf/annualreport/AnnualReport2021-22.pdf

# Editors and Contributors

## Editors

**Dr Jasim Ahmad**, Ph.D. (Edu), M.Ed., M.Sc. (Zoology), UGC-NET (Edu), is a Professor at the Institute of Advanced Studies in Education, Jamia Millia Islamia. He also holds the position of Honorary Director of Centre for Distance and Online Education (CDOE) of JMI. Prof. Ahmad has a teaching and research experience of around 25 years; his areas of interests include Science Education, Educational Psychology, Research Methodology and Teacher Education. He has published eleven books and has to his credit around 70 research papers and articles published in journals, around 50 research papers in conferences, 15 chapters in edited books and 16 SLM units, more than 100 invited talks, around 80 workshops, and coordinated several training programmes. 14 Ph.D. degrees and around 50 PG. dissertations have been awarded under his guidance. He has been awarded with the 'Proud Indian Eminent Professor Award 2022' in Teacher Education by IMRF, Andhra Pradesh on the occasion of India's 73rd Republic Day.

**Dr Aerum Khan**, MSc Botany, B.Ed, MA Education, MA Sociology, DCA, Ph.D. (Botany), Ph.D. (Education) is Associate Professor, Science Education at Dept of TT & NFE (IASE), F/o Education, JMI, New Delhi. She has done courses on *Qualitative Research Methods* from University of Amsterdam, *Feminism and Social Justice* from University of California, Santa Cruz, *Introduction to Philosophy* from The University of Edinburgh, *Psychological First Aid* from Johns Hopkins University, *The Science of Well-being* from Yale University, and *Gender and Sexuality: Diversity and Inclusion in the Workplace* from University of Pittsburgh. She has worked with NCERT, New Delhi, SCERT Delhi. She has been a Visiting Faculty for SOL-Delhi University, IGNOU (continued) and NIOS, and has been Academic Consultant for the British Council. Got published more than 70 articles, chapters and research papers in Botany and Education in National and International journals. She has delivered more than 350 invited talks in different programs. She was the core member of the development team of NCERT for MOOCs for school education on SWAYAM. She has been the Academic Coordinator for the UGC funded project e-PG Pathshala for the subject of Education, joint venture of CIET-NCERT and University of Allahabad. The first online PG level MOOC in Education created by her and team was launched by UGC on the SWAYAM platform on 1 August 2017. She received the MoE sponsored training for SWAYAM Course Coordinators at Chennai, jointly conducted by IIT Bombay, IIM Bangalore, NIEPA Delhi and NITTTR Chennai on the nomination of UGC. In March 2020 she was invited by IIT Madras and JNU, New Delhi to develop video lectures for UG level for National telecast through Swayam Prabha Channels of MoE-GoI, under which she developed 168 video lectures in 5 phases. She is the recipient of the 'Inspiring Woman Awards 2021' from 'Fourth Screen Education' for outstanding and remarkable services in the field of Education.

**Dr Ansar Ahmad,** Ph.D. (Education), M.Phil., M.Ed., M.A. (Geography), PGD in Disaster Management, Certificate in "Remote Sensing & GIS Technology and Application for UT & Government Officials" from ISRO, Indian Institute of Remote Sensing, Dehradun, is Assistant Professor at the Department of Teacher Training & Non-Formal Education (IASE), Faculty of Education, Jamia Millia Islamia, New Delhi. Earlier he worked as Assistant Professor of Education at Miranda House and Shyama Prasad Mukherjee College, University of Delhi. He has 12 years of Teaching and Research Experience; his area of interests includes Social Science Education (with super specialization of Geography Education), Educational Administration and Measurement & Evaluation. He is a recipient of the International Teacher's Pride Award 2021. Dr. Ahmad is founding editor of a peer reviewed multidisciplinary research journal 'Council for Teacher Education Foundation (CTEF).' He is credited to have published many Research Papers and Articles in various National and International Journals, 5 Books/Chapters and 4 Units/ Blocks of SLM. He has delivered 75 Invited Lectures/Talks and attended 50 Workshops and Training programmes. He has been Co-Convener and Organizing Secretary of National and International Conferences, successfully coordinated various Workshops, In-Service Training Programme and Refresher Course for College and University Professors and School Teachers at UGC-Human Resource Development Centre.

## Contributors

**Amanpreet Kaur**, Research Scholar, Department of Education, Panjab University, Chandigarh. amansehgal84@yahoo.com

**Ambrin Khanam**, Research Scholar, Department of Teacher Training & Non-formal Education (IASE), Jamia Millia Islamia, New Delhi. ambrin288@gmail.com

**Anwesha Rai**, B.El.Ed Scholar, Department of Elementary Education, Lady Shri Ram College for Women, New Delhi. anwesha.lsr@gmail.com

**Ashoshika Bhadoria**, Lecturer (Political Science), Directorate of Education, Govt. of NCT, Delhi. ashoshika.bhadoria@gmail.com

**Ashu Threja Malhotra**, Assistant Professor, Department of Elementary Education, Miranda House. New Delhi. ashu.threja@mirandahouse.ac.in

**Ayushi Sinha,** B.El.Ed Scholar, Department of Elementary Education, Lady Shri Ram College for Women, New Delhi. ayushisinha.090203@gmail.com

**Bashir Ahmad Khan** (ICSSR Fellow), Research Scholar, Department of Teacher Education, Central University of Haryana. kbashirku2011@gmail.com

**Dori Lal**, Associate Professor, Department of Teacher Training and Non-formal Education (IASE), Jamia Millia Islamia, New Delhi. dl.jamia@gmail.com

**Kaushik Sarkar**, Research Scholar, Department of Education, Sikkim University, Gangtok, Sikkim. kaushiksarkar018@gmail.com

**Kiran Joshi**, Assistant Professor, Department of Teacher Education, Mewar Institute of Management, Ghaziabad. drkiranjoshi.edu@gmail.com

**Kothai Nayagi N**, Research Scholar, Department of Education, University of Delhi. kothainayaginatarasan@gmail.com

**Masooda Haseeb**, Assistant Professor, Department of Education, Janhit Institute of Education and Information, Greater Noida. zia.sana@gmail.com

**Meera**, Professor, Department of Library and Information Science, Faculty of Arts, University of Delhi, Delhi. meeradlis@gmail.com

**Mohd Haroon Salmani**, Research Scholar, Department of Teacher Training and Non-Formal Education, Jamia Millia Islamia, New Delhi. mohdh6600@gmail.com

**Mohammad Kaif Farooqui**, Research Scholar Department of Education, AMU Aligarh. kaifalig18@gmail.com

**Mohd Zia Ul Haq Rafaqi**, Assistant Professor, University of Kashmir, South Campus Anantnag. mzrafiqi@uok.edu.in

**Mridula Bhardwaj**, Ph.D. Scholar, Department of Teacher Training & Non-formal Education (IASE), Jamia Millia Islamia, New Delhi and Assistant Professor, DIET Pitampura, New Delhi. mridulabhardwaj72@gmail.com

**Muddam Yochitha Reddy**, An alumna of Indira Gandhi National Open University, New Delhi. myochireddy64@gmail.com

**Pooja Jain**, Research Scholar, Ph.D., Department of Library and Information Science, University of Delhi & Assistant Librarian, Library and Documentation Division, NCERT, New Delhi. poojajain18nov@gmail.com

**Pradeep Gusain**, Lecturer, Dr. B.R Ambedkar School of Specialized Excellence, Directorate of Education, GNCTD, New Delhi. prys2023@gmail.com

**Priti Sangray**, Research Scholar, Sikkim University, Gangtok. pritisangray28@gmail.com

**Priyanka Singh**, Research Scholar, Amity Institute of Education, Amity University, Noida. priyanka.singh8@s.amity.edu

**Raisa Khan**, Assistant Professor, Department of Teacher Training & Non-formal Education (IASE), Faculty of Education, Jamia Millia Islamia, New Delhi. rkhan9@jmi.ac.in

**Reena Kumari**, Research Scholar, Department of Education, Panjab University, Chandigarh. rr9410096@gmail.com

**Roohi Fatima**, Professor, Department of Teacher Training & Non-formal Education (IASE), Jamia Millia Islamia, New Delhi. dr.roohiazam@yahoo.co.in

**Sajid Jamal**, Professor, Department of Education, AMU, Aligarh.

**Shadma Absar**, Assistant Professor, National Centre for School Leadership, NIEPA, New Delhi. drshadmaabsar@gmail.com

**Shaista Tanveer**, Department of Educational Studies, Jamia Millia Islamia, New Delhi. shaista.012020@gmail.com

**Shama Norien Major**, Assistant professor, Department of Elementary Education, Lady Shri Ram College for Women, New Delhi. majornoriens@gmail.com

**Shumaila Saif Siddiqui**, Principal, Aishabai College of Education, Mumbai. drshumaila.siddiqui27@gmail.com

**Soumya Priyadarsani**, Research Scholar, Department of Teacher Training & Non-formal Education, Jamia Millia Islamia, New Delhi. psoumyapanigrahi@gmail.com

**Tashnim Ferdaus**, Research Scholar, Department of Teacher Training & Non-formal Education, Jamia Millia Islamia, New Delhi. ferdaustashnim@gmail.com

**Vandana Laishram**, Senior Research Fellow, Department of Education, Panjab University, Chandigarh. laishramv375@gmail.com